CIVIL PROCEDURE 2016

FIRST SUPPLEMENT
TO THE
2016 EDITION

D1328990

Up-to-date generally to 25 May 2016.

SWEET & MAXWELL

THOMSON REUTERS

Published in 2016 by Thomson Reuters (Professional) UK Limited (Registered in England &
Wales, Company No 1679046.
Registered Office and address for service: 2nd Floor, 1 Mark Square, Leonard Street, London
EC2A 4EG) trading as Sweet & Maxwell.
Typesetting by Sweet & Maxwell electronic publishing system.
Printed and bound in the UK by CPI Group (UK) Ltd, Croydon, CR0 4YY.
For further information on our products and services, visit
http://www.sweetandmaxwell.co.uk.

No natural forests were destroyed to make this product; only farmed timber was used and
replanted.

British Library Cataloguing in Publication Data
A catalogue record for this book is available from the British Library

ISBN–978–0–41405–679–4

Publisher's Note

Civil Procedure 2016 published on 29 March 2016. The First Cumulative Supplement contains updating material for both Volumes of *Civil Procedure 2016* and brings the work up-to-date to 25 May 2016.

The First Supplement updates *Civil Procedure* in the following respects:

- The inclusion of the Senior Master's Practice Notes on: Transfers for Enforcement to the High Court (December 2015); Applications for Transfers for Enforcement of Possession Orders to the High Court (March 2016); and Civil Recovery Claims under CPR Part 8 (April 2016)
- The addition of an editorial table to PD6A to demonstrate a comparison of deemed dates of service for the Claim Form and Particulars of Claim
- Updated commentary in respect of the Legal Aid, Sentencing and Punishment of Offenders Act 2012 (Commencement No.12) Order 2016 (SI 2016/345)
- Updated Court and Procedural Guides
- Updated and new commentary on case law including: *Deutsche Bank AG v Unitech Global Ltd*; *Dubai Financial Group LLC v National Private Air Transport Services*; *EB v Secretary of State for the Home Department*; *In re L (A Child)*; *Kennedy v Cordia (Services) LLP*; *Kernkraftwerke Lippe-Ems GmbH v Hauptzollamt Osnabruck*; *Littlestone v MacLeish*; *OOO Abbott v Econowall UK Ltd*; *R. (C) v Secretary of State for Justice*; *R. (Holmcroft Properties Ltd) v KMPG LLP*; *R. (McKenzie) v Director of the Serious Fraud Office*; *R. (Wasif) v Secretary of State for the Home Department*; *Re Kenyan Emergency Group Litigation*; *Sarpd Oil International Ltd v Addax Energy SA*; *Sellar-Elliott v Howling*; *Sobrany v UAB Transtira*; *Swindon BC v Webb*; *Thomas Cook Belgium NV v Thurner Belgium GmbH*; *Tubelike Ltd v Visitjourneys.com Ltd*; and *Winkler v Shamoon*.
- Plus a host of further commentary updates.

Civil Procedure News will continue to keep you abreast of developments for the remainder of the subscription year.

We welcome feedback from subscribers—please email *whitebook@sweetandmaxwell.co.uk* with any comments or suggestions.

The White Book Team
May 2016

PREFACE

On p.xiii of the 2016 edition of the *White Book*, in the preliminary pages, the date of Lord Justice Jackson's preface is printed as "January 12, 2015". This is incorrect and should state "11 December 2015".

The publishers apologise for the error.

List of Editors

EDITOR-IN-CHIEF

THE RIGHT HONOURABLE LORD JUSTICE JACKSON

Lord Justice of Appeal; Honorary Fellow of Jesus College, Cambridge

GENERAL EDITORS

SENIOR MASTER B. FONTAINE

Senior Master of the Senior Courts in the Queen's Bench Division and Queen's Remembrancer; Central Authority for the Hague Conventions on Service and Taking of Evidence; Central Body under the EC Service and Evidence Regulations; Former Member of the Civil Procedure Rule Committee

PROFESSOR I. R. SCOTT Q.C. (Hon)

Emeritus Professor, University of Birmingham; Honorary Bencher of Gray's Inn

EDITOR OF CIVIL PROCEDURE NEWS

DR J. SORABJI

Barrister; Principal Legal Adviser to the Lord Chief Justice and the Master of the Rolls; UCL Judicial Institute

SENIOR EDITORIAL BOARD

SENIOR COSTS JUDGE A. GORDON-SAKER

Senior Courts Costs Office

THE RIGHT HONOURABLE LORD JUSTICE HAMBLEN

Lord Justice of Appeal

ROBERT N. HILL

Recorder, Deputy District Judge and Regional Costs Judge, North Eastern Circuit; Former District Judge and Former Member of the Civil Procedure Rule Committee

HIS HONOUR JUDGE NIC MADGE

Inner London Crown Court and Central London Civil Justice Centre

EDITORS

JONATHAN AUBURN

Barrister, 11 King's Bench Walk

DR SIMON AUERBACH

Recorder and Employment Judge, Central London Employment Tribunal

MR REGISTRAR BAISTER

Chief Bankruptcy Registrar of the High Court

DR STUART BARAN

Barrister, Three New Square

V. C. BELL

Barrister, High Court Chancery Chambers

HIS HONOUR JUDGE NIGEL BIRD

Manchester Civil Justice Centre

DISTRICT JUDGE SUZANNE BURN

A District Judge on the South Eastern Circuit; Former Member of the Civil Procedure Rule Committee

MARTIN CHAMBERLAIN Q.C.

One of Her Majesty's Counsel

SARA COCKERILL Q.C.

One of Her Majesty's Counsel

MASTER DAVID COOK

A Master of the Senior Courts, Queen's Bench Division

THE HONOURABLE MR JUSTICE COULSON

Judge of the Queen's Bench Division of the High Court; Presiding Judge of the North Eastern Circuit; Member of the Civil Procedure Rule Committee

REGISTRAR DERRETT

A Bankruptcy Registrar of the High Court

MASTER R. EASTMAN
A Master of the Senior Courts, Queen's Bench Division
LAURA FELDMAN
Senior Associate (Barrister), Eversheds
M. GIBBON Q.C.
One of Her Majesty's Counsel, Maitland Chambers
JOAN GOULBOURN
Of the Public Guardianship Office
DISTRICT JUDGE MICHAEL HOVINGTON
Manchester County Court; Member of the Civil Procedure Rule Committee
R. JAY
Solicitor
E. JEARY
Of the Court Funds Office
MASTER JERVIS KAY Q.C.
Admiralty Registrar and a Master of the Senior Courts, Queen's Bench Division; One of Her Majesty's Counsel
CHRISTOPHER KNIGHT
Barrister, 11 King's Bench Walk
DISTRICT JUDGE M. LANGLEY
A District Judge of the Central London County Court
THE HONOURABLE MR JUSTICE LEWIS
Judge of the Queen's Bench Division of the High Court; Presiding Judge, Wales
SARA MASTERS Q.C.
One of Her Majesty's Counsel
MASTER VICTORIA MCCLOUD
A Master of the Senior Courts, Queen's Bench Division
DISTRICT JUDGE SIMON MIDDLETON
Truro Courts of Justice and Bodmin County Court
KARON MONAGHAN Q.C.
One of Her Majesty's Counsel
HELEN MOUNTFIELD Q.C.
One of Her Majesty's Counsel
JOHN O'HARE
Formerly a Master of the Senior Courts Costs Office
HIS HONOUR JUDGE RICHARD PARKES Q.C.
A Circuit Judge on the South Eastern Circuit
EDWARD PEPPERALL Q.C.
One of Her Majesty's Counsel, St Philips Chambers; Member of the Civil Procedure Rule Committee
MASTER N. PRICE
A Master of the Senior Courts, Chancery Division
MASTER ROBERTS
A Master of the Senior Courts, Queen's Bench Division; Member of the Civil Procedure Rule Committee
DISTRICT JUDGE RICHARD ROBINSON
Principal Registry of the Family Division
DISTRICT JUDGE PHILIP ROGERS
A District Judge on the South Eastern Circuit
C. SANDERS
Solicitor
IAN SEWELL
Costs Clerk, Supreme Court of the United Kingdom
DR J. SORABJI
Barrister; Principal Legal Adviser to the Lord Chief Justice and the Master of the Rolls; UCL Judicial Institute

CONTENTS

CONTENTS

TABLE OF CASES

TABLE OF STATUTES

TABLE OF INTERNATIONAL AND EUROPEAN LEGISLATION, TREATIES AND CONVENTIONS

SECTION A   CIVIL PROCEDURE RULES 1998

PART 1

OVERRIDING OBJECTIVE

Encouraging co-operation between parties

Replace the second paragraph with:

Various provisions in the CPR encourage party co-operation once proceedings have been **1.4.4** commenced. A good illustration is provided by r.29.4 which states that the court may approve without a hearing proposals agreed by the parties for the management of proceedings on the multi-track and give directions in the terms proposed. Other illustrations include r.15.5 (agreement extending period for filing defence) and r.26.4 (agreement to request stay to allow for settlement of case), and r.35.7 (agreement on single joint expert). The efforts made by the parties to resolve their dispute is a factor to which the court should have regard in deciding the amount of costs (r.44.4(3)(a)). In *Hertsmere Primary Care Trust v Rabindra-Anandh* [2005] EWHC 320 (Ch); *The Times*, April 25, 2005, Lightman J. disapproved of a party's failure to cooperate with his opponents by his declining to respond to their request for him to explain to them the basis upon which he asserted that their offer did not comply with the provisions of Pt 36. See further Vol.2 Section 11 (Duty of the Parties), subs.E (para.11-15) and *OOO Abbott v Econowall UK Ltd* [2016] EWHC 660 (IPEC), 23 March 2016, unrep. (HHJ Hacon).

PART 2

APPLICATION AND INTERPRETATION OF THE RULES

Words and expressions defined in r.2.3(1)

"filing"

After "meant lodging in a court office a document having those effects (see) now r.9.2).", replace "Practice Direction 4 (Court Forms" with:

Practice Direction 5A (Court Documents)   **2.3.9**

Delete paragraph 2.4.5 "The County Court Legal Advisers Pilot".

The County Court Legal Advisers Pilot

Replace with:

Practice Direction 51K provides for a pilot scheme whereby certain types of order may be made **2.5.4** by legal advisers in relation to money claims commenced in the County Court Money Claims Centre or County Court Business Centre under authority from the Designated Civil Judges for Northampton & Leicester Trial Centre and Greater Manchester Civil Justice Centre and Manchester Outer. The scope of the jurisdiction is set out in the schedule to the Practice Direction and the pilot runs for a period of 12 months, from 1 October 2015 to 30 September 2016.

PART 3

THE COURT'S CASE AND COSTS MANAGEMENT POWERS

I.   Case Management

Extending or shortening time limits

Replace the sixth paragraph with:

3.1.2   As to extending time limits in consent orders, see *Siebe Gorman & Co Ltd v Pneupac Ltd* [1982] 1 W.L.R. 185; [1982] 1 All E.R. 377, CA; *Ropac Ltd v Inntrepreneur Pub Co* [2001] C.P. Rep 31; [2001] L. & T.R. 10; *Zappia Middle East Construction Co Ltd v Clifford Chance (Extension of Time)* [2001] EWCA Civ 1387; and *Placito v Slater* [2003] EWCA Civ 1863; [2004] 1 W.L.R. 1605, CA and *Safin (Fursecroft) Ltd v Badrig* [2015] EWCA Civ 739. In *Siebe Gorman* the Court of Appeal made the point that when an order is expressed to be made "by consent" it is ambiguous. One meaning is that the words evidence a real contract between the parties (i.e. a contract excluding the jurisdiction of the court to extend time) in which case the court would only interfere with such an order on the same grounds as it would with any other contract. The other meaning is that the words mean "the parties hereto not objecting". In the latter case there is no real contract and the order can be varied by the court in the same circumstances as any other order. In *Ropac*, Neuberger J. held that given the overriding objective under r.1.1, the court had jurisdiction under r.3.1(2)(a) and r.3.9 to extend a time limit even where this was contrary to an agreement between the parties. This was a wider jurisdiction than under the RSC. However, he added that the court should place very great weight on what the parties have agreed and should be slow, save in unusual circumstances, to depart from what the parties have agreed. In *Safin (Fursecroft) Ltd v Badrig's Estate* [2015] EWCA Civ 739, the Court of Appeal reviewed the many cases cited above and held that, not only is there jurisdiction under the CPR to extend any time limits in a consent order, including an order which resolved the substantive dispute between the parties and even where the parties have stated expressly that time is of the essence, but also that the discretion is not limited to the existence of "unusual circumstances". Rather, the weight to be given to the fact of the parties' agreement will depend on all the circumstances, of which the fact that the agreement was one disposing of the substantive dispute rather than a case management decision will always be highly important and often decisive.

Add new paragraph after the sixth paragraph:

In *Safin* the Court of Appeal neither approved nor disapproved the case law on the power of the court to discharge or vary undertakings given to the court. *Di Placito v Slater* [2003] EWCA Civ 1863; [2004] 1 W.L.R. 1605, in which the Court of Appeal considered *Eronat v Tabbah* [2002] EWCA Civ 950 and especially the observations of Mance LJ at paragraphs [20] and [21] of that case, is authority that the discretion of the court to discharge or modify a time limit contained in a voluntary undertaking can only be exercised if there are "special circumstances".

Making orders subject to conditions

After the fourth paragraph beginning "In Huscroft v P&O Ferries (above)", add new paragraph:

3.1.4   In *Deutsche Bank AG v Unitech Global Ltd* [2016] EWCA Civ 119, 3 March 2016, CA, unrep., the Court of Appeal (1) noted that the *Huscroft v P&O Ferries* case (above) provides authority for the proposition that, where there is a specific rule in the CPR which deals with a particular type of application, r.3.1(3) cannot be relied upon as a means of circumventing the requirements of that specific rule, (2) explained that, where on an application for summary judgment under Part 24 the court makes a conditional order requiring a party to pay money into court and providing that "that party's claim will be dismissed or his statement of case struck out if he does not comply", the court's power to make such an order is not derived from any specific rule in Part 24 but is derived from r.3.1(3), and (3) held, accordingly, that the court below erred in considering the claimant's application for a conditional order, first in reliance on Part 24 and then, separately, under r.3.1(3). (See further para.24.6.6 below.)

Varying or revoking final orders

Add new paragraph at end:

3.1.12   The court's power under r.3.1(7) to vary or revoke an order could not be used to support a second application to set aside a default judgment under r.13.3; see: *Samara v MBI & Partners UK Ltd* [2016] EWHC 441 (QB), applying *Roult*.

Early neutral evaluation

Replace the second paragraph with:

3.1.20   ENE is a form of dispute resolution which has been developed by judges seeking to further the overriding objective by actively managing cases, such that they help the parties settle the whole or part of the case (see in particular the decision of HH Judge Birss as he then was in *Fayus Inc v Flying Trade Group Plc* [2012] EWPCC 43; and see *Frey v Labrouche* [2012] EWCA Civ 881 at [41] in which Lord Neuberger made it clear that judges are permitted to express preliminary views as to points at issue). The court's decision whether or not to conduct ENE is not dependent in any way on the consent of the parties. It is simply part of the court's inherent jurisdiction to control proceedings. However, if all parties seek ENE, the court will usually give directions for it unless it decides that ENE would not be appropriate in that case (see, for instance the guidance given in The Chancery Guide 2016 para.18.7, see Vol.2, para.1A-139).

After the second paragraph (beginning with "ENE is a form") add new paragraph:
If ENE takes place, the decision whether to accept the evaluation given by the court is entirely dependent upon the consent of the parties. The provisional views expressed by the court are not by themselves binding upon the parties unless they consent to the making of an order giving effect to them (see *Seals v Williams* [2015] EWHC 1829 (Ch); [2015] 4 Costs L.O. 423, Norris J).

Improper collateral purpose

Add new paragraph at end:
In *Sobrinho v Impresa Publishing SA* [2016] EWHC 66 (QB); [2016] E.M.L.R. 12, Dingemans J, it **3.4.3.4.1** was held that although the meaning of the words complained of in a newspaper article, which was the subject of libel proceedings brought by an international banker against a Portugese publishing company, implied illegality on the part of the banker, publication of the article had not caused serious harm to the banker's reputation in England and Wales. The claimant's reputation had been so effectively restored by the reporting of his and other evidence to a Parliamentary inquiry in Portugal that the pursuit of the instant proceedings was "not worth the candle" and was an abuse of process, *Jameel* applied.

Other forms of abuse

Add new paragraph at end:
In *Lewis v Ward Hadaway (A Firm)* [2015] EWHC 3503 (Ch), it was held that the issuing of claim **3.4.3.6** forms deliberately understating the value of claims in order to defer paying higher court fees was an abuse of process. However, in the circumstances, and having regard to the overriding objective, it was held that it would be disproportionate to strike out the claims which were arguable and very substantial. To strike out the claims would be to enable the defendant to avoid claims entirely without a trial on the merits. The full fees had been paid before the claims forms were served.

Claim "totally without merit"

Replace the third paragraph with:
In *R. (Grace) v Secretary of State for the Home Department* [2014] EWCA Civ 1091; [2014] 1 W.L.R. **3.4.10** 342, the Court of Appeal stated that the proper meaning of "totally without merit" is simply "bound to fail". The court made the point that no judge would certify an application as totally without merit unless he was confident that the case was truly bound to fail. *Grace* was followed in *R. (Wasif) v Secretary of State for the Home Department* [2016] EWCA Civ 82. However, in *Wasif*, the court warned that an application should not be labelled as being totally without merit merely because it was unsuccessful. The court should distinguish between an unsuccessful application in respect of which some rational argument could be raised and an unsuccessful application in support of which no rational argument could be raised. Whilst it might be said that both types of claim were "bound to fail", the making of a "totally without merit" certificate was appropriate only in the latter case (see [15] to [17]).

Effect of rule in general terms

Replace the last paragraph with:
It should be noted that r.3.9 comes into play, not merely where a party has failed to comply **3.9.1** with any rule, etc., but only where a sanction is imposed as a result of that failure. The rule in its current form was first implemented in April 2013 (see further, paras 3.9.2 and 3.9.3, below). The new wording gave rise to an avalanche of new cases in respect of which the Court of Appeal has now clearly re-stated how the courts should deal with applications under r.3.9 (the *Mitchell/Denton* principles, as to which see paras 3.9.3 to 3.9.4.4, below). These principles now underscore the court's approach to rule-compliance in all circumstances whether or not r.3.9 itself is engaged (see further on this, paras 3.9.5 ("Effect of *Mitchell/Denton* principles on applications to set aside default judgments") and 3.9.7 ("Effect of *Mitchell/Denton* principles in all cases of non-compliance").

The first stage: assess seriousness and significance of breach

Add new paragraph at end:
British Gas Trading Ltd v Oak Cash and Carry Ltd [2016] EWCA Civ 153, involved an unless order **3.9.4.1**

following a failure to file a pre-trial checklist. The Court of Appeal held that in assessing the seriousness or significance of the breach of an unless order it was also necessary to look at the underlying breach. It was not possible to look at an unless order in isolation. The reference in the first sentence of paragraph 27 in *Denton* to "unrelated failures" is a reference to earlier breaches of rules or orders which the applicant has committed during the course of the litigation. The phrase "the very breach" in para.27 of *Denton*, when applied to an unless order, means: the failure to carry out the obligation which was (a) imposed by the original order or rule and (b) extended by the unless order. Jackson LJ, giving the leading judgment, added that the very fact that a party has failed to comply with an unless order (as opposed to an 'ordinary' order) is undoubtedly a pointer towards seriousness and significance. However, it was acknowledged that not every breach of an unless order is serious or significant. See 3.9.4.3 for the court's consideration of the third stage.

The Third Stage: all the circumstances of the case, including r.3.9 (1)(a) and (b)

Add new paragraph at end:

3.9.4.3   In *British Gas Trading Ltd v Oak Cash and Carry Ltd* [2016] EWCA Civ 153 (noted in para.3.9.4.1, above), the Court of Appeal regarded the defendant's lack of promptness in applying for relief from sanction as the critical factor for consideration at the third stage. Had the application been made promptly, it would have been granted. However, when the delay in applying for relief was added to all the other factors, it could be seen that the defendant's default had substantially disrupted the progress of the action. The application for relief was refused.

Effect of Mitchell/Denton principles on applications to set aside default judgments

Add new paragraphs at end:

3.9.5   In *Gentry v Miller* [2016] EWCA Civ 141, a road accident claim was notified to the defendant's insurer in April 2013. On 8 August 2013 the claimant obtained judgment in default of an acknowledgment of service and later, on 17 October 2013, at an unopposed hearing, the damages payable were assessed at £75,089. The insurer was informed as to that assessment in late October 2013. On 25 November 2013 the defendant's insurer made a set aside application under r.13.3 in respect of the default judgment. On 10 February 2014 the solicitors nominated by the insurer made a further application to cease acting for the defendant and for an order joining the insurer as a second defendant in order to allege that the claim was fraudulent. After some further proceedings, including an application made under r.39.3, the orders sought in the February application were made, the default judgment was set aside on an application under r.13.3 and the judgment for £75,089 was set aside under r.39.3 (judgment at trial obtained in the absence of a party). The claimant's first appeal as to these set asides were heard and dismissed. On the claimant's second appeal, the Court of Appeal reinstated both the default judgment and the judgment for £75,089. It was held that the *Mitchell/Denton* principles were relevant to the application to set aside a default judgment and also to the application under CPR r.39.3 once the express requirements of those rules had been considered (see [23] and [24]).

As to r.13.3 the insurer had shown real prospects of success but could not show that it had acted promptly once it knew or ought to have known of the default judgment. It had inexcusably delayed action for more than 2 months. The defendant's insurer first knew of the possibility of a claim in April 2013 and of the commencement of proceedings in July 2013 and knew or ought to have known of the default judgment on 19 September 2013 if not earlier, but did not make a set aside application until 25 November 2013 (see [31]). As to r.39.3 the court must first consider the three mandatory requirements of CPR r.39.3(5), before considering the question of whether relief from sanctions is appropriate, applying the *Mitchell/Denton* principles. The promptness of the application is a pre-condition under CPR r.39.3(5)(a). In this case the insurer had not applied promptly but had delayed for approximately 4 months, from October to February (see [40]).

Had the court had to apply the *Mitchell/Denton* principles, questions of delay would also have been considered at the outset but not in respect of the failure to apply promptly. The sanction from which relief was sought in respect of the default judgment would have been the failure to file an acknowledgment of service. The sanction from which relief was sought in respect of the judgment for £75,089 would have been the failure to attend the trial. The promptness of the application would have been considered only at stage three (as part of all the circumstances). On the facts, the insurer's allegations of fraud would not have been a determinative factor under the *Mitchell/Denton* principles. Thus, as to the fraud allegation, the insurer would have to pursue what remedies it could by way of a new fraud action (see [41]).

3.9.6.4   *Change title of paragraph:*

Breach which does not imperil future hearing dates or otherwise disrupt the case in hand or litigation generally

Add new paragraph at the beginning:

In *Denton* the Court of Appeal accepted that, in many cases, a court might conclude that a breach is not serious or significant if it does not imperil future hearing dates and does not otherwise disrupt this case or litigation generally. Nevertheless it declined to adopt this as a test of seriousness and significance, holding that some breaches are serious even though they are incapable of affecting the efficient progress of litigation, e.g. a failure to pay court fees (see judgment at [26] and see *Joshi and Welch Ltd v Taj Foods Ltd* [2015] EWHC 3905 (QB), Green J).

No good reason for breach

Replace first paragraph with:

Case examples of reasons held not to be good reasons explaining a failure to comply with a rule, **3.9.6.9**
practice direction or order include the following: "...overlooking a deadline will rarely be a good reason" ([41]); "...well-intentioned incompetence, for which there is no good reason, should not usually attract relief from a sanction unless the default is trivial" ([48]). See also *Newland Shipping & Forwarding Ltd v Toba Trading FZC* [2014] EWHC 210 (Comm); [2014] 2 Costs L.R 279; Hamblen J (the loss of legal representation as a result of a dispute over fees payable in respect of it); *British Gas Trading Ltd v Oak Cash & Carry* [2014] EWHC 4058 (QB) (upheld on appeal; [2016] EWCA Civ 153), McGowan J (personal difficulties suffered by the applicant's solicitor whose wife was subject to ongoing medical problems, where the solicitor was a member of a firm large enough to enable work to be delegated to other fee earners with sufficient experience and skill to ensure that tasks were properly completed).

Replace the third paragraph with:

The fact that a litigant was awaiting a funding decision by the Legal Aid Agency does not, by itself, amount to a good reason for missing a deadline; it is no more than a factor which may be taken into account (*R. (Kigen) v Secretary of State for the Home Department* [2015] EWCA Civ 1286; [2016] 1 W.L.R. 723). To hold otherwise would place those who apply for and obtain legal aid in a better position than those who, through no fault of their own, are forced to represent themselves (Moore-Bick LJ at [18]).

Relevance of "all the circumstances"

In the second paragraph, replace "Abdulle v Commissioner of Police of the Metropolis [2015] EWCA Civ 1260" with:

Abdulle v Commissioner of Police of the Metropolis [2015] EWCA Civ 1260; 2016 1 W.L.R. 898 **3.9.6.11**

Replace the fourth paragraph with:

The fact that the non-compliance has caused the loss or adjournment of a trial date is often fatal to the grant of relief (see for example *British Gas Trading Ltd v Oak Cash & Carry Ltd* [2016] EWCA Civ 153, trial date lost because a trainee solicitor filed a directions questionnaire in mistake for a listing questionnaire, thereby breaching an unless order; the loss of the trial date was regarded as a matter of grave concern bearing in mind the impact that it would have not only on the conduct of this case but also on other cases awaiting dates for hearings).

Add new paragraph at end:

Allegations of fraud do not give rise to any exemption from of disapplication of the *Mitchell/Denton* principles even where those allegations have real prospects of success (*Gentry v Miller* [2016] EWCA Civ 141, noted in para.3.9.5, above).

Delete paragraph 3.9.6.13 "Other non-compliance cases governed by Mitchell/Denton principles".

Delete paragraph 3.9.6.14 "Non-compliance cases not governed by Mitchell/Denton principles".

Replace title and paragraph with: **3.9.7**

Effect of Mitchell/Denton principles in all cases of non-compliance
The *Mitchell/Denton* principles now underscore the court's approach to rule-compliance generally whether or not a particular failure to comply with a rule, practice direction or court order has resulted in the imposition of an express sanction. As to applications to strike out a statement of case under r.3.4(2)(c) see *Walsham Chalet Park Ltd v Tallington Lakes Ltd* [2014] EWCA Civ 1607; [2015] C.P.Rep 16, noted in para.3.4.1, above. As to applications to set aside default judgments, see para.3.9.5, above. As to out-of-time applications for extensions of time (implied sanction cases) see *Elliott v Stobart Group Ltd* [2015] EWCA Civ 449 and *R. (Hysaj) v Secretary of State for the Home Department* [2014] EWCA Civ 1633; [2015] 1 W.L.R. 2472 noted in para.3.9.6.7. As to applications to amend statements of cases, see *Hague Plant Ltd v Hague* [2014] EWCA Civ 1609, noted in paras 16.4.1 and 17.3.5, below. As to applications under r.39.3 to set aside a judgment at trial made in the applicant's absence, see *Gentry v Miller* [2016] EWCA Civ 141 noted in para.3.9.5. The *Mitchell/Denton* principles do not apply to in-time applications for extensions of time (see para.3.9.6.2), there being no non-compliance in such cases. As yet there is no caselaw stating whether or not the *Mitchell/Denton* principles affect the court's approach to cases falling within r.3.10 (General power of the court to rectify matters where there has been an error of procedure) as to which, see paras 3.10.1 to 3.10.3, below.

II. Costs Management

Costs management to be prospective not retrospective

Add new paragraph at end:

3.12.2   In *Sarpd Oil International Ltd v Addax Energy SA* [2016] EWCA Civ 120, the Court of Appeal was concerned with the role of costs budgets in determining the scope of an order for security for costs. The court described how the costs budgeting regime operates and stated that although a costs budget set out the incurred costs element and the estimated costs element, under CPR PD3E para.7.4 the court did not formally approve the incurred costs element but only the estimated costs element; and it was only in relation to that approved estimated costs element that the court would not depart from the approved budget "unless satisfied that there is good reason to do so" r.3.18(b). However, the court could still comment on the incurred costs element of costs budgets, as well as take them into account when considering the reasonableness and proportionality of items in the estimated costs element. Those comments will carry significant weight when exercising its general discretion as to costs at the end of a trial. Therefore, depending on the court's comments, the practical effect of a comment on already incurred costs might be similar to the effect of formal approval of the estimated costs element in a cost budget. Significantly, Sales LJ, giving the judgment of the court, stated that parties coming to the first CMC to debate their respective costs budgets therefore know that that is the appropriate occasion on which to contest the costs items in those budgets, both in relation to the incurred costs elements in their respective budgets and in relation to the estimated costs elements.

Effect of rule

Replace with:

3.14.1   This rule is explicit and the consequences of failure to comply Draconian; the defaulting party is deemed to have filed a budget comprising only the applicable court fees. Rule 3.18 provides that, when assessing costs on the standard basis where a costs management order has been made, the court will not depart from an approved or agreed budget unless satisfied that there is "a good reason to do so". It would seem that, when assessing costs, the court may also depart from a deemed budget if satisfied that there is "a good reason to do so". In one respect r.3.14 is narrower than it appears: it is not engaged if a party merely fails to exchange a budget with another party. The sanction of a deemed budget is applied only if a party fails to file a budget with the court. However, in another respect, the rule is much wider than it appears: in *Mitchell v News Group Newspapers Ltd* [2013] EWCA Civ 1537; [2014] 1 W.L.R. 795; [2013] 6 Costs L.R. 1008, CA, the Court of Appeal confirmed that r.3.14 applies not only to parties who fail to file a budget at all, but also to parties who fail to file a budget within the time prescribed by r.3.13 (see judgment at [30]). In *Mitchell* the Court of Appeal stated that the merit of this rule is that it sets out a stark and simple default sanction which applies unless relief from sanctions is appropriate (as to which see para.3.9.3, above). In that case, the failure to file a costs budget in time had caused the cancellation of a hearing in another case and the Master's decision to refuse to grant relief from sanctions was upheld. In other cases, where the consequences of breach were not so material, the late service of a costs budget was held to be neither serious nor significant and relief from sanctions was granted (see for example *Utilise TDS Ltd v Cranstoun Davies* [2014 EWHC 834 (Ch) (45 minutes delay), *Azure East Midlands Ltd v Manchester Airport Group Property Developments Ltd* [2014] EWHC 1644 (TCC) (2 days delay) and *Murray v BAE Systems Plc*, 22 December 2015, unrep., HH Judge Peter Gregory, (7 days delay)).

Approving budgets and withholding approval

To the end of the first paragraph, add:

3.15.2   In *Group Seven Ltd v Nasir* [2016] EWHC 620 (Ch), Morgan J directed the parties to review their budgets having regard to a miscellany of points set out in his written judgment.

PRACTICE DIRECTION 3D—MESOTHELIOMA CLAIMS

"Mesothelioma"

Replace the fourth paragraph with:

3DPD.1.1   In May 2002 a special list for asbestos related illness claims was set up at the Royal Courts of Justice (RCJ), which is now conducted by Master Eastman, Master Fontaine, Master Davison, Master Gidden and some deputy masters of the Queen's Bench Division, and administered by staff there (contact: qb.asbestos@hmcts.gsi.gov.uk). Over the years, an efficient practice has been developed in that list to resolve claims for damages for mesothelioma (most of which are made against former employers) quickly and wherever possible, to provide compensation during the lifetime of the victim of exposure either by interim payment or full assessment of damages. Experience in that list has shown that in over 95 per cent of claims, there is no real prospect of success of any defence and that if liability can be eliminated as an issue at an early stage, by pro-active use of the court's case management powers, then almost all claims can be quickly timetabled and managed to settlement of the issue of quantum. Experience has also shown that in many claims in which life expectancy is short and which need to be dealt with expeditiously, where there is some probability of a real prospect of a defence being shown which relates to exposure and breach of duty, the alleged victim'sevidence should be taken on deposition and recorded on a DVD and a transcript made available, in case death occurs before any sort of trial can be arranged and the victim's evidence is lost.

"At the first case management conference the court will …"

Replace with:

It is the practice in all mesothelioma claims for the court not only to order an early CMC but **3DPD.6.5** also at that first CMC wherever possible to set the date for (and timetable to) an assessment of damages, on the supposition that the defendant will not be, or has not been, able to show cause. If the defendant does show cause that date or one as near to it as possible can be used for a trial. Directions will be issued based upon **PF 52A** (April 2016 edition) and no other standard form.

PART 6

SERVICE OF DOCUMENTS

I. Scope of this Part and Interpretation

"claim" "claim form"

Replace the third paragraph with:

For date of service of a claim form see r.6.14. Where the particulars of claim are contained in a **6.2.3** separate document and are not served with the claim form, the particulars of claim are not "a claim form" for the purposes of Pt 6 and the deemed service provisions in r.6.26 will apply to the particulars of claim when served in the United Kingdom. The combined effect of rr.6.3, 6.14, 7.5(1) and 6.26 is that where the Claim Form and Particulars of Claim are separate, but delivered together, the only method of service that would give the same date of deemed service for both Claim Form and Particulars of Claim is service by first class post, or by document exchange or other service that provides delivery on the next business day. See table in Note 6APD.10. Unless the context of the method of service, "of necessity" means that the claim form served will be a copy of the original sealed by the court, as for example service by fax or other electronic means, for service to be valid, an original claim form sealed by the court must be served: *Hills Contractors and Construction Ltd v Struth* [2013] EWHC 1693 (TCC); [2014] 1 W.L.R. 1 (Ramsey J). (Though see the earlier first instance decision in *Weston v Bates* [2012] EWHC 590 Q.B., 15 March 2012, unrep.).

II. Service of the Claim Form in the Jurisdiction or in specified circumstances within the EEA

Effect of rule (r.6.5)

Replace the second paragraph with:

Personal service is one of the "methods of service" for the service of claim forms listed in **6.5.1** r.6.3(1). In the CPR the most important of the provisions stating that service of documents (whether documents in the form of originating process or some other form) should be by the method of personal service are those found in Part 81 relating to applications and proceedings in relation to contempt of court and the service of certain documents (including court orders) in such applications and proceedings. The appropriate form of originating process for proceedings falling within Section III of Part 81 (Committal for interference with the due administration of justice) is Part 8 claim form. Rule 81.14(1) states that the claim form must be served personally on the respondent "unless the court otherwise directs".

Practice and supporting evidence

Add new paragraph at end:

There is a warning for practitioners in the drafting of an order under r.6.15 in *Dubai Financial* **6.15.2** *Group LLC v National Private Air Transport Services* [2016] EWCA Civ 71 where the CA held,

Longmore J dissenting, that the requirement in r.6.15(4)(c) that an order "must" specify the period for filing an acknowledgement of service, behoved the judge to specify a date for that, and if a defendant was never under a valid obligation to acknowledge service, either as specified by the Rules or by an order of court, then judgment in default could not be entered against it because it was not in default at all.

Retrospective operation—"steps already taken"

Add new paragraphs at end:

6.15.5   But note that in *OOO Abbott v Econowall UK Ltd* [2016] EWHC 660 (IPEC) it was held that applications under r.6.15 were to be considered in the light of *Abela v Baadarani* [2013] UKSC 44; 1 W.L.R. 2043, and the court rejected the defendants' contention that the case of *Bethel Construction Ltd* (see above) meant that the requirements of CPR r.7.6(3) were to be imported into r.6.15 in cases concerning failure to serve a claim form in time. The case involved conduct falling short of the overriding objective, which, together with the fact that the defendants knew the content of the claim form by delivery of a photocopy of the unsigned claim form, amounted to sufficient collectively to authorise service retrospectively, deemed by delivery of the unsigned photocopy claim form.

In *Barton v Wright Hassall LLP* [2016] EWCA Civ 177 the CA considered the correct approach when considering for the purposes of r.6.15(2) whether steps taken by a claimant to bring a claim form to defendant's attention, but falling short of compliance should be deemed to count as 'good service'. The CA dismissed an application by a litigant in person for an order for alternative service where the claim form had been attempted to be served by email, the claimant mistakenly thought that service by email was permitted, where the defendant's solicitors conduct could not be criticised, they had done nothing to encourage the claimant to believe that he had effected good service and the claimant had received correspondence with the correct address for service. At para.19 the court summarises the authorities and current state of the law regarding validation of service.

In *Gee 7 Group Ltd v Personal Management Solutions Ltd*[2016] EWHC 891 (Ch); 6 April 2016, unrep. (Arnold J, Ch. D.) the court held that, even looked at cumulatively, the factors relied upon for seeking a retrospective order for alternative service, namely (a) the claim form being brought to the defendants' attention; (b) the limitation period not expiring and therefore the ability to issue another claim form; (c) the absence of prejudice if service was treated as effective; (d) the assertion that the claimants thought they were entitled to serve the defendants' solicitors; and (e) no denial of authority by the defendants' solicitors, were not good enough reasons for authorising service by an alternative method.

Service abroad of domestic process

Add new paragraph at end:

6.15.7   In *Maughan v Wilmot* [2016] EWHC 29 (Fam) involving the equivalent provision to r.6.15 in the FPR, permission had been granted to serve by email on the applicant husband because he had been travelling between a number of countries when service was attempted. The husband applied to set aside default judgment on the grounds that the Hague Convention on Service applied and the court should be reluctant to order service by alternative means where the convention or a bilateral treaty applied. The application was refused, holding that a good reason not to serve under the Convention and grant an order for alternative service would be, as here, delay and inability to pin down the defendant's location.

Effect of rule (r.6.18)

Add new paragraph at end:

6.18.1   In *Tanir v Tanir* [2015] EWHC 3363 (QB) the operation of the deeming provision in r.6.18(2) was considered. Because in the instant case it was far from certain on the evidence that the court ever had served the claim form by post, it was held that the claimant could not rely on the rule and a default judgment was set aside.

III.   Service of Documents other than the Claim Form in the United Kingdom or in specified circumstances within the EEA

Effect of rule (r.6.22)

Replace the third paragraph with:

6.22.1   Personal service is one of the "methods of service" for the service of documents (other than claim forms) listed in r.6.20(1). An example of provisions in the CPR requiring service by the method of personal service of such documents is r.71.3 (expressed as subject to the court's power to dispense with service); note also r.65.3 (service of applications for housing injunctions), Practice Direction (Interim Injunctions) para.7.4 (service of search orders) (see para.25APD.7 below). In Part 81 (Applications and proceedings in relation to contempt of court) numerous rules provide for personal service of documents; see rr.81.6, 81.7(1) and (2), 81.15(5), 81.22, 81.23(1), 81.26(4), 81.34(2) and 81.35. Where those provisions take effect it is commonly further provided that, by rule or by court order, either that service may be dispensed with or that it may effected by an alternative method; see rr.81.8, 81.15(6), 81.24 and 81.26(5).

In the fourth paragraph, after "other stipulated method.", replace "Examples are" with:
An example is

IV. Service of the Claim Form and other Documents out of the Jurisdiction

Service of claim form in Scotland or Northern Ireland—permission not required where court has power to determine claim under the 1982 Act (r.6.32(1))

Replace the third paragraph (where the citation for Cook v Virgin Media Ltd has changed) with:
In *Cook v Virgin Media Ltd* [2015] EWCA Civ 1287; [2016] I.L.Pr. 6, the Court of Appeal **6.30.7** explained that the several rules in Sch.4 do not mirror the Judgments Regulation, but reproduce provisions of the Regulation with modifications, tailored to make them appropriate to UK domestic law (para.30). The rules set out in Sch.4 apply in relation to the international jurisdiction of the UK courts, as well as where there is no international question of jurisdiction (e.g. in cases where there is simply a question of whether the English courts or the Scottish courts have jurisdiction) (ibid).

Principles upon which permission to serve outside the jurisdiction is granted

Rule 6.36 and para.3.1 of 6BPD

Replace the fourth paragraph (where the citation for Brownlie v Four Seasons Holdings Inc has changed) with:
In *CH Offshore Ltd v PDV Marina SA* [2015] EWHC 595 (Comm) the court rejected a defendant's **6.37.15.1** argument that a third party was a necessary and property party under CPR PD 6B para.3.1(4). There was no single investigation to be carried out in respect of the main claim and the third party claim, and they were not bound by a common thread. They arose under very different contracts which gave rise to different and separate issues and were not back-to-back. In *Brownlie v Four Seasons Holdings Inc* [2015] EWCA Civ 665; [2015] C.P. Rep. 40 the CA held that consequential loss suffered in England as a result of an accident abroad is insufficient to found English jurisdiction. Such loss does not constitute "damage ... sustained within the jurisdiction" for the purposes of the tort jurisdiction gateway in CPR PD 6B para.3.1(9)(a). This gateway has to be interpreted consistently with the European regime on jurisdiction and applicable law. The judgment also contains clarification on the standard of proof: see *Canada Trust Co v Stolzenberg* above. It follows *Erste Group Bank AG (London) v JSC (VMZ Red October)* [2015] EWCA Civ 379, where a differently constituted CA doubted whether it was correct to interpret "damage" for the purposes of the tort jurisdictional gateway as extending to consequential loss, and expressly stated that it had "serious reservations as to whether those first instance cases were right" in relation to the first instance decisions of *Booth v Phillips* [2004] EWHC 1437 (Comm); [2004] 1 W.L.R. 3292, *Cooley v Ramsey* [2008] EWHC 129 (QB) (see para.6.37.43 below). The effect of those decisions is to reverse the trend of those first instance decisions in widening the test for the jurisdictional gateway under CPR PD 6B para.3.1(9)(a).

PRACTICE DIRECTION 6A—SERVICE WITHIN THE UNITED KINGDOM

Add new paragraph 6APD.10.1:

Editorial note
Comparison of deemed dates of service for Claim Form and Particulars of Claim when **6APD.10.1** Particulars of Claim are served separately from Claim Form.

METHOD OF SERVICE CPR 6.3 and 6.26	DEEMED DATE OF SERVICE OF CLAIM FORM CPR 6.14 and 7.5(1); 6.5(3)	DEEMED DATE OF SERVICE OF PARTICULARS OF CLAIM CPR 6.26
First Class Post, document exchange or other service that provides delivery on the next business day	The second business day after completion of the step. e.g. posted, left with, delivered to or collected by the relevant document delivery service on Monday, deemed served on Wednesday (unless Monday is a Bank Holiday, then deemed service on Thursday); or posted, left with, delivered to	The second day after it was posted, or left with, delivered to or collected by the relevant service provider, provided that day is a business day, if not the next business day after that day. e.g. posted, left with, delivered to or collected by the relevant document delivery service on Monday, deemed

	or collected by the relevant document delivery service on Friday, deemed served on the following Tuesday (unless Monday is a Bank Holiday, then deemed service on Wednesday).	served on Wednesday posted, left with, delivered to or collected by the relevant document delivery service on Friday, deemed served on the followingMonday (unless Monday is a Bank Holiday, then deemed service on Tuesday).
Delivery of the document or leaving it at the relevant place	Second business day after delivering to or leaving at the relevant place. e.g. delivered /left on Monday, served on Wednesday; (unless Monday is a Bank Holiday, then deemed service on Thursday) delivered/left on Friday, deemed served on Tuesday (unless Monday is a Bank Holiday, then deemed service on Wednesday).	If delivered/left at permitted address on a business day before 4pm, on that day, or in any other case, the next business day. e.g. delivered/left 4pm Monday, deemed served Monday (unless Monday is a Bank Holiday, then deemed service on Tuesday); delivered/ left 5pm Monday, deemed served Tuesday delivered/left 4pm Friday, deemed served Friday; delivered/left 5pm Friday, deemed served the following Monday (unless Monday is a Bank Holiday, then deemed service on Tuesday).
Personal Service	Second business day after leaving claim form in accordance with r.6.5 (3). e.g. left on Monday, deemed served on Wednesday (unless Monday is a Bank Holiday, then deemed service on Tuesday); left on Friday, deemed served on the following Tuesday (unless Monday is a Bank Holiday, then deemed service on Wednesday).	If served personally before 4.30pm, on a business day, on that day, or in any other case, the next business day. e.g. personally delivered 4pm Monday, deemed served Monday (unless Monday is a Bank Holiday, then deemed service on Tuesday); personally delivered 5pm Monday, deemed served Tuesday personally delivered 4pm Friday, deemed served Friday; personally delivered 5pm Friday, deemed served the following Monday (unless Monday is a Bank Holiday, then deemed service on Tuesday).
Fax	Second Business day after transmission of the fax is completed. e.g. transmission of fax completed on Monday, deemed served on Wednesday (unless Monday is a Bank Holiday, then deemed service on Thursday); transmission of fax completed on Friday, deemed served on the following Tuesday (unless Monday is a Bank Holiday, then deemed service on Wednesday).	If transmission of the fax is before 4.30pm on a business day, on that day, or in any other case, the next business day. e.g. transmitted 4pm Monday, deemed served Monday (unless Monday is a Bank Holiday, then deemed service on Tuesday); transmitted 5pm Monday, deemed served Tuesday; transmitted 4pm Friday, deemed served Friday; transmitted 5pm Friday, deemed served the following Monday (unless Monday is a Bank Holiday, then deemed service on Tuesday).
Email or other Electronic Method	Second Business day after sending the email or other electronic transmission. e.g. transmission on Monday, deemed served on Wednesday	If electronic transmission is before 4.30pm on a business day, on that day, or in any other case, the next business day. e.g. transmitted 4pm

	(unless Monday is a Bank Holiday, then deemed service on Thursday); transmission on Friday, deemed served on the following Tuesday (unless Monday is a Bank Holiday, then deemed service on Wednesday).	Monday, deemed served Monday (unless Monday is a Bank Holiday, then deemed service on Tuesday); transmitted 5pm Monday, deemed served Tuesday; transmitted 4pm Friday, deemed served Friday; transmitted 5pm Friday, deemed served the following Monday (unless Monday is a Bank Holiday, then deemed service on Tuesday).

NOTES ON RULES OF JURISDICTION IN JUDGMENTS REGULATION (RECAST)

A. INTRODUCTION

2. Scope and exclusions

Replace the last paragraph (where the citation for Cook v Virgin Media Ltd has changed) with:

In *Cook v Virgin Media Ltd* [2015] EWCA Civ 1287; [2016] I.L.Pr. 6, a case in which a claimant **6JR.5** domiciled in Scotland brought a claim in an English court against a company situated in England for damages for personal injuries arising from an accident in Scotland, the Court of Appeal explained (referring to a leading text) that the Regulation does not have any role where (as in the instant case) the matter "is demonstrably wholly internal to the United Kingdom", so that the only jurisdictional question which may arise is as to the part of or a place within the United Kingdom which has jurisdiction (para.25).

(b) Exclusion of arbitration (art.1.2(d))

Replace the seventh paragraph (where the citation for Gazprom OAO has changed) with:

In *Claxton Engineering Services Ltd v TXM Olaj-Es Gazkutato Kft* [2011] EWHC 345 (Comm); **6JR.7** [2011] 1 Lloyd's Rep. 510 (Hamblen J), it was explained that the anti-suit injunction granted in the Front Comor case was found by the ECJ to be incompatible with the Judgments Regulation because it interfered with the court of another Member State's deciding on its own jurisdiction under the Regulation. The judge held that an injunction restraining an arbitration in another Member State (Hungary) was not incompatible because it did not interfere with the court of a Member State deciding on its own jurisdiction; it interfered with an arbitration (albeit foreign arbitration), and arbitration is outside the scope of the Judgments Regulation. The Judgments Regulation governs conflicts of jurisdiction between courts of Member States. Arbitral tribunals are not courts of a State. In the case of *Gazprom OAO* (C-536/13) EU:C:2015:316; [2015] 1 W.L.R. 4937; [2015] 1 Lloyd's Rep. 610; [2015] I.L.Pr. 31, the ECJ ruled that where an arbitral tribunal in one Member State (State A) makes an award prohibiting a party from bringing certain claims before the courts of Member State (State B), the Judgments Regulation does not preclude the courts of State B from recognising and enforcing, or refusing to recognise or enforce, such injunctive arbitral award.

C. SPECIAL JURISDICTION: PERSON MAY BE SUED IN ANOTHER MEMBER STATE

1. Special jurisdiction—general (arts 7 and 8)

(a) Special jurisdiction—particular matters (art.7)

(i) Matters relating to contract (art.7(1))

Replace the eleventh paragraph with:

"Obligation in question" does not include a quasi-contractual obligation to make restitution **6JR.15** (*Kleinwort Benson Ltd v Glasgow City Council* [1999] 1 A.C. 153, HL). Nor does it include a claim of a co-insurer for contribution against a co-insurer in a case of double insurance: *XL Insurance Co SE (formerly XL Insurance Co Ltd) v AXA Corporate Solutions Assurance* [2015] EWHC 3431 (Comm) (Judge Waksman QC). On the other hand, the obligation in question could be the obligation to make full disclosure on placement of reinsurance in London (*Agnew v Lansforsakringsbolagens AB* [2001] 1 A.C. 223; [2000] Lloyd's Rep 317; [2000] 1 All E.R. 737, HL).

(ii)   Matters relating to tort, delict or quasi-delict (art.7(2))

To the end of the fifth paragraph (beginning "In a case of negligent mis-statement"), add:

6JR.16   In *Kolassa v Barclays Bank Plc* (C-375/13) [2015] C.E.C. 753; [2015] I.L.Pr. 14 a claim was brought against the bank on the basis of alleged mistakes and wrongful information in a prospectus issued by it. The CJEU ruled that under Art.5(3) (now Art.7(2)) the court where the investor was domiciled and had its bank account had jurisdiction as this was the place where the loss occurred.

2.   Special Jurisdiction—Insurance, Consumer and Individual Employee Contracts (arts 10 to 23)

(a)   Jurisdiction in matters relating to insurance (arts 10 to 16)

Replace the fourth paragraph with:

6JR.26   Article 11(1)(b) states that an insurer domiciled in a Member State may be sued, not only in the courts of the Member State where he is domiciled, but also in another Member State, in the case of actions brought by the policyholder, the insured or a beneficiary, in the courts for the place where the plaintiff is domiciled. Article 13(2) states that art.11 shall apply to actions brought "by the injured party directly against the insurer, where such direct actions are permitted". Article 13(3) adds that, if the law governing such direct actions provides that the policy holder or the insured may be joined as a party, then "the same court shall have jurisdiction over them". These provisions acknowledge that the national laws of Member States may differ as to whether or not actions by injured parties directly against the insurers of the persons who injured them are permitted, and that, if such actions are permitted, that the detailed substantive and procedural provisions governing such direct actions may differ. In *Hoteles Pinero Canarias SL v Keefe* [2015] EWCA Civ 598; [2016] 1 W.L.R. 904, the Court of Appeal held that under Art.11(3) (now Art.13(3)) a claimant could bring a claim in tort against the owner of a hotel in circumstances where the claimant also had a direct claim against the company's insurer as there was no requirement that the claim against the hotel's owner concerned the underlying policy or some other insurance dispute.

After the fourth paragraph (beginning with "Article 11(1)(b) states") add new paragraph:

A direct right of action against insurers in road traffic cases was required to be introduced into the laws of all Member States (insofar as it did not already exist) by Directive 2000/26/EC of the European Parliament and Council of 16 May 2000. In the United Kingdom, the direct claim for these purposes was first provided for by the European Communities (Rights against Insurers) Regulations 2002 (SI 2002/3061). A simple question arises: if a person (C) domiciled in Member State A is injured in a car accident in Member State B, where the other driver and that driver's insurers (D) are domiciled in Member State B, can C bring an action against D in the courts of Member State A? In *Odenbreit v FBTO Schadeverzekeringen NV* (C-463/06) [2007] E.C.R. I-11321; [2008] 2 All E.R. (Comm) 763; [2008] I.L.Pr. 12, the European Court of Justice ruled that the answer to this question was "yes", provided, as art.11(2) (now art.13(2)) states, such a direct action is "permitted". That settles the question of jurisdiction. (The question as to what law the court of Member State A should apply to the determination of the action is, of course, a different matter.) In a given case, the question whether or not a direct action is "permitted" is to be determined in accordance with the lex causae (not the lex fori) (*Maher v Groupma Grand Est* [2009] EWCA Civ 1191; [2010] 1 W.L.R. 1564; *Jones v Assurances Generales de France (AGF) SA* [2010] I.L.Pr. 4 (Judge Birtles)).

(b)   Jurisdiction over consumer contracts (arts 17 to 19)

Add new paragraph at end:

6JR.27   In *Hobohm v Benedikt Kampik Ltd & Co KG* (C-297/14) EU:C:2015:844; [2016] 2 W.L.R. 940 a consumer, domiciled in Germany, entered into a brokerage contract with an intermediary in Spain to buy a holiday apartment in Spain being built by a German developer and marketed in Germany via a prospectus written in German. The developer encountered financial difficulties and the intermediary proposed to the consumer to finish the work in the apartment and for that purpose a transaction management contract was concluded in Spain between the consumer and the intermediary. The consumer brought a claim for sums paid under the transaction management contact before the German courts on the basis of the special provisions relating to consumer contracts. Jurisdiction was challenged on the basis that although the brokerage contract was a consumer contract, the transaction management contract was not. The CJEU held that where a contract which was not a consumer contract was closely linked to a previous contract that was a consumer contract, the consumer could rely upon art.16(1) (now art.18(1)), and that a sufficient link was established where (i) the parties to both contracts were the same in law and fact, (ii) the economic objective of the contracts was identical and (iii) the second contract complemented the first in that it made it possible to achieve the objectives of the first contract.

(c) Jurisdiction over individual contracts of employment (arts 20 to 23)

Replace the ninth paragraph (where the citation for Petter v EMC Europe Ltd has changed) with:

6JR.28 A member of a group of companies that does not directly employ the relevant employee may be treated as an employer for the purposes of arts 20 to 23 the Judgments Regulation (*Samengo-Turner v J & H Marsh & McLennon (Services) Ltd* [2007] EWCA Civ 723; [2007] 2 All E.R. (Comm) 813; [2007] I.L.Pr. 52; *Petter v EMC Europe Ltd* [2015] EWCA Civ 828; [2016] I.L.Pr. 3 (where held that, as a stock award agreement between an American company and their employee (employed through a UK subsidiary) fell within the Regulation, the court was bound to disregard the agreement's foreign exclusive jurisdiction clause, assume jurisdiction, and grant an anti-suit injunction).

D. EXCLUSIVE JURISDICTION: JURISDICTION REGARDLESS OF THE DOMICILE OF THE PARTIES (ART. 24)

2. Rights in immovable property

Add new paragraph at end:

6JR.30 In *Komu v Komu* (C-605/14) EU:C:2015:833; [2016] 4 W.L.R. 26, the CJEU held that an action concerning a number of Finnish domiciled parties for the termination of the co-ownership of properties in Spain fell within the exclusive jurisdiction of the Spanish Court under (what is now) Art.24(1).

E. PROROGATION OF JURISDICTION (ARTS 25 AND 26)

4. Stay of proceedings where court seised on basis of exclusive jurisdiction agreement

Jurisdiction derived where defendant enters appearance (art.26)

Replace the second paragraph with:

6JR.39 Article 26 states that, apart from jurisdiction derived from other provisions of the Regulation, a court of a Member State before which a defendant enters an appearance "shall have jurisdiction". (By entering an appearance the defendant is deemed to have submitted to the jurisdiction.) The article adds that this rule shall not apply where another court has exclusive jurisdiction under art.24 (Exclusive jurisdiction) (see para.6JR.29 above). (Jurisdiction based on submission to one court does not trump, as it were, jurisdiction based on a rule of jurisdiction conferring exclusive jurisdiction on another court.) And it shall not apply where the defendant entered appearance "to contest the jurisdiction". Jurisdiction is not conferred on a court under art.26 where a defendant enters an appearance, not only for the purpose of making submissions contesting the court's jurisdiction, but additionally for the purpose of making other submissions (including submissions as to the merits of the claim). For a period uncertainty on this latter point was caused by the fact that the comparable article in the 1968 Convention, as amended (art.18), contained the phrase "solely to contest the jurisdiction". Whether or not a Defendant "enters an appearance" is a question of national procedural law provided that does not undermine the effective operation of the Regulation, see *Deutsche Bank AG London Branch v Petromena ASA* [2015] EWCA Civ 226; [2015] 1 W.L.R. 4225. For what might or might not constitute submission to the jurisdiction, see *Winkler v Shamoon* [2016] EWHC 217 (Ch), 18 February 2016, unrep.

F. Priority of Jurisdiction—Lis Pendens and Related Actions

Degree to which proceedings must be "related"

Replace the last paragraph (where the citation for Maxter Catheters SAS v Medicina Ltd has changed) with:

6JR.46 In *Maxter Catheters SAS v Medicina Ltd* [2015] EWHC 3076 (Comm); [2016] 1 W.L.R. 349 it was explained (1) that an *action en référé* brought in a French court is to be distinguished from an *action au fond*, and that the former action is a summary procedure most often used to prevent imminent harm, danger or unlawful activity, (2) that for the purposes of art.30 the *action en référé* does not appear to be relevant because it is not designed to produce a judgment on the merits, and (3) that in the instant case because the former action was not designed to resolve the substantive dispute between the parties it did not constitute proceedings parallel to proceedings in English court which gave rise to a risk of inconsistent judgments. However, the judge further explained (para.37) that under the Judgments Regulation the mere fact that the court in country A granted provisional relief will not mean that the court in country B where substantive proceedings were later commenced will be the court first seised, because, if the proceedings before the court in country A can, although they commenced with the grant of provisional relief, proceed to a determination of the substantive issue between the parties (as in an English action), then the court of country A can be regarded as the court first seised.

PART 11

DISPUTING THE COURT'S JURISDICTION

Effect of Part 11

Replace the fourth paragraph (where the citation for Cook v Virgin Media Ltd has changed) with:

11.1.1 In *Cook v Virgin Media Ltd* [2015] EWCA Civ 1287; [2016] I.L.Pr. 6, a claimant (C) domiciled in Scotland brought a claim in the English County Court against a company (D) situated in England for damages for personal injuries arising from an accident in Scotland. D filed an acknowledgment of service but made no application to stay or strike out the proceedings on forum non conveniens grounds, and made no application under r.11(1) for a declaration as to jurisdiction. On its own initiative, the court stayed the proceedings on the ground that Scotland was the most convenient forum for the claim, and after hearing submissions, in exercise of case management powers, struck out the claim on that ground. The Court of Appeal dismissed C's appeal, holding that the lower court had power, under r.3.1(2)(f), to stay or, under r.3.1(2)(m), to strike out C's claim, and expressed the opinion that the better course would be to stay rather than to strike out (especially where the defendant has admitted liability). In reaching its decision the Court rejected C's submission (made in reliance on the decision of the Court in *Hoddinott v Persimmon Homes (Wessex) Ltd* [2007] EWCA Civ 1203; [2008] 1 W.L.R. 806, CA), to the effect that (1) because D had not applied for a declaration under r.11(1), they were to be treated as having accepted the English court's jurisdiction, and (2) in those circumstances the English court should exercise that jurisdiction. The Court explained (distinguishing Hoddinott) that in the instant case the County Court was not considering whether it should decline jurisdiction under r.11, but was acting of its own initiative and exercising its case management powers in accordance with the overriding objective. The court was not prevented by D's failure to make an application under r.11(1) from exercising those powers or from exercising them in the way it did.

Replace the ninth paragraph with:

However it is inconsistent with an intention to challenge the jurisdiction that a defendant should seek an extension of time for their defence, advance a defence on the merits in reliance of a purported settlement and threaten to strike out the claim if the claimant refuses to discontinue it, *Global Multimedia International Ltd v ARA Media Services* [2006] EWHC 3612 (Ch); [2007] 1 All E.R. (Comm) 1160. The rule is strict: the application must be promptly made and be supported by evidence (r.11(4)). There is, however, power to extend time for compliance: see *Sawyer v Atari Interactive Inc* [2005] EWHC 2351 (Ch); [2006] I.L.Pr. 8, paras 42–48; *Polymer Vision R & D Ltd v Van Dooren* [2011] EWHC 2951 (Comm), [2012] I.L.Pr. 14, para 74 (Beatson J) (where the authorities are examined). A request by a defendant for an extension of time for service of a defence cannot be construed as also being a request for an extension of time for making an application to contest the jurisdiction. A request for an extension of time for service of a defence is capable of amounting to a submission to the jurisdiction. Where waiver by conduct is asserted the question is whether a reasonable person in the shoes of the claimant would have understood the defendant's conduct as waiving any irregularity as to service. Furthermore, r.11(5) carries with it a presumption of waiver; *Hoddinott v Persimmon Homes (Wessex) Ltd* [2007] EWCA Civ 1203; [2008] 1 W.L.R. 806. A defendant cannot rely upon r.3.4 to avoid the Part 11 regime: *Burns-Anderson Independent Network Plc v Wheeler* [2005] EWHC 575. If the application is successful the court will grant a declaration (see r.11(6)); if the application is not successful the acknowledgment of service ceases to have effect but the defendant may file a further acknowledgment which does then amount to a submission to the jurisdiction (see r.11(7) and (8)). If a defendant wishes to appeal against a decision rejecting its jurisdiction challenge, it should ask for an extension of time for filing a second acknowledgement of service sufficient for an application for permission to appeal or an appeal to be determined, and should not file a second acknowledgement of service as the latter will be treated as a submission to the jurisdiction, see *Deutsche Bank AG London Branch v Petromena ASA* [2015] EWCA Civ 226; [2015] 1 W.L.R. 4225. For what might or might not constitute submission to the jurisdiction, see *Winkler v Shamoon* [2016] EWHC 217 (Ch), 18 February 2016, unrep.

After the ninth paragraph (beginning with "However it is inconsistent") add new paragraph:

The periods set out in r.6.35 for the service of a defence run during the time provided for a defendant to make an application under Pt 11 with the consequence that, where a challenge is not pursued, the time for service of the defence may have expired unless extended by agreement or order; see *Flame SA v Primera Maritime (Hellas) Ltd* [2009] EWHC 1973 (Comm). Not every issue of jurisdiction has to be disposed of at this stage and the court may postpone a question of jurisdiction to a later stage where it is convenient to do so; as for instance, where the justiciability of an issue may be disputed (*Kuwait Airways Corp v Iraqi Airways Co* [1995] 1 W.L.R. 1147; [1995] 3 All E.R. 694, HL). Although not expressly stated in Pt 11, the relief granted by the court may relate to only part of the case (*Kuwait Airways Corp* above).

PART 12

DEFAULT JUDGMENT

"judgment in default of an acknowledgment of service"

Replace the second paragraph with:

12.3.1 Where a claimant has issued an application for default judgment (being unable simply to file a request) and the defendant has filed an acknowledgment of service, but did so after the period for doing so fixed by r.10.3 had expired and after the application for default judgment had been issued, the claimant is not prevented from obtaining default judgment by the defendant's late filing of an acknowledgment of service, because the question whether the conditions in r.12.3(1) are satisfied has to be judged at the time when the claimant's application is made (*Taylor v Giovani Developers Ltd* [2015] EWHC 328 (Comm), 6 February 2015, unrep. (Popplewell J), where the defendant's application for an extension of the period for filing of its acknowledgment of service was refused). In *Almond v Medgolf Properties Ltd* [2015] EWHC 3280 (Comm); 19 May 2015, unrep. Phillips J agreed with Popplewell J in *Taylor v Giovanni Developers* that on an application for default judgment, the question as is not whether the conditions in r.12.3(1) are satisfied must be considered at the date of the issue of the application. Where the acknowledgment of service is filed after the period for doing so fixed by r.10.3 had expired but before after the claimant's application for default judgment had been issued, it seems the same position obtains. That is, the defendant's late filing of the acknowledgment is ineffective to prevent the entry of default judgment unless the defendant applies for and obtains an extension of the relevant period (*Taylor v Giovani Developers Ltd*, op cit, a point doubted but not resolved in *ESR Insurance Services Ltd v Clemons* [2008] EWHC 2023 (Comm), 11 August 2008, unrep. (Blair J). Phillips J in *Almond v Medgolf Properties Ltd* said that he has some doubt as to whether default judgment could be entered where an acknowledgment of service had been filed late but before the application for default judgment had been issued. See further paras 10.2.1 and 11.1.1 above.

PART 13

SETTING ASIDE OR VARYING DEFAULT JUDGMENT

Effect of rule

Add new paragraph at end:

13.3.1 In *Samara v MBI & Partners UK Ltd* [2016] EWHC 441 (QB), 4 March 2016, unrep. Cox J held that a decision made by a judge under r.13.3 was a final decision and could not be the subject of a second application to set aside judgment or a further challenge by reference to r.3.1(7). The only way forward for a dissatisfied party is to appeal.

PART 16

STATEMENTS OF CASE

Editorial introduction

To the end of the last paragraph, add:

16.0.1 In *Sobrany v UAB Transtira* [2016] EWCA Civ 28, issues arose as to insurance taken out in support of credit hire agreements. In its Defence the defendant referred to the issue of only one insurance policy. However, when being cross-examined, the claimant stated that two policies had been issued. The Court of Appeal upheld the trial judge's decision to allow the defendant to advance arguments on the basis of this evidence. Although, generally speaking a defendant should not be permitted to advance a positive case inconsistent with its pleading, different considerations applied where a defendant sought to rely on evidence the claimant had in effect volunteered.

Defence of tender before claim

Replace with:

16.5.6 The expression "defence of tender before claim" is defined in the Glossary. The defence may be raised in response to any money claim, whether or not a specified amount is claimed. Where the defendant wishes to rely on this defence they must make a payment into court of the amount they say was tendered (r.37.3). Reliance upon this defence will often reap substantial advantages in costs for the defendant if the claimant cannot later prove an entitlement to a sum larger than was tendered. In all cases, whether claims for debts or damages, the court may treat this defence as akin to a pre-action offer to settle and therefore may make an order that the claimant should pay rather than receive costs incurred in the period after the date the tender was made. However, in damages actions, the claimant may still be entitled to an order for his costs incurred before the date of tender (contrast the common law defence of "tender before action", available in debt cases only, which, if successful, leads to an order dismissing the claim with costs against the claimant: see *RSM Bentley Jennison (A Firm) v Ayton* [2015] EWCA Civ 1120; [2016] 1 W.L.R. 1281, CA and the cases cited therein).

PART 17

AMENDMENTS TO STATEMENTS OF CASE

Late amendments

Replace the fifth paragraph with:

17.3.7 The relevant authorities on late amendment were examined and applied in *Brown v Innovatorone Plc* [2011] EWHC 3221 (Comm), 28 November 2011, unrep. (Hamblen J): relevant factors include the history as regards the amendment and the explanation as to why it was being made late; the prejudice which would be caused to the applicant if the amendment was refused; the prejudice which would be caused to the resisting party if the amendment was allowed; whether the text of the amendment was satisfactory in terms of clarity and particularity (see [5]–[14] of judgment). In *Hawksworth v Chief Constable of Staffordshire* [2012] EWCA Civ 293, CA, unrep., the Court of Appeal stated, obiter, that it might appropriate to permit an amendment at trial in respect of a matter which, although not raised in the pleadings, had nevertheless been raised in some of the witness statements and experts' reports served pre-trial (and see further on this case, and *Sobrany v UAB Transtira* [2016] EWCA Civ 28, both noted in para.16.0.1, above). In *Dany Lions Ltd v Bristol Cars Ltd* [2014] EWHC 928 (QB) (amendment sought two days before trial) Andrews J refused to allow amendments prompted by a reappraisal of the merits of the case by newly instructed counsel and stated that the practice on late amendments should also take account of the stricter views as to defaults in compliance with rules which were indicated by the Court of Appeal in *Mitchell v News Group Newspapers Ltd* [2013] EWCA Civ 1537; [2014] 1 W.L.R. 795; [2014] 2 All E.R. 430.

To the end of the sixth paragraph (beginning "The principles relevant to the determination"), add:
  Davidson v Seelig [2016] EWHC 549 (Ch), 15 March 2016, unrep. (Henderson J) at para.43).

PART 19

PARTIES AND GROUP LITIGATION

I. Addition and Substitution of Parties

"evidence" (r.19.4.(3))

Replace with:

19.4.3 See Practice Direction, para.1.3 (see para.19APD.1), Pt 32 and the Practice Direction to Pt 32 (see para.32PD.1). In *Allergan Inc v Sauflon Pharmaceuticals Ltd* [2000] All E.R. (D.) 106, Ch D, Pumfrey J refused an application to join a party as a second defendant where the claimant failed to plead a good arguable case. In *Pece Beheer BV v Alevere Ltd* [2016] EWHC 434 (IPEC) HH Judge Hacon stated that, in most cases, in order to show a good arguable case for this purpose, the correct test to be applied is that which would be applied in an application to strike out a claim against a defendant pursuant to CPR r.3.4(2)(a) or (b) (as to which, see further paras 3.4.2 and 3.4.3, above).

II.   Representative Parties

Claim form and application for permission to continue

Replace the third paragraph (where the citation for Hook v Sumner has been changed) with:

An applicant for permission under s.261 has to establish a prima facie case for the giving of **19.9A.1** permission to bring the claim in respect of a cause of action which arises from some negligence, default, breach of duty or breach of trust by a director of the company in whom that cause of action is vested. As to the meaning of the term "prima facie" in this context, see *Bhullar v Bhullar* [2015] EWHC 1943 (Ch). In deciding whether to grant permission the court must consider a range of factors including the strength of the claim and the amounts or value at stake (*Stainer v Lee* [2010] EWHC 1539 (Ch); [2011] B.C.C. 134). Normally a company should be the only party entitled to enforce a cause of action belonging to it, and that a member should only be able to maintain proceedings in relation to alleged wrongs done to the company only in exceptional circumstances (*Bamford v Harvey* [2012] EWHC 2858 (Ch); [2013] Bus. L.R. 589; *Cinematic Finance Ltd v Ryder* [2010] EWHC 3387 (Ch); [2012] B.C.C. 797). The availability of an alternative remedy is an important factor for the court to consider, but it was not an absolute bar to a grant of permission; the possibility of an alternative remedy did not mean that it was inevitable that a person seeking a derivative action would be denied permission (*Hughes v Weiss* op cit; *Parry v Bartlett* [2011] EWHC 3146 (Ch); [2012] B.C.C. 700 (bringing an "unfair prejudice" petition under Companies Act 2006, s.994 was inappropriate where the company was not trading and its shares had no value); *Cullen Investments Ltd v Brown* [2015] EWHC 473 (Ch) (Mark Anderson QC) (derivative action sought as a precautionary response to the defendant's defence in a personal action which denied that he owed relevant duties to anyone other than the company); *Hook v Sumner* [2015] EWHC 3820 (Ch), 27 November 2015, QB, HH Judge David Cooke (the claimant was entitled not to proceed by way of an unfair prejudice petition because he did not want his shares to be bought out by the majority).

III.   Group Litigation

Note

Add new paragraph at end:

In *Schmidt v Depuy International Ltd* [2016] EWHC 638 (QB) the court declined to make a GLO in **19.10.1** a number of product liability claims against the same manufacturer, even though it accepted that there were common or related issues of fact and law and a large enough group of claimants, because it concluded that the claims within the group, when subjected to scrutiny, were atypical, would not benefit from a GLO, and were not likely to be informative to the court in respect of other GLOs made in respect of other manufacturers of similar products.

Editorial note

Replace the fifth paragraph (where the citation for T (formerly H) v Nugent Care Society (formerly Catholic Social Services) has changed) with:

Subsection (e): cut-off dates only limit entry to the group litigation. They have no bearing on **19.13.1** limitation and do not preclude an individual from seeking the court's permission to join the group at a later date or to issue separate proceedings (subject to the overriding objective and proportionality). See *T (formerly H) v Nugent Care Society (formerly Catholic Social Services)* [2004] EWCA Civ 51; [2004] 1 W.L.R. 1129.

Add new paragraph at end:

In *Pearce v Secretary of State for Energy and Climate Change* [2015] EWHC 3775 (QB) Turner J extended a cut off date but observed that cut off dates were essential in GLOs to secure the good case management of the claims within its scope. The parties depend upon some level of certainty as to the cut off date in order to decide how to deploy their resources and when. Accordingly extensions to the cut off date should not be regarded as the norm. However if a mechanistic approach were taken whereby the cut off date were to regarded as sacrosanct, there is a risk that unexpected developments may give rise to a situation such as in the instant case, an accumulation of residual applications by claimants who had not met the cut off date, which would have the potential to further disrupt the progress of the GLO. Those competing matters had to be balanced.

PART 21

CHILDREN AND PROTECTED PARTIES

Effect of rule

Add new paragraph at end:

21.10.2   In *R. (C) v Secretary of State for Justice* [2016] UKSC 2; [2016] 1 W.L.R. 444, the Supreme Court stated that it is necessary to draw a distinction between ordinary civil proceedings in which a mental patient may be involved (not always as a protected party), and proceedings relating to a patient detained in a psychiatric hospital, or otherwise subject to compulsory powers, under the Mental Health Act 1983. The Supreme Court held that there should be no presumption of anonymity in every case in proceedings concerning powers under the 1983 Act. The question in all these cases is that set out in r.39.2(4): is anonymity necessary in the interests of the mental patient? A balance has to be struck to be struck between the public's right to know and who the principal actors are. An anonymity order should be made if in the absence of such an order the therapeutic enterprise involving the patient might be put in jeopardy.

PART 22

STATEMENTS OF TRUTH

Form of statement of truth

To the end of the last paragraph, add:

22.1.16   The definition of "budget" in the CPR Glossary was added by the Civil Procedure (Amendment) Rules 2013 (SI 2013/262) r.21(a) with effect from 1 April 2013, and para.2.2A was inserted in Practice Direction 22 by Update 60, with effect from the same date. The form of words in para.2.2A was substituted by Update 69 with effect from 22 April 2014, but the definition of "budget" in the Glossary was not amended in the light of this substitution. The result is that the Glossary definition is misleading.

PART 23

GENERAL RULES ABOUT APPLICATIONS FOR COURT ORDERS

Application "totally without merit"

Replace the third paragraph with:

23.12.2   Under r.23.12, consideration by the court of the question whether it is appropriate to make a civil restraint order (CRO) is triggered by a finding that the application was totally without merit (TWM). The least severe of the several forms of CRO may not be made unless at least two applications made by the party have been found to be TWM. The questions (1) whether the court should record a finding of TWM and (2) whether it is appropriate to make a CRO are distinct and raise different considerations. In *R. (Grace) v Secretary of State for the Home Department* [2014] EWCA Civ 1091, [2014] 1 W.L.R. 3432, CA, a High Court judge on paper dealt with and dismissed an application under r.54.4 for permission to proceed with a judicial review claim and, in accordance with r.23.12(a), recorded the fact that the application was totally without merit with the result that, by operation of r.54.12(7), the applicant was barred from requesting that the dismissal of the application be re-considered at a hearing. (No question of whether it was appropriate to make a CRO arose.) The Court of Appeal held that, in these circumstances, the proper test for determining whether an application is totally without merit was whether it was "bound to fail"; it was not necessary for it to be shown that the application was abusive or vexatious. Subsequently, in *R. (Wasif) v Secretary of State for the Home Department* [2016] EWCA Civ 82, 9 February 2016, CA, unrep., the Court recognised the continuing difficulty about the proper approach to be taken by the High Court or the Upper Tribunal in considering whether to certify an application for permission to apply for judicial review as TWM and gave further guidance (see further para.3.4.10 above and para.54.12.1 below).

PART 24

Summary Judgment

A conditional order

After "so (see para.4.", replace "3" with:
4

Add new paragraph at end:
The court's power to make a conditional order on a summary judgment application is not limited to cases in which the respondent raises a case (claim or defence) as to which success, although possible, is improbable. In *Deutsche Bank AG v Unitech Global Ltd* [2016] EWCA Civ 119, 3 March 2016, CA, unrep., summary judgment had been sought in respect of a loan agreement; the defendants, challenging the validity of that agreement, sought an order for rescission which, if granted, would inevitably be on terms that they must refund to the claimants the original sums borrowed. In those circumstances the Court of Appeal held that the lower court could have made a conditional order even though the defendant's case for rescission could not be said to have been improbable. The Court of Appeal held that paras 4 and 5 of Practice Direction 24 are not exhaustive of the court's options as to the orders it may make on an application for summary judgment; the relevant power to impose conditions, as to payments into court or otherwise, is not found in Part 24, but is contained in r.3.1(3) (referred to in the parenthesis following r.24.6). See further para.3.1.4 above.

Setting aside order for summary judgment

Replace the first paragraph with:
The orders the court may make on an application for summary judgment include: (1) judgment on the claim, (2) the striking out or dismissal of the claim, (3) the dismissal of the application, (4) a conditional order (Practice Direction (The Summary Disposal of Claims), para.5.1; see para.24PD.5 below). Where the applicant or any respondent to an application for summary judgment fails to attend the hearing of the application, the court may proceed in their absence. Where, in the absence of the applicant or any respondent, an order is made at the hearing, r.23.11 would appear to have the effect of enabling the court on the application of the absent party (or of its own initiative) to re-list the application for further consideration. However if, at the hearing of the application, the court gives summary judgment against the absent party, the question which then arises is whether that party may apply to the court to have the judgment set aside or varied. Under the former summary judgment rules contained in the RSC (and applied in county courts by operation of CCR Ord.9 r.14(5)), it was expressly provided that any judgment given against a party who did not appear at the hearing of an application for summary judgment could be set aside or varied by the court on such terms as it thought just (RSC Ord.14 r.11, see also RSC Ord.86 r.7). The purpose of this rule was to reverse the effect of the decision of the Court of Appeal in *Spira v Spira* [1939] 3 All E.R. 924, CA, and to remove the anomaly that, although every other judgment (including a judgment at trial) given in the absence of a defendant could be set aside (at least in certain circumstances), a summary judgment could not, though it could be made the subject of an appeal. CPR Pt 24 contains no such express provision and the omission is not made good by CPR r.39.3(3), as it is confined to the setting aside of a judgment given at trial in the absence of a party (see further para.39.3.8 below). Further, the matter is not dealt with by r.23.11, which is confined to orders made on applications (including, as suggested above, orders made on summary judgment applications other than summary judgment, e.g. conditional orders.) However, it seems to be readily assumed that the position is retrieved by Practice Direction (Summary Disposal of Claims), para.8.1 which states that, if an order for summary judgment under Pt 24 is made against a respondent who does not appear at the hearing of the application, the respondent may apply "for the order to be set aside or varied" (see para.24PD.8 below). In this context "order" includes judgment on the claim (ibid., para.5.1(1)). On the hearing of an application the court "may make such order as it thinks just" (ibid., para.8.2). It is not always easy to tell whether particular paragraphs in practice directions supplementing CPR rules are attempting (1) merely to narrate what the rules they are supplementing say, or (2) to put an authoritative gloss on those rules. In *Tubelike Ltd v Visitjourneys.com Ltd* [2016] EWHC 43 (Ch), 22 January 2016, unrep. (Chief Master Marsh), it was stated that, although the matter is not entirely free from doubt, para.8.1 of Practice Direction 24 is intended to supplement the rules in Part 24 and to give the court a power it would not otherwise have if an order is made in the absence of a party (para.20).

After the first paragraph (beginning with "The orders the") add:
Other CPR provisions permitting applications to set aside or vary judgments given in the applicant's absence set out the criteria which the court must apply (e.g., r.3.6(2) (application must be made promptly) and r.39.3(5) (application must be made promptly, good reason shown for absence

and reasonable prospects of success) and see also the *Mitchell/Denton* criteria in applications under r.3.9 and r.13.3). Practice Direction 24 does not provide any guidance about the criteria the court should apply in applications under para 8.1. In *Tubelike Ltd v Visitjourneys.com Ltd* (see above), Chief Master Marsh considered that an application under para.8.1 was analogous to an application under r.39.3 (failure to attend the trial) and so had regard to the r.39.3(5) factors (summarised above) "without being a slave to the requirements of that rule" and to the provisions of the overriding objective (r.1.1, above).

Replace "See further paras 39.3.8 and 40.9.2." with:
   See further paras 3.1.9.2 (above) and 39.3.8 and 40.9.2 (below).

PART 25

INTERIM REMEDIES AND SECURITY FOR COSTS

I. Interim Remedies

Orders in relation to relevant property (r.25.1(1)(c))

Inspection of relevant property (r.25.1(1)(c)(ii))

Add new paragraph at end:

25.1.18   The powers of the court under sub-para.(ii) of r.25.1(1)(c), and also under sub-paras (i) and (iv), were exercised in *Orb arl v Ruhan* [2015] EWHC 3638 (Comm), 14 December 2015, unrep. (Walker J). The circumstances were unusual. It was alleged that a computer hacker, having been employed to "drop" child pornography onto the computer system of the claimants for the purpose of causing injury to them, and to prejudice the fair trial of ongoing proceedings, was now offering the same materials to the claimants in return for a cash payment. The claimants wished to inspect the materials, but were concerned that to have or to access such materials would of itself be a criminal offence. The Court authorised the claimants, their lawyers and their computer experts to take custody of, preserve, inspect and experiment upon the specified materials including by interrogating the data, making appropriate reports to the police and prosecuting authorities.

Freezing injunction (formerly Mareva injunction) (r.25.1(1)(f))

Example of order to restrain disposal of assets

Replace the first paragraph with:

25.1.25.6   The example of an order for a freezing injunction annexed to Practice Direction 25A (Interim Injunctions) (see para.25APD.10 below) may be adapted for either worldwide or domestic relief. The content of the example may be modified as appropriate in any case. Any departure from the standard wording must be drawn to the attention of the judge hearing the without notice application. It is expressly provided that the court may, if it considers it appropriate, require the applicant's solicitors, as well as the applicant, to give undertakings (ibid. paras 6.1 and 6.2). The examples, modified in certain respects, are also contained in App.5 to the Admiralty and Commercial Courts Guide (see Vol.2, para.2A-162).

Varying, clarifying or revoking order

In the first paragraph, replace "para.25PFD.10" with:

25.1.25.9   para.25APD.10

Search order (formerly Anton Piller order) (r.25.1(1)(h))

Jurisdiction—county courts

After "High Court judge", add:

25.1.27.2   or a judge of the Court of Appeal

Discharge of injunction for material non-disclosure

Replace the third paragraph with:

25.3.6   In deciding what should be the consequences of any breach of duty it is necessary for the court to take account of all the relevant circumstances, including the gravity of the breach, the excuse or explanation offered, and the severity and duration of the prejudice occasioned to the defendant, including whether the consequences of the breach were remediable and had been remedied; above all, the court has to bear in mind the overriding objective and the need for proportionality (see r.1.1) (*Memory Corporation Plc v Sidhu (No.2)* [2000] 1 W.L.R. 1443, CA). For summary of the authorities on the exercise of the court's discretion to continue or re-grant the order, notwithstanding serious non-disclosure, see *Alphasteel Ltd v Shirkhani* [2009] EWHC 2153 (Ch), July 30, 2009, unrep (Teare J) (where the freezing order was limited to assets within the jurisdiction). The principles about how the court should respond to a breach of the duties of an ex parte applicant were examined in *Dar Al Arkan Real Estate Development Co v Al Refai* [2012] EWHC 3539 (Comm), 12 December 2012, unrep. (Andrew Smith J) at paras 148 & 149. See also *Metropolitan Housing Trust v Taylor* [2015] EWHC 2897 (Ch), 19 October 2015, unrep. (Warren J) at paras 36 & 37.

Effect of rule

Replace the first paragraph with:

25.6.1 For extended commentary on interim payments, see Vol.2, Section 15 Interim Remedies, subs.E, paras 15-99 to 15-132.

Replace the fourth paragraph with:

Contrary to what is said in this rule, "interim payment" is not defined by r.25.1(1)(k). That paragraph merely repeats part of the definition of interim payment given by the Senior Courts Act 1981 s.32(5) and leaves out the final phrase "to or for the benefit of another party to the proceedings" (cf. RSC Ord.29 r.9), a part of the definition that was crucial to the decision in *Securities and Investments Board v Scandex Capital Management A/S* [1998] 1 W.L.R. 712; [1998] 1 All E.R. 514, CA. In *Deutsche Bank AG v Unitech Global Ltd* [2016] EWCA Civ 119, 3 March 2016, CA, unrep., the Court of Appeal explained that section 32 only sets out a rule-making power in respect of orders for interim payments, and that it is r.25.1(1)(k) which provides the jurisdiction for the court to make such an order.

Evidence

Add new paragraph at end:

25.6.4 An application for an interim payment order must be decided by the court on the basis of the evidence before it; see further Vol.2 para.15-101.

Effect of rule

In the second paragraph, after "for further information", add:

25.7.1 as to the test to be applied

II. Security for costs

Amount of security

Replace the first paragraph with:

25.12.7 The amount of security awarded is in the discretion of the court, which will fix such sums as it thinks just, having regard to all the circumstances of the case (r.25.13(1)(a)). The court's exercise of that discretion is quintessentially a matter of case management with which an appeal court should be slow to interfere (*Stokors SA v IG Markets Ltd* [2012] EWCA Civ 1706). In some cases the amount of security may be limited to the extra burden or risk involved in seeking to enforce orders for costs subsequently obtained (see further, para.25.13.5). In other cases the amount of security may relate to the total costs likely to be incurred in opposing the claim or appeal. In cases in which a costs management order has been made (as to which, see para.3.12.1, above) the defendant's approved or agreed costs budget will be a strong guide as to the likely costs order to be made after trial, if the claim fails; this budget should be used as the relevant reference point (in relation to the incurred costs elements and also the estimated costs elements) for considering the amount which should be ordered for security for costs (*Sarpd Oil International Ltd v Addax Energy SA* [2016] EWCA Civ 120). Security is not always awarded on a full indemnity basis. If the application is made late, security may be limited to future costs only or refused altogether (and see further, para.25.12.6 "Ideal time for applying", above). In other cases one of the factors for the court to consider is the possibility that the proceedings may soon settle. In such a situation it may will be sensible to make an arbitrary discount of the costs estimated as likely future costs, but there is no hard and fast rule. Each case has to be decided on its own circumstances, and it may not always be appropriate to make such a discount. For a pre-CPR authority on this point, see *Procon (Great Britain) Ltd v Provincial Building Co Ltd* [1984] 1 W.L.R. 557, [1984] 2 All E.R. 368, CA. However, today, a frequently preferred alternative to discounting is for the court to order security for the whole costs, to be paid in instalments as the action progresses.

Replace the second paragraph with:

The amount of security allowed often takes into account costs incurred in complying with a pre-action protocol. However, as to the costs of a failed mediation incurred pre-action, see *Lobster Group Ltd v Heidelberg Graphic Equipment Ltd* [2008] EWHC 413 (TCC); [2008] 2 All E.R. 1173. If as a result of the claim the defendant commences third party proceedings (an "additional claim" as to which, see para.20.7, above) and it is likely that, if the claim fails, the claimant will also be required to pay all the costs of the third party proceedings, the amount of security to be awarded may also take into account all such costs incurred or to be incurred by the defendant and by the third party (*Sarpd Oil International Ltd v Addax Energy SA* [2016] EWCA Civ 120).

PART 26

CASE MANAGEMENT—PRELIMINARY STAGE

26.11.1 *Change title of paragraph:*

Effect of rule

Replace with:
   By the Civil Procedure (Amendment No.8) Rules 2013 (SI 2013/3112), r.26.11 was substituted with effect from 1 January 2014. The former rule required an application for a claim to be tried by a jury to be made within 28 days of service of the defence. That rule is preserved by para.(1) of the rule as replaced for a claim other than a claim for libel and slander, for which different provision is made in para.(2); see further Vol.2 para.9A-258.

26.11.2 *Change title of paragraph:*

Senior Courts Act 1981 s.69 and County Courts Act 1984 s.66

PART 29

THE MULTI-TRACK

Fixing the trial date

In the fourth paragraph (beginning "The Queen's Bench Guide"), replace "once affixed date" with:

29.2.6   once a fixed date

PART 31

DISCLOSURE AND INSPECTION OF DOCUMENTS

(c) Legal Professional Privilege generally

Use of an independent lawyer to review seized material

Replace with:

31.3.30.2   Where a search is undertaken pursuant to a search warrant, an independent lawyer should be present to assess claims made for legal professional privilege: *R. v Customs and Excise Commissioners Ex p. Popely* [1999] S.T.C. 1016; *R. v Middlesex Guildhall Crown Court ex p. Tamosius* [2000] 1 W.L.R. 453. There is a range of guidance covering the process of determining the status of potentially privileged documents, including the Attorney General's Guidelines on Disclosure (2013), Attorney General's Supplementary Guidelines on Digitally Stored Material (2011), and the Serious Fraud Office's Operational Handbook. An independent lawyer should be used to determine whether seized material is protected by legal professional privilege, as this involves close consideration of the content and context of a document or communication. However that does not mean that an independent lawyer must, as a matter of law, be used for the preliminary sift of paper or electronic material, identifying documents, files or communications as potentially attracting legal professional privilege, but without close consideration of the content and context: *R. (McKenzie) v Director of the Serious Fraud Office* [2016] EWHC 102 (Admin); [2016] 1 W.L.R. 1308, D.C. para.40. The latter case also upheld the legality of the guidance in the Serious Fraud Office's Operational Handbook.

"... under any Act for disclosure before proceedings have started"

Replace the sixth paragraph with:

31.16.1 Applications for pre-action disclosure pursuant to s.33(2) of the Senior Courts Act 1981 and CPR r.31.16 must be made prior to the commencement of proceedings, as the court does not have jurisdiction to make such an order once proceedings have been issued: *Personal Management Solutions Ltd v Gee 7 Group Wealth Limited* [2015] EWHC 3859 (Ch), paras 14-18. However pre-action disclosure under CPR r.31.16 may be ordered even where there already are other extant proceedings covering related issues, where the pre-action disclosure relates to some different causes of action not raised in the extant proceedings: *Anglia Research Services Ltd v Finders Genealogists Ltd* [2016] EWHC 297 (QB).

Rule 31.16(3)(a), (b) and (d)

After the sixth paragraph (beginning "In Black v Sumimoto"), add as a new paragraph:

31.16.4 In *Ittihadleh v Metcalfe* [2016] EWHC 376 (Ch) the Court exercised its discretion to refuse pre-action disclosure as the parties had entrenched such positions of hostility towards each other that the prospects of any disclosure, whatever it might reveal, enabling the dispute to be resolved without proceedings, was negligible and probably non-existent, and thus even though the disclosure sought was not unduly onerous, the remaining factors all weighed heavily and determinatively against making such an order.

Note

Replace the last paragraph with:

31.20.1 Permission of the court is still required even where an inadvertently disclosed document indicates that there might have been serious non-disclosure of relevant documents by a party: *Property Alliance Group Ltd v The Royal Bank of Scotland Plc* [2015] EWHC 3341 (Ch); [2016] 4 W.L.R. 3 (Birss J).

PART 35

EXPERTS AND ASSESSORS

Expert evidence at trial

Add new paragraph at end:

35.0.5 *Kennedy v Cordia (Services) LLP* [2016] UKSC 6 was a personal injury claim by a home carer who slipped on snow over ice on an ungritted sloping path to a client's home. An engineer with expertise in health and safety prepared a report for the Claimant, criticised the risk assessment carried out by the Defendant, which omitted falls in bad weather, and for not offering the Claimant anti-slip footwear attachments. The first instance court found for the Claimant but the appeal court concluded that permission should not have been given for the expert as health and safety was not a recognized area of scientific expertise, and that the Defendant had taken adequate steps to protect the Claimant. The Supreme Court thoroughly reviewed the law on the admissibility of expert evidence in civil claims, and how courts should police performance of expert's duties, and concluded that this expert's report did assist the court because the expert had direct experience of carrying out risk assessments and had conducted helpful research into how this particular risk could have been avoided. The appeal was allowed.

Personal injury and clinical negligence cases

Add new paragraph at end:

35.1.2 *Kennedy v Cordia (Services) LLP* [2016] UKSC 6 provided a helpful summary of the role of liability expert evidence in personal injury claims and concluded health and safety experts could assist the court in slipping accident at work claims.

PART 36

OFFERS TO SETTLE

I.   Part 36 Offers to Settle

Scope of Pt 36

36.2.3

Replace the second paragraph (where the citation for Van Oord UK Ltd v Allseas UK Ltd has changed) with:
Counterclaims and other additional claims—Rule 36.2(3)(a) now clarifies that Part 36 offers can be made in respect of counterclaims and other additional claims. This was always the case (see *AF v BG* [2009] EWCA Civ 757; [2009] All E.R. (D) 249; [2010] 2 Costs L.R. 164, CA) but the clarification is welcome in view of the difficulty perceived in the old rules in *F&C Alternative Investments (Holdings) Ltd v Barthelemy (Costs)* [2011] EWHC 2807 (Ch); [2012] Bus. L.R. 891, Ch D (Sales J); overturned on appeal: [2012] EWCA Civ 843; [2013] 1 W.L.R. 548; [2012] 4 All E.R. 1096, CA. The matter is put beyond doubt by the signpost at the end of this rule to rr.20.2 to 20.3 and by the wording of the new form **N242A**. When making an offer in a case concerning a counterclaim or other additional claim, it is important to make clear whether it is intended to be a claimant's or a defendant's offer. By way of example, a counterclaiming defendant may wish to make a claimant's offer (where the offer is to accept some payment on the counterclaim) or a defendant's offer (where the offer is to pay some money on the claim). Such offer may be limited to the counterclaim or claim; alternatively it may take the other adverse claim into account: see rr.36.5(1)(d) to (e). See also the guidance notes on form **N242A** and *Van Oord UK Ltd v Allseas UK Ltd* [2015] EWHC 3385 (TCC); [2016] 1 Costs L.O. 1, 30 November 2015 (Coulson J).

Costs to be determined by the court—paras (4) to (6)

36.13.3

Replace the second paragraph (where the citation for Dutton v Minards has changed) with:
In one case (that of late acceptance of an offer relating to the whole claim under r.36.13(4)(b)) express provision is made. First, in the absence of agreement, the court must, "unless it considers it unjust", make the costs orders specified by r.36.13(5). Secondly, r.36.13(6) provides that in deciding whether it would be unjust to make such orders the court will consider the matters listed in r.36.17(5). These rules are rather more elaborate than the comparable provisions that applied before 6 April 2015, which simply provided that the default orders would be made "unless the court orders otherwise". There is, however, no change to the proper approach since paras (5)–(6) codify the decisions in *PGF II SA v OMFS Co 1 Ltd* [2013] EWCA Civ 1288; [2014] 1 W.L.R. 1386; [2014] 1 All E.R. 970, CA; *SG (A Child) v Hewitt (Costs)* [2012] EWCA Civ 1053; [2013] 1 All E.R. 1118; [2012] Costs L.R. 937, CA; *Lumb v Hampsey* [2011] EWHC 2808 (QB), 11 October 2011, unrep. (Lang J); *Dutton v Minards* [2015] EWCA Civ 984; [2015] 6 Costs L.R. 1047, 16 July 2015. See also *Purser v Hibbs* [2015] EWHC 1792 (QB), 19 May 2015, unrep. (HHJ Maloney QC) for confirmation that the new rules codify *Lumb*.

"more advantageous" (r.36.17(2))

36.17.2

Replace the last paragraph with:
Where the defendant makes a payment to the claimant after the date of the Part 36 offer (not being an interim payment made generally on account of the claim) such that the value of the claim is reduced, the Part 36 offer becomes more attractive: *LG Blower Specialist Bricklayer Ltd v Reeves* [2010] EWCA Civ 726; [2010] 1 W.L.R. 2081; [2011] 2 All E.R. 258, CA. See, contra, *Littlestone v MacLeish* [2016] EWCA Civ 127; [2016] 2 Costs L.O. 275; *Times*, 15 April 2016, in which Briggs LJ doubted Blower, holding that a later payment was made on account of both the claim generally and the Part 36 offer.

Indemnity costs (r.36.17(4)(b))

36.17.4.2

Replace the first paragraph with:
Rule 36.17(4)(b) requires the court to award the claimant costs on an indemnity basis. Such order is likely to be more favourable to the claimant than would otherwise be the case. The costs to which the claimant is entitled under r.36.17(4)(b) are those which would, on the application of the principles set out in r.44.2, be awarded, disregarding the effect of the Part 36 offer (*Kastor Navigation Co Ltd v AGF MAT (Costs)* [2003] EWHC 472 (Comm); *The Times*, 29 March 2003, affirmed on this point by the Court of Appeal [2004] EWCA Civ 277; [2004] Lloyd's Rep. 199; [2005] 2 All E.R. (Comm) 720, CA. See, however, *Greenwich Millennium Village Ltd v Essex Services Group Plc* [2014] EWHC 1099 (TCC); [2014] T.C.L.R. 4 (Coulson J), at para.29). See, contra, *Webb v Liverpool Women's NHS Foundation Trust* [2016] EWCA Civ 365; 14 April 2016, unrep.: (1) the successful claimant is entitled to all of his costs on an indemnity basis, unless it would be unjust to do so, (2) the court should not first consider the costs that would have been awarded under Pt 44, (3) Kastor

distinguished. Where the offeror is treated as having filed a costs budget limited to court fees, or is otherwise limited in his recovery of costs to such fees, "costs" in r.36.17(4)(b) has the meaning given in r.36.23.

"considers it unjust to do so" (r.36.17(5))

Replace the fifth paragraph (where the citation for Yentob v MGN Ltd has changed) with:

In *Yentob v MGN Ltd* [2015] EWCA Civ 1292; [2015] 6 Costs L.R. 1103, the Court of Appeal **36.17.5** upheld a decision of Mann J to depart from the usual order in a phone-hacking case upon the claimant failing to obtain a judgment more advantageous than the newspaper's Part 36 offer on the grounds that only limited admissions had been made and it was unlikely that the defendant would have agreed to make a statement in open court pursuant to para.6.1 of the Practice Direction to Pt 53. In a passage that was approved on appeal, Mann J cautioned, at para.43,

> "In what I might call a more normal case, it seems to me that the desire to have a trial in order to have a finding of a judge in public as to what happened is unlikely to be a legitimate objective in Part 36 terms so as to justify a claimant refusing to accept a Part 36 offer and insisting on going to trial."

Rule 36.17(5)(e)—a genuine attempt to settle proceedings

To the end of the last paragraph, add:

In *Jockey Club Racecourse Ltd v Willmott Dixon Construction Ltd* [2016] EWHC 167 (TCC); [2016] 4 **36.17.5.1** W.L.R. 43; [2016] 1 Costs L.R. 123, a 95% offer was effective in an open-and-shut case.

Add new paragraph 36.17.7:

"... upon judgment being entered" (r.36.17(1))

These words should not be interpreted narrowly. Where, for example, an offer is made "net of **36.17.7** CRU benefits", it may not be possible to determine whether the offer has been effective immediately on entering judgment: *Crooks v Hendricks Lovell Ltd* [2016] EWCA Civ 8; [2016] 1 Costs L.O. 103.

Add new paragraph 36.21.2:

Editorial note

The provisions of Pt 36 trump those of Pt 45, accordingly indemnity costs are recoverable under **36.21.2** r.36.17(4) in Section IIIA cases: *Broadhurst v Tan* [2016] EWCA Civ 94; [2016] 2 Costs L.O. 155.

Add new paragraph 36.22.1.1:

"... without regard to any liability for recoverable amounts" (r.36.22(3))

Where the offer is made "net of CRU benefits" see *Crooks v Hendricks Lovell Ltd* [2016] EWCA Civ **36.22.1.1** 8; [2016] 1 Costs L.O. 103.

PART 37

MISCELLANEOUS PROVISIONS ABOUT PAYMENTS INTO COURT

Defence of tender before claim

Replace the last paragraph (where the citation for RSM Bentley Jennison (A Firm) v Ayton has been changed) with:

Ever since the CPR were introduced, the Glossary has defined "a defence of tender before **37.2.1** claim" as "a defence that, before the claimant started proceedings, the defendant unconditionally offered to the claimant the amount due or, if no specified amount is claimed, an amount sufficient to satisfy the claim" (see Glossary at Section E). Such definition purports to extend the defence of tender before claim to unliquidated claims. However, r.2.2 provides that the Glossary is "a guide to the meaning of certain legal expressions ... but is not to be taken as giving those expressions any meaning in the Rules which they do not have in the law generally." In *RSM Bentley Jennison (A Firm) v Ayton* [2015] EWCA Civ 1120; [2016] 1 W.L.R. 1281; [2016] P.N.L.R. 10, the Court of Appeal confirmed that the defence remains limited to debt actions, notwithstanding the definition offered in the Glossary.

PART 39

MISCELLANEOUS PROVISIONS RELATING TO HEARINGS

Anonymity of party or witness (r.39.2(4))

Replace with:

39.2.11   The power of the court to order that the identity of any party or witnesses must not be disclosed is a broad power and the "interests" involved may include, although they are not limited to, privacy and confidentiality. The question whether a court should grant anonymity to a party or witness is separate from the question whether the court should sit in private. Obviously, the two questions may arise in the same practical context. Where a court sits in private but gives judgment in public, and there is a continuing need to protect the interests which justified the hearing being held in private in the first place, the court may "anonymise" the judgment by identifying parties or witness by letter only (e.g AB v CD; witness X). This may be done, for example, where a court considers that, by naming the parties or witnesses, the court itself would infringe their art.8 Convention rights as to privacy and family life and therefore act unlawfully under the Human Rights Act s.6 (*Re Guardian News and Media Ltd* [2010] UKSC 1; [2010] 2 W.L.R. 325, SC, at [28] per Lord Rodger). The question of whether a court should grant an order under r.39.2(4), or any other anonymity order, is not a matter of the judge's discretion, but is a matter of obligation under the Human Rights Act 1998 s.6 and ECHR art.8. The test to be applied is whether there is sufficient general public interest in publishing a report of proceedings that identifies the party to justify any resulting curtailment of that party's art.8 rights. (*AMM v HXW* [2010] EWHC 2457 (QB), 7 October 2010 unrep. (Tugendhat J) (where anonymity order made together with interim injunction in proceedings for injunction restraining publication of information which claimant claimed to be private)). In *Secretary of State for the Home Department v AP (No.2)* [2010] UKSC 26; [2010] 1 W.L.R. 1652, S.C., an individual (D) subject to a control order appealed successfully to the Supreme Court against conditions as to place of residence imposed by the order which had been upheld by the Court of Appeal. An anonymity order, protecting D from being identified, had been in force throughout the proceedings. By the time the Court's judgment was handed down, D was no longer subject to a control order, but was on bail pending deportation with a residence condition imposed. The Supreme Court ordered that the anonymity order should be continued after judgment and that the judgment and any reports of it should not reveal the identity of D. In the circumstances, the public interest in publishing a full report of the proceedings and judgment had to give way to the need to protect D from violence and did not justify curtailing his right to respect for his private and family life. In *R. (C) v Secretary of State for Justice* [2016] UKSC 2; [2016] 1 W.L.R. 444, SC, the Supreme Court held that there is no presumption of anonymity of the identity of a mental patient detained or otherwise subject to compulsory powers in every case of proceedings under the Mental Health Act 1983. The question in all these proceedings is (as r.39.2(4) provides): is anonymity necessary in the interests of the mental patient? Cases have arisen where the court has anonymised its written judgment even after a public hearing. See further *Revenue and Customs Commissioners v Banerjee (No.2) (Note)* [2009] EWHC 1229 (Ch); [2009] 3 All E.R. 930 (Henderson J.) (where party's application for anonymity in judgment following public hearing refused), and authorities referred to there. The power of the court referred to in r.39.2(4) goes beyond the "anonymising" of judgments and includes apower to make orders restraining others (including the press) from disclosing the identities of parties and witnesses (see *Re Guardian News and Media Ltd.*, op cit, at [30] per Lord Rodger).

PART 40

JUDGMENTS, ORDERS, SALE OF LAND ETC.

I.   *Judgments and Orders*

Effect of judgment before entry—altering judgment

Add new paragraph at end:

40.2.1   Where a party shows that consent to an order has been obtained by fraud the order should not be perfected but set aside and the hearing or case reopened: *Sharland v Sharland* [2015] UKSC 60; [2015] 3 W.L.R. 1070, SC, and see Setting aside consent judgments and orders, below at para.40.6.3.

Altering draft judgment

To the end of the sixth paragraph, add:

40.2.1.0.2   In *Quan v Bray* [2015] EWCA Civ 1401, 14 December 2015, CA, unrep., the Court of Appeal, after handing down a judgment giving a wife permission to appeal to the Court from a decision of a Family Division judge made in proceedings involving her and her husband, dismissed an application by the husband to reconsider that judgment in which he alleged there were factual errors. The Court stressed that in giving permission an appeal court is neither confirming nor rejecting any of the findings within the judgment at first instance.

Setting aside consent judgments and orders

Add new paragraph at end:

Where before an order is perfected a party shows that her consent has been obtained by fraud, **40.6.3** then the order should not be perfected, but the case should be reopened unless the fraud would not have influenced a reasonable person and the court should not in reopening the case deal with it on the basis only of the material then before it, but the case should be reheard: *Sharland v Sharland* [2015] UKSC 60; [2015] 3 W.L.R. 1070, SC.

Effect of rule

Replace with:

The provenance of this rule is CCR Ord.22 (Judgments and Orders) r.8 (Certificate of judg- **40.14A.1** ment) (see 2013 edition of the *White Book* Vol.1, para.cc22.8). For further explanation see para.40.9A.1 above. Rule 83.19 (Creditor's request for transfer to the High Court for enforcement) applies where the creditor makes a request for a certificate of judgment under r.40.14A(1) in the circumstances provided for in that rule. As to transfer to High Court from County Court of possession orders for purposes of enforcement, see commentary in 83.13.1 and 83.19.2, and on County Courts Act 1984 ss.41 and 42 (Vol.2 para.9A-481.1).

Practice Note—(Chancery Division—Production of Orders for Masters and Judges)

Add new paragraph at beginning:

Editorial note

See now Chancery Guide, Ch.22, Vol.2 paras 1A–192—202. **40PN.0.1**

PART 44

General Rules about Costs

I. General

Reasons

To the end of the paragraph, add:

The reasons for a judge's costs order made at the end of a trial may be largely discernible from **44.2.4** the transcript of the judgment, but where counsel are not sure they should seek from the judge a note of the reasons for the order (*Darougar v Belcher* [2002] EWCA Civ 1262, 25 July 2002, CA, unrep., at para.7 per Keene LJ).

Offers to settle (r.44.2(4)(c))

Add new paragraph at end:

In a case where r.36.14 applies (claimant fails to obtain a judgment more advantageous than a **44.2.13** defendant's Part 36 offer or judgment against the defendant is at least as advantageous to the claimant as the proposals contained in a claimant's Part 36 offer), an issue-based or proportionate costs order may only be made if it would be unjust to make the order provided by the rule. In such a case the court does not exercise its discretion under r.44.2: *Webb v Liverpool Women's NHS Foundation Trust* [2016] EWCA Civ 365.

PART 45

FIXED COSTS

IIIA.   Claims Which No Longer Continue Under the RTA or EL/PL Pre-Action Protocols—Fixed Recoverable Costs

Add new paragraph 49.29B.1:

Part 36 offers

45.29B.1   Where a claim no longer continues under the protocol pursuant to r.45.29A(1), r.36.14 applies with the modifications set out in r.36.14A. If judgment is entered against the defendant on terms at least as advantageous to the claimant as the proposals contained in the claimant's Part 36 offer, r.36.14(3) will apply. The claimant will be awarded fixed costs to the last staging point provided by r.45.29C and Table 6B and, unless the court considers it unjust, costs assessed on the indemnity basis from the date on which the relevant period expired: *Broadhurst v Tan* [2016] EWCA Civ 94.

IV.   Scale Costs For Claims in the Intellectual Property Enterprise Court

Effect of rule

To the end of the sixth paragraph (beginning "Rule 45.31(1) imposes"), add:

45.31.1   Where a defendant had succeeded on its counterclaim but part of the claim had been adjourned, the defendant asked for its costs of the counterclaim to be assessed. The court held that it could not assess the costs until all of the issues, including the adjourned claim, had been resolved: *Global Flood Defence Systems v Johan Van Den Noort Beheer BV* [2016] EWHC 189 (IPEC).

PART 48

PART 2 OF THE LEGAL AID, SENTENCING AND PUNISHMENT OF OFFENDERS ACT 2012 RELATING TO CIVIL LITIGATION FUNDING AND COSTS: TRANSITIONAL PROVISION IN RELATION TO PRE-COMMENCEMENT FUNDING ARRANGEMENTS

2.   Savings provisions in the 2012 Act and commencement order

After the third paragraph (beginning "Article 3 of SI 2013/77"), add as a new paragraph:

48.0.2.4   Article 2 of the Legal Aid, Sentencing and Punishment of Offenders Act 2012 (Commencement No.12) Order 2016 (SI 2016/345) brought into force, on 6 April 2016, s.44 and s.46 in relation to insolvency proceedings, thereby removing the exclusion of those proceedings from the commencement of those sections effected by art.4 of SI 2013/77. (The transitional provisions in s.44(6) and s.46(3) of the 2012 Act have effect in respect of the provisions commenced by this Order.)

Replace the first sentence of the last paragraph with:

It is expected that, in due course, s.44 and s.46 will be brought into force in relation to proceedings of the types which remain covered by the saving provisions.

Effect of CPR Pt 48

Replace the second paragraph with:

48.0.3   As indicated above, the significant amendments made by s.44 and s.46 of the 2012 Act relate to what are defined in r.43.2(1)(k), as it stood before 1 April 2013, as a "funding arrangement", specifically, a CFA providing for the payment of a success fee, an insurance policy taken out against the risk of costs liability, and an agreement with a membership organisation to meet legal costs. The draftsman has met the considerable challenges posed in the drafting of Part 48 by distinguishing between a funding arrangement as defined by r.43.1(1)(k), made in relation to insolvency-related proceedings, publication or privacy proceedings, or a mesothelioma claim, and a funding arrangement so defined but entered into in relation to other proceedings. Both forms of funding arrangement are defined as a "pre-commencement funding arrangement". In relation to proceedings other than insolvency-related proceedings, publication or privacy proceedings, or a mesothelioma claim, "pre-commencement" means a funding arrangement made before 1 April 2013. In relation to insolvency-related proceedings, publication or privacy proceedings, or a mesothelioma claim,"pre-commencement" means a funding arrangement made at any time before s.44 and s.46 of the 2012 Act come into force; that is to say, at any time before 1 April 2013, or during the subsequent period in which the savings provisions in the 2012 Act and the commencement order explained above may continue to have effect. As noted above (para.48.0.2.4), in relation to insolvency-related proceedings, those saving provisions ceased to have effect on 6 April 2016. In respect of insolvency-related proceedings, s.44 and s.46 came into force on 6 April 2016.

Add new paragraph 48.2.2:

The relevant date for insolvency-related proceedings

In respect of insolvency-related proceedings, s.44 and s.46 came into force on 6 April 2016: **48.2.2** Legal Aid, Sentencing and Punishment of Offenders Act 2012 (Commencement No.12) Order 2016 (SI 2016/345) art.2.

PART 44

[BEFORE APRIL 1, 2013] GENERAL RULES ABOUT COSTS

Rule 44.3(4)(c)—offers to settle

Add new paragraph at end:

Where a case had settled on terms offered by the defendants 6 months earlier but which offer **44x.3.20** was withdrawn after 21 days for no good reason, the appropriate order was that the claimant should have his costs to the date of the offer with no order as to costs thereafter: *Patience v Tanner* [2016] EWCA Civ 158.

GENERAL PRINCIPLES AND CASE LAW RELATING TO COSTS AND THEIR ASSESSMENT

Liquidation

Add new paragraph at end:

In misfeasance proceedings brought by liquidators against the directors, the **48GP.74** court concluded that a disputed entry in the company's accounts was genuine. The directors sought their costs of that issue. The court decided that overall the liquidators had won the proceedings and the validity of the entry was not a freestanding allegation which it had been unreasonable for them to pursue. The directors had failed to engage with the litigation and had failed to explain the entry. Accordingly they should pay the costs of that issue: *Bishop v Fox*, 9 February 2016, unrep., Proudman J.

PART 51

TRANSITIONAL ARRANGEMENTS AND PILOT SCHEMES

Shorter and Flexible Trials Pilot Schemes

To the end of this paragraph, add:

As to the court's discretion to transfer an existing case into or out of the Shorter Trials Scheme, **51.2.16** see *Family Mosaic Home Ownership Ltd v Peer Real Estate Ltd* [2016] EWHC 257 (Ch); [2016] 4 W.L.R. 37 (Birss J)).

Pilot for Insolvency Express Trials

Replace "para.51OPD.1 below" with:

51.2.17   para.51PPD.1 below).

Add new paragraphs at end:

The aim of the Insolvency Express Trials (IET) pilot scheme is to provide litigants in the Bankruptcy and Companies Court with a speedy, streamlined procedure, and an early date for the trial or disposal of simple applications by the bankruptcy registrars with consequential costs savings for the parties. Use of the IET pilot scheme is voluntary: applicants can decide which of their cases (if any) should proceed under the scheme, but there is provision for the respondent to object and for the court to remove an application from the IET list if it thinks fit. The scheme applies to simple applications which require limited directions and disclosure (only one directions hearing is envisaged) and can be disposed of finally in no more than two days. The trial date given will be a fixture and will not be capable of being be vacated by consent; and an adjournment will only be granted in exceptional circumstances. If sufficient time has been allowed in the time estimate judgment will generally be given at the trial. If judgment is reserved it will generally be handed down within four weeks of the trial. Costs will either be assessed summarily or detailed assessment may be ordered.

The costs management provisions of the CPR do not apply, but there is a costs cap, at present fixed at £75,000. This was fixed before the abolition of the insolvency exemption from the Legal Aid, Sentencing and Punishment of Offenders Act 2012 (see para.48.0.2.4 above) which otherwise removed the ability to recover CFA uplifts and after-the-event insurance premiums. It is hoped that the present figure can be reduced as a result.

Practitioners should note that the IET list operates alongside and in addition to the regimes created by Practice Direction 51N—Shorter and Flexible Trials Pilot Schemes (see para.51.2.16 above).

Comments and suggestions from users of the IET scheme should be sent to the chief registrar or may be made via the Bankruptcy and Companies Court Users' Committee.

PART 52

APPEALS

I.   General Rules about Appeals

Approach of appeal court to costs appeals

52.1.4   *Delete the fourth paragraph (beginning "That dictum has been adopted").*

After the sixth paragraph (beginning "Where the issue on the appeal"), add as a new paragraph:

In *Patience v Tanner* [2016] EWCA Civ 158, 22 March 2016, CA, unrep., the Court explained the approach that an appeal court should take to an appeal against a costs order made by a trial court where the proceedings settled prior to trial.

Requirement for permission

Replace the second paragraph (where the citation for Michael Wilson & Partners Ltd v Emmott has changed) with:

52.3.1   An appeal from the High Court to the Court of Appeal invoking the Court's so-called "residual jurisdiction" (see Vol.2 paras 2E-268 and 9A-55.1) is an "appeal" for the purposes of the Senior Courts Act 1981 s.16(1), and it follows from that that such an appeal is an appeal for which permission to appeal is required by r.52.3 (*Michael Wilson & Partners Ltd v Emmott* [2015] EWCA Civ 1285; [2016] 1 W.L.R. 857, CA).

The effect of refusal of permission

Add new paragraph at end:

52.3.8   Where a judge of the High Court grants a defendant's application to discharge a freezing order against it, and refuses permission to appeal, the judge has power to order that the discharge should take effect only after a prescribed period, sufficient to enable it to protect its position by making an application to the Court of Appeal for a freezing order pending an appeal to that Court (supplemental judgment in *Metropolitan Housing Trust Ltd v Taylor* [2015] EWHC 2897 (Ch), 23 October 2015, unrep. (Warren J)). See further Vol.2 para.15-9.1.

Application for permission to appeal "totally without merit"-reconsideration

Replace the second paragraph with:

52.3.8.1

Sub-rules (4A) and (4B) were originally added to r.52.3 by the Civil Procedure (Amendment) Rules 2006 (SI 2006/1689) for the purpose of enabling the Court of Appeal to make an order to the effect that a person refused permission to appeal may not request the decision to be reconsidered at a hearing. Such an order may be made if the appeal court considers that the application is "totally without merit". Sub-rule (4A) was significantly modified by the Civil Procedure (Amendment No.2) Rules 2012 (SI 2012/2208) for the purpose of extending the powers of the Court of Appeal in this respect to judges sitting at other levels in the appellate hierarchy and dealing with applications for permission to appeal. In this way, High Court Judges, Designated Civil Judges, and some Specialist Civil Judges have the jurisdiction to refuse an application for permission to appeal on the papers, and if they conclude that the appeal is "totally without merit", there is no right to a further oral hearing.

Add new paragraphs at end:

In circumstances where sub-rule (4A) of r.52.3 applies the judge "may make" an order that the person seeking permission to appeal may not request the decision to be reconsidered at a hearing; the loss of the right to a hearing is not an automatic consequence. This may be contrasted with the position where an applicant's application for permission to apply for judicial review is certified as TWM and r.52.15 or r.52.15A governs the applicant's application to the Court of Appeal for permission to appeal; in that event the application will be determined on paper without a hearing (see para.52.15.1 below).

No authoritative test has emerged for determining whether an application for permission to appeal should be certified as "totally without merit". In *R. (Grace) v Secretary of State for the Home Department* [2014] EWCA Civ 1091; [2014] 1 W.L.R. 3432, CA, and *R. (Wasif) v Secretary of State for the Home Department* [2016] EWCA Civ 82, 9 February 2016, CA, unrep., the Court of Appeal has given guidance on the approach to be adopted in the quite different context of applications for permission to apply for judicial review (see further para.54.12.1 below).

Permission will be granted more sparingly to appeal against case management decisions

Replace the last paragraph (where the citation for Abdulle v Commissioner of Police of the Metropolis has changed) with:

52.3.9

In *Abdulle v Commissioner of Police of the Metropolis* [2015] EWCA Civ 1260; [2016] 1 W.L.R. 898, CA the Court of Appeal re-affirmed that it would not lightly interfere with case management decisions of lower courts and stressed that that approach applied to decisions to grant or refuse relief from sanctions under r.3.9 and to decisions on whether to strike out under r.3.4(2)(c).

The role of respondents in relation to permission applications

Replace the first paragraph with:

52.3.17

In relation to appeals to the Court of Appeal the role of the respondent to an appeal is affected by provisions in Practice Direction 52C (Appeals to the Court of Appeal) as significantly amended by Update 79 with effect from 6 April 2015; in particular, by para.19 (Respondent's actions when served with the appellant's notice), and by para.20 (Respondent's costs of permission applications) (see paras 52CPD.19 and 52CPD.20 below). (Initially those directions reflected guidance given by the Court in *Jolly v Jay* [2002] EWCA Civ 277, 7 March 2002, CA, unrep.) It may be noted that, as amended, para.19(1)(a) states that a respondent "is permitted, and is encouraged" to file and serve "a brief statement" of any reasons why the appellant should be refused permission to appeal. (Before 6 April 2015, it was provided that a respondent "need not take any action" until notified that permission to appeal had been granted.)

Delete the second and third paragraphs.

Statutory time limits for filing notice of appeal

Replace the last paragraph (where the citation for Szegfu v Hungary has changed) with:

52.4.1.1

In relation to appeals under s.26(4) of the Extradition Act 2003, para.21.1(c) of PD52D stated that the appellant must serve a copy of the notice of appeal on the CPS, if they are not a party to the appeal, in addition to the persons to be served under r.52.4(3) "and in accordance with that rule". With effect from 6 October 2014, and subject to transitional provisions, rules of court for appeals to the High Court in extradition proceedings were included in Section 3 of Pt.17 in the Criminal Procedure Rules 2014 (SI 2014/1610) and by CPR Update 75 the whole of para.21.1 was omitted from PD52D. Cases dealing with the point that the court had no jurisdiction to extend the times limits for service of notices of appeal as required by para.21.1 are: *R. (Bajorek Sawczuk) v Poland* [2014] EWHC 1108 (Admin), 21 March 2014, unrep. (Collins J); *Bugyo v Slovakia* [2014] EWHC 4230 (Admin), 21 November 2014, unrep. (Blake J). Amendments made to Extradition Act 2003 effected by the Anti-social Behaviour, Crime and Policing Act 2014 s.160 altered the provisions imposing time limits on appeals for all cases in which notice of appeal was given on or after

15 April 2015. The effect of s.26(5) (as amended) is to require the High Court to refuse to entertain an application in a case in which notice was given outside a specified period of seven days unless the person concerned shows that he did everything reasonably possible to ensure that notice was given as soon as it could be given (*Szegfu v Hungary* [2015] EWHC 1764 (Admin); [2016] 1 W.L.R. 322, DC).

Date when time starts to run

52.4.2

In the last paragraph, replace "21 days" with:
28 days

Skeleton argument

52.4.5

At the end of the first paragraph, replace "para.5.3" with:
para.1(1)

To the end of the third paragraph (beginning "As to form and content"), add:
An appeal may be struck out and dismissed where the appellant fails to comply with the practice direction as to the preparation and filing of skeleton arguments (e.g. *Vaux v Solicitors Regulation Authority* [2015] EWHC 1365 (Admin), 31 March 2015, unrep., where the directions were reinforced by case management directions given by the appeal court).

At the end of the fifth paragraph (beginning "The cost of preparing a skeleton"), replace "para.5.1(4)" with:
para.5.1(5)

Imposition of conditions

52.9.4

To the end of the fifth paragraph (beginning "In Société Générale SA v SAAD"), add:
In *Goldtrail Travel Ltd v Aydin* [2016] EWCA Civ 20, 21 January 2016, unrep. (Patten LJ) it was explained that, in deciding whether to impose the condition that the appellant should pay the judgment debt into court, there is no absolute bar against the court's taking into account the position of other entities or persons "close to the appellant", in particular, for example, where the appellant is a corporation, by taking into account that it has "wealthy owners" who could, if they were so minded, pay the judgment debt on its behalf.

II. Special Provisions Applying to the Court of Appeal

Skeleton and supplementary skeleton arguments

52.12.1.4

In the first paragraph, replace "Practice Direction 52A para.5.1(4)" with:
Practice Direction 52A para.5.1(5)

Application for permission to appeal against refusal of permission below

52.15.1

Add new paragraph at end:
In *R. (Wasif) v Secretary of State for the Home Department* [2016] EWCA Civ 82, 9 February 2016, CA, unrep., the Court of Appeal explained (para.7) that it is established that one consequence of certain provisions in r.52.15 (Judicial review appeals from the High Court) and r.52.15A (Judicial review appeals from the Upper Tribunal) is that, where an application for permission to apply for judicial review has been certified by the court or tribunal below as "totally without merit", a judge of the Court of Appeal is precluded from directing that an application for permission to appeal be heard orally, even if the judge believes that in the particular circumstances of the case a hearing would be desirable. The Court (1) commented that it is surprising, and sometimes inconvenient, that the hands of a judge of the Court of Appeal should be tied in this way by a decision taken at first instance, and (2) doubted whether this was the rule-makers' intention.

Effect of rule

52.15A.1

Replace the third paragraph with:
An application for permission to appeal may be considered by an appeal court at an oral hearing or on paper. Paragraph (2) of this rule states, categorically, that in the circumstances provided for therein "the application will be determined on paper without an oral hearing". In this respect, r.52.15A accords with r.52.15.

PART 53

Defamation Claims

Direction to elect whether or not to make offer of amends

At the end of the paragraph, replace "53PD.37" with:
53PD.27

PRACTICE DIRECTION 53—DEFAMATION CLAIMS

Pleading the meaning

Replace the last paragraph with:
   Note that by s.1(1) of the Defamation Act 2013, a statement is not defamatory unless its publica- **53PD.6** tion has caused or is likely to cause serious harm to the reputation of the claimant. For the require-ments of s.1(1), see *Cooke v MGN* [2014] EWHC 2831 (QB); [2015] W.L.R. 895, *Lachaux v Independent Print Ltd* [2015] EWHC 2242 (QB); [2016] 2 W.L.R. 437; [2015] E.M.L.R. 28, *Theedon v Nourish Training (t/a CSP Recruitment)* [2015] EWHC 3769 (QB); [2016] E.M.L.R. 10, and *Sobrinho v Impresa Publishing SA* [2016] EWHC 66 (QB); [2016] E.M.L.R. 12. Proof that the words complained of have caused or are likely to cause serious harm to reputation may be achieved by inference, but the claimant would be wise to plead all relevant circumstances, including the extent and nature of publication, the sort of people to whom the words were published, altered behaviour on the part of those who knew him, and adverse social media responses: see generally *Lachaux* at [101]ff. The bar is higher for bodies trading for profit, because by s.1(2) harm to reputation is not in their case "serious harm" unless they can show at least the likelihood of serious financial loss.

Damages

Replace the second paragraph (where the citation for Lachaux v. Independent Print Ltd has changed) with:
   However, in the light of Defamation Act 2013 s.1(1), the claimant must in every case show that **53PD.24** publication of the words complained of has caused or is likely to cause serious damage to his or her reputation. (A higher threshold still applies to bodies trading for profit: s.1(2): harm to the reputa-tion of a body that trades for profit is not "serious harm" unless it has caused or is likely to cause the body serious financial loss). It therefore appears that, whether or not Parliament envisaged it, the common law presumption of damage has been swept away: *Lachaux v Independent Print Ltd* [2015] EWHC 2422 (QB); [2016] 2 W.L.R. 437; [2015] E.M.L.R. 28 at [60].

Offer of amends and s.1, Defamation Act 2013

Replace the paragraph (where the citation for Lachaux v. Independent Print Ltd has changed) with:
   A defendant who wishes to resist a claim on the basis that it fails to meet the threshold of serious **53PD.28.1** harm to reputation created by s.1 should not serve a defence before taking the serious harm point. If the application to determine the threshold issue fails, because no defence has been served the defendant can still consider making an offer of amends (*Lachaux v Independent Print Ltd* [2015] EWHC 2422 (QB); [2016] 2 W.L.R. 437; [2015] E.M.L.R. 28 at [169]).

PART 54

Judicial Review and Statutory Review

Related sources

Replace list with:
- Senior Courts Act 1981 s.31 (Vol.2, para.9A-101.)
- CPR Pt 8
- CPR r.52.15 (judicial review appeals)
- Nationality, Immigration and Asylum Act 2002
- Tribunals, Courts and Enforcement Act 2007
- Criminal Justice and Courts Act 2015.

I.   Judicial Review

Against whom does judicial review lie

Replace the fourth paragraph with:

54.1.2   The current approach is conveniently summarised in the decision of the Divisional Court in *R. v Insurance Ombudsman Bureau Ex p. Aegon Life Insurance Ltd*, *The Times* 7 January 1994. The court held that judicial review would not lie against a body whose birth and constitution owed nothing to any exercise of governmental power; a body could be classed as public only if it had been woven into the fabric of public regulation or into a system of governmental control, or was integrated into a system of statutory regulation or, but for its existence, a governmental body would assume control. Judicial review did not lie against a body whose powers derived from the agreement of the parties and when private law remedies were available against the body concerned. The Insurance Ombudsman Bureau fell into the latter category because it was a body whose jurisdiction was dependent on the contractual consent of its members and its decisions were of a private law arbitrative nature. The application of these principles is not always easy in practice. In *R. (Holmcroft Properties Ltd) v KMPG LLP* [2016] EWHC 323 (Admin), the Divisional Court was dealing with a system whereby the Financial Conduct Authority was concerned with redress for alleged mis-selling of certain financial products by a particular bank. An agreement was entered into whereby a non-statutory body (a limited liability partnership) was appointed as an independent reviewer to report on the progress of the redress scheme and offers of redress to individual customers needed the approval of the independent reviewer. A decision of the independent reviewer was held not to be amenable to judicial review. Although woven into the regulatory framework, the scheme of redress was essentially voluntary and the independent reviewer's powers were confirmed by contract. See generally, Ch.2 of Lewis, *Judicial Remedies in Public Law* (5th edn).

Time limits and delay

Replace the sixth paragraph with:

54.5.1   A court may grant an extension of time under CPR Pt 3.1(2)(a) (previously, RSC Ord.53 itself provided that the court could extend the time if there was good reason to do so). The likelihood is that the courts will continue to apply the previous case law on RSC Ord.53 on whether there was a good reason for extending the time in deciding whether or not to grant an extension of time under CPR r.3.1 in a judicial review claim. The courts have always recognised that public law claims are unlike ordinary civil litigation and require strict adherence to the time limits contained in the rules governing judicial review (*R. v Institute of Chartered Accountants in England and Wales Ex p. Andreou* (1996) 8 Admin L.R. 557). The courts are likely to require that there is a good reason or adequate explanation for the delay and that extending the time limit will not cause substantial hardship or substantial prejudice or be detrimental to good administration. Under the former provisions of RSC Ord.53 r.4 the courts refused to accept that there was good reason for extending the time for making a judicial review application where the delay was the fault of the applicant's lawyers (*R. v Secretary of State for Health Ex p. Furneaux* [1994] 2 All E.R. 652). The courts have accepted that there was good reason for the delay if the applicant was unaware of the decision provided that they applied expeditiously once they became aware of it (*R. v Secretary of State for the Home Department Ex p. Ruddock* [1987] 1 W.L.R. 1482; *R. v Secretary of State for Foreign and Commonwealth Affairs Ex p. World Development Movement Ltd* [1995] 1 W.L.R. 386 at p.402). The fact that the claim raises issues of general public importance may be a reason for extending the time-limit (*R. v Secretary of State for the Home Department Ex p. Ruddock* [1987] 1 W.L.R. 1482; *Re S (Application for Judicial Review)* [1998] 1 F.L.R. 790). In the past, delay arising out of the need to obtain legal aid was regarded as a sufficient justification for delay: see *R. v Stratford-upon-Avon DC Ex p. Jackson* [1985] 1 W.L.R. 1319. The Court of Appeal has now indicated, in a different context, that delay arising out of the need to obtain legal aid is unlikely, of itself, to justify compliance with relevant procedural rules: see *R. (Kigen) v Secretary of State for the Home Department* [2015] EWCA Civ 1286; [2016] 1 W.L.R. 723, CA. The Court of Appeal was dealing with an application for an extension of time for filing a request for reconsideration of a refusal of permission to apply for judicial review in the Upper Tribunal under the relevant statutory procedural rules but similar principles are likely to apply to a failure to comply with other provisions of the CPR: see *Kigen* at para.6.

Reconsideration of a refusal of permission

Replace the last paragraph with:

54.12.1   Applications for a request for reconsideration must be filed within even days of service of the reasons for refusal of permission: see r.54.12(4). The Court of Appeal has indicated the appropriate approach to consideration of applications for an extension of time in the context of applications to renew in the Upper Tribunal (where the relevant rules provide for requests to made within nine days). The court should consider the seriousness and significance of the failure to comply with the rule, whether there is a satisfactory explanation for the failure and all the other circumstances. Delay arising out of the need to obtain legal aid is unlikely of itself to be a satisfactory explanation. Similar principles are likely to apply to applications for reconsideration in the Administrative

Court. See *R. (Kigen) v Secretary of State for the Home Department* [2015] EWCA Civ 1286; [2016] 1 W.L.R. 723, CA at paras 6, 20, 25 to 29 and 32.

Interlocutory applications

To the end of the first paragraph, add:

54.16.2
See also *Jedwell v Denbighshire CC* [2015] EWCA Civ 1232 (justice required permitting cross-examination to determine whether reasons given for an earlier decision were an ex post facto justification of the decision or gave an account the reasons existing at the time for taking the decision).

PART 64

Estates, Trusts and Charities

Related sources

Replace the first list with:

64.0.2
- Part 8 (Alternative Procedure for Claims)
- Part 23 (General Rules about Applications for Court Orders)
- Part 40 (Judgments, Orders, Sale of Land etc.)
- Part 52 (Appeals)
- Part 57 (Probate and Inheritance)
- Chancery Guide 2016 (Vol.2 para.1A–0)

Replace the second list with:
- **CH13** Executor's or administrator's account
- **CH14** Order stating results of proceedings on usual accounts and inquiries in administrative claim
- **CH38** Order for distribution of Lloyd's Estate
- **CH39** Lloyd's Estate form of witness statement

I. Claims Relating to the Administration of Estates and Trusts

Applications under r.64.2(a) to determine any question arising in the administration of the estate of a deceased person or execution of a trust

Replace with:

64.2.1
Examples of claims under r.64.2(a) are set out in PD 64 para.1. Applications for directions by trustees or personal representatives must be made by Pt 8 claim form. The proceedings will normally be heard in private (BPD 64 para.3r.39.2(3)(f) and PD 39, para.1.5). The court will always consider whether such applications can be dealt with on paper without a hearing. If the trustees consider it appropriate they may apply to the court under r.8.2A for permission to issue the claim form without naming any defendants (BPD 64 para.4.2 Chancery Guide 7.15-7.16). Detailed guidance as to the procedure for applying to the court for directions in relation to the administration of a trust are given in the Practice Direction, BPD 64; see also Chancery Guide, paras 29.10–29.12.

Prospective Costs Orders in relation to applications under r.64.2(a)

At the end of the first paragraph, replace "para.25.9" with:

64.2.2
paras 29.18–29.19.

Beddoe applications under 64.2(a)

To the end of the paragraph, add:

64.2.3
(See also Chancery Guide para.29.17.)

Other more usual forms of application under 64.2(a)

Replace with:

64.2.4
These include: absence of power (the sanctioning of acts being done by trustees which they themselves have no power to do); purchase by trustees of part of the trust estate; orders for partial distribution to known beneficiaries; kin inquiries; and Benjamin orders (authorising the distribution of the fund on the footing that a beneficiary predeceased the testator or intestate (*Re Benjamin, Neville v Benjamin* [1902] 1 Ch. 723).

Applications for permission to distribute the estate of a deceased Lloyd's name

Replace with:

64.2.5   These are made under r.64.2(a). The procedure for this is governed by a Practice Statement dated 25 May 2001 ([2001] 3 All E.R. 765), following *Re Yorke (deceased)* [1997] 4 All E.R. 907, which enables the personal representatives of a deceased Lloyd's name to distribute the estate on the footing that no, or no further, provision need be made for Lloyd's creditors. The application must be made by Pt 8 claim form, which may be issued without naming any other party. Directions may be given without a hearing. The Practice Statement includes a form of witness statement and draft order, both of which should accompany the claim form. If the deceased was involved in underwriting activities through a limited liability vehicle, this should be drawn to the court's attention. (See Chancery Guide paras 29-41 and Forms **CH38** (Order for distribution of Lloyd's Estate) and **CH39** (Lloyd's Estate form of witness statement)).

Administration orders—r.64.2(b)

Replace the second and third paragraphs with:

64.2.6   Administration actions are of two kinds: creditor's administration actions and beneficiary's administration actions. Normally, a creditor's administration action is for the administration of a deceased person's estate. A beneficiary's administration action in respect of the estate of a deceased person or a trust may be brought by a beneficiary or by the executors, administrators or trustees as the case may be. All the executors, administrators or trustees must be made parties and any of them who does not consent to being joined as a claimant must be made a defendant.

Where the estate is insolvent the proceedings should be commenced by a creditor as claimant against the personal representative as defendant. The personal representative is not entitled to commence proceedings against a creditor who is unwilling to be made a defendant. In such a case the proper course is for the personal representative to present a petition under the Insolvency Act 1986. But, it would seem that the proceedings would be properly constituted if brought against a creditor who was willing to be joined as a defendant (*Re Bradley* [1956] Ch. 615; [1956] 3 All E.R. 113). Where the usual order has been made for administration in a beneficiary's action, and, by reason of insolvency, beneficiaries are no longer interested, the action must be reconstituted and carried on by creditors as claimants. See *Re Van Oppen* [1935] W.N. 51; 179 L.TJ. 255. The application is then treated on the same footing as any other application for a creditor's administration order in case of insolvency and is dealt with by the Master without reference to the judge.

Variation of Trusts Act 1958—r.64.2(c)

Replace with:

64.2.7   Applications under the Variation of Trusts Act must be made by Pt 8 claim form (CPR r.64.3) and will normally be heard in private (CPR r.39.2(3)(f)). Applications under the Variation of Trusts Act may be heard by a judge or a Master, following the changes in 2015 to PD2B. District Judges may not make final orders under s.1.1 of the Variation of Trusts Act, except in certain circumstances, without the consent of their Supervising Judge (PD2B para.7B 2(b)). If the application is to be heard by a judge, it will be listed in the General list. The previous practice of listing these applications before a Judge without reference to the Master no longer applies (see Chancery Guide para.21.18). However, the Master will normally exercise jurisdiction and hear the case, unless it is appropriate for some reason (eg particular complexity) to refer the matter to the Judge. In every case a certificate of readiness, signed by the advocates for all the parties, must be lodged, stating that the evidence is complete and has been filed, the application is ready for hearing, and giving the estimated length of the hearing. Practice Direction 64 para.4 sets out the requirements as to the evidence that must be filed where any children or unborn beneficiaries will be affected by a proposed arrangement under the Act. A written opinion of the advocate who will appear at the hearing may be required, particularly in complicated cases. (See also Chancery Guide, paras 29.22–29.27). Attention is drawn to CPR r.64.4(2), which specifies the parties to be joined in such proceedings.

Administration of Justice Act 1985 s.48—r.64.2(d)

Replace with:

64.2.8   Claims under s.48 of the Administration of Justice Act (power of the High Court to authorise action to be taken in reliance on written legal opinion as to the construction of a will or trust document) must be made by Pt 8 claim form (CPR r.64.3) without naming the defendant under CPR r.8.2A and no separate application for permission under r.8.2A need be made (PD 64 para.5).The legal opinion must be given by a person who has a 10-year High Court qualification within the meaning of s.71 of the Courts and Legal Services Act 1990. The claim should be supported by a witness statement or affidavit stating the names of all persons affected by the order sought, the surrounding circumstances admissible and relevant to construction of the document, details of the qualification and experience of the writer of the opinion, the approximate value of the fund or property in question and the details of any dispute known to exist. There should be exhibited to the witness statement or affidavit copies of all relevant documents, instructions to the writer of the opinion, the opinion itself and a draft order. The Master will consider whether the evidence is complete and, if it is, will either deal with the matter or, if appropriate, send it to the Judge. If the Master or judge directs service of notices under r.19.8A and any acknowledgment of service is received, the claimant should apply to the Master, on notice to the parties who acknowledged service, for directions (see Chancery Guide, paras 29.28–29.34).

II. Charity Proceedings

Editorial introduction

At the end of the last paragraph, replace "para.25.10" with:
   paras 29.20–29.21.

64.5.1

PART 68

REFERENCES TO THE EUROPEAN COURT

Effect of rule

After the first paragraph, add as a new paragraph:
   In *Kernkraftwerke Lippe-Ems GmbH v Hauptzollamt Osnabruck* (C-5/14) EU:C:2015:354; [2016] 2 **68.2.1** W.L.R. 369, ECJ, the German Finance Court referred to the ECJ the question whether art.267 of TFEU must be interpreted as meaning that a national court which has doubts as to whether national legislation is compatible with both EU law and with the constitution of the Member State concerned loses the right or, as the case may be, is exempt from the obligation to submit questions to the ECJ concerning the interpretation or validity of that law, on the ground that parallel proceedings in the Finance Court had been stayed pending the conclusion of a reference to the German Federal Constitutional Court for a ruling on the constitutionality of that legislation. The ECJ ruled that in these circumstances a national court neither loses the right, nor is exempt from submitting questions to the ECJ.

PART 71

ORDERS TO OBTAIN INFORMATION FROM JUDGMENT DEBTORS

"produce at court documents in his control" (r.71.2(6))

Replace with:
   The concept of "control" of documents for the purposes of the information-gathering exercise **71.2.9** under Pt 71 to enable enforcement of a judgment is different from control in the context of disclosure. Under Pt 71, a person may have sufficient control to be required to produce a document if he is likely to have "a real say" as to whether or not to produce the document (*North Shore Ventures Ltd v Anstead Holdings Ltd* [2012] EWCA Civ 11, 18 January 2012, CA, unrep., per Toulson LJ at [35]). If there are reasonable grounds to infer that the true nature of the relationship with a third party (such as a trustee) is that there is some understanding or arrangement by which the latter is to shelter assets or follow instructions, the judge may be entitled to infer that such assets and related documents are under the control of the person being examined (ibid at [38-40]). This is consistent with the approach of the court to provision of information in orders ancillary to freezing orders: the court can make an order under r.25.1(1)(g) for provision of information about relevant assets. Such orders provide to the claimant an opportunity of investigating the truth of the claim, for example, that assets are held on trust or by a third party for the defendant, in order to avoid sophisticated or wily operators from making themselves immune to the court's orders (see *JSC Mezhdunarodniy Promyshlenniy Bank v Pugachev* [2015] EWCA Civ 139; 2016 1 W.L.R. 160, CA, at [58]).

PART 74

ENFORCEMENT OF JUDGMENTS IN DIFFERENT JURISDICTIONS

Forms

74.0.2   *Replace list with:*
- **PF 154** Order for permission to register a foreign judgment
- **PF 156** Evidence in support of application for registration of a Community Judgment
- **PF 157** Order for registration of a Community judgment
- **PF 160** Order for registration of a Judgment of another contracting state
- **PF 163** Evidence in support of application for a certified copy of a judgment for enforcement in another contracting state
- **PF 165** Evidence in support of application for registration in the High Court of a Judgment of a court in another part of the United Kingdom containing non-money provisions

I.   Enforcement in England and Wales of Judgments of Foreign Courts

Public policy

Add new paragraph at end:

74.10.5   In *Meroni v Recoletos Ltd* (C-559/14) Advocate General Kokott delivered the Opinion that a freezing injunction from another member state did not infringe art.34(1) of the 2001 Brussels Regulation (public policy) where any third party affected had the right to apply to the original court to vary or discharge the judgment. The appeal against enforcement of the freezing injunction in Latvia was on the basis that the party affected by the order had not been party to the English proceedings, which was alleged to be contrary to its right to a fair trial. The Opinion, which is likely to be followed by the ECJ, confirms the limited scope of public policy as a ground for resisting enforcement of a judgment from another EU member state.

PART 81

APPLICATIONS AND PROCEEDINGS IN RELATION TO CONTEMPT OF COURT

The Committal Practice Direction—purpose and scope

Replace the last paragraph with:

81.0.2.1   Paragraph 1 of the Committal PD states that it applies to all proceedings for committal for contempt of court, including contempt in the face of the court, whether arising under any statutory or inherent jurisdiction. This wide scope is significantly affected by paras 7 to 17 of the Practice Guidance. Thus para.8 of the Practice Guidance (see para.B17A-004 below) states that the Committal PD does not apply to orders made on a written reference to a High Court judge or circuit judge under the procedure set out in paras.8(1) and 8(2) of CPR r.71.8 (Judgment debtor's failure to comply with order) and CPR PD71, paras 6 and 7 (see, respectively, para.71.8.1 and para.71PD.6 above), but for reasons given there does apply to any hearing under r.71(8)(4)(b). In terms, para.9 of the Practice Guidance states that the Committal PD applies to the attachment of earnings procedure under CCR Ord.27 r.7 and 7A as it does to CPR r.71.8. The effect of that was that the Committal PD only applied to the adjourned hearing referred to in CCR Ord.27 r.7B and to any further hearing to deal with a suspended committal order made under that provision. With effect from 6 April 2016, CCR Ord.27 was revoked and replaced by Pt 89 with the result that rr.7, 7A and 7B in Ord.27 referred to in the Guidance now stand as rr.89.7, 89.8 and 89.9 (see further para.89.8.2 below). Further, para.11 et seq of the Practice Guidance modifies the effect of the Committal PD in its application to proceedings under the Policing and Crime Act 2009 and the Antisocial Behaviour, Crime and Policing Act 2014.

II.   Committal for breach of a judgment, order or undertaking to do or abstain from doing an act

Effect of notice of order

Replace with:

81.8.2   The court may dispense with personal service of a mandatory or a prohibitory judgment or order if it thinks just to do so. Where the judgment or order is prohibitory, the court may dispense with personal service if satisfied that the respondent has had notice of it. The court's discretion is a wide one (*Davy International Ltd v Tazzyman* [1997] 1 W.L.R. 1256, CA). Modern cases in which the relevant authorities were examined include: *Benson v Richards* [2002] EWCA Civ 1402, *The Times*, 17 October 2002, CA; *Hydropool Hot Tubs Ltd v Roberjot* [2011] EWHC 121 (Ch), 4 February 2011, unrep. (Arnold J); *Gill v Darroch* [2010] EWHC 2347 (Ch), 22 July 2010, unrep. (Vos J). In *Sports Direct International Plc v Rangers International Football Club* [2016] EWHC 85 (Ch), 22 January 2016, unrep. (Peter Smith J), where the failure to serve the order personally was not mere oversight, the judge was not persuaded that in the circumstances he should exercise his discretion and dispense with the requirements of personal service retrospectively. Paragraph 16.2 of Practice Direction 81 refers to the court's power to waive procedural defects. In *JSC Mezhdunarodniy Promyshlenniy Bank v Pugachev* [2016] EWHC 192 (Ch), 8 February 2016, unrep. (Rose J) concluded that, in the circumstances, it was in the interests of justice to waive the requirement for personal service (and thereby to dispense retrospectively with the requirements for a penal notice). In *Khawaja v Popat* [2016] EWCA Civ 362, 14 April 2016, CA, the Court of Appeal rejected the contemnor's submission that the judge was wrong to have waived the requirement of personal service, holding that the question is whether injustice has been caused, not whether the circumstances were sufficiently exceptional to justify that course. On the question whether failure to effect personal service is defect that can be waived, see further para.81.10.2 below. Where the court finds, in a case where the respondent has persistently failed to comply with a mandatory order, that there is no doubt at all that the respondent knew perfectly well what the order said and what its consequences were, any view other than that it was just to dispense with personal service would be an encouragement for persistent offenders to use technicalities to defeat the purpose of such orders (*Benson v Richards* op cit at [38]). Where a prohibitory order with a penal notice attached is made, the court has power to include in the order a method of service alternative to personal service. In committal proceedings, if the court is satisfied that the order was properly served through the alternative method stipulated within the order it may dispense with personal service (*Serious Organised Crime Agency v Hymans* [2011] EWHC 3599 (QB), 18 October 2011, unrep. (Kenneth Parker J)).

Effect of rule

To the end of the second paragraph (beginning "The proposition that the lack"), add:
See also *In re L (A Child)* [2016] EWCA Civ 173, 22 March 2016, CA, unrep., at para.60 per Sir **81.9.1** James Munby P.

Application notice under Part 23

Replace the eighth paragraph with:
An order for committal for breach of a judgment or order to do or abstain from doing an act is **81.10.2** more than a form of execution available to one party to enforce an order against another, because the court itself has a very substantial interest in seeing that its orders are upheld. Where an application is made to commit a defendant for contempt of court, it is obviously important that great care is taken by the applicant to ensure that all the procedural requirements in this Section of Pt 81 are met. However, committal orders ought not to be set aside on purely technical grounds which having nothing to do with the justice of the case, because that would have the effect of undermining the system of justice and the credibility of court orders. (See *Nicholls v Nicholls* [1997] 1 W.L.R. 314, CA, *Bell v Tuohy* [2002] EWCA Civ 423; [2002] 1 W.L.R. 2703, CA, and authorities referred to there.) Accordingly, para.16.2 of Practice Direction 81 states that the court may waive any procedural defect in the commencement (or conduct) of a committal application if satisfied that no injustice has been caused to the respondent by the defect. As a practical matter, procedural defects are more likely to emerge through the applicant's failure to comply fully with the requirements of rr.81.4 and 81.5, rather than with the terms of r.81.10. In the Family Procedure Rules 2010, the comparable provision to para.16.2 of PD 81 is para.13.2 of PD 37. For a discussion of the authorities relevant to application of that provision, see *W v H* [2015] EWHC 2436 (Fam), 21 August 2015, unrep. (Parker J).

VI.   Committal for making a false statement of truth (rule 32.14) or disclosure statement (rule 31.23)

Permission where collateral criminal proceedings

Replace (where the citation for First Capital East Ltd v Plana has changed) with:
It is conceivable that, in a given case, the material facts relevant to an application to commit a **81.18.2.1** person for contempt of court may also expose that person to other forms of legal liability, in particular, for a criminal offence. In principle, where contempt proceedings have been taken and completed, any subsequent criminal charge cannot be met by a plea of autrefois acquit or autrefois convict. Conversely, the fact that criminal proceedings have been taken against a person is no bar to a committal application on the same facts (see Vol.2 para.3C-25). But where permission to proceed with the committal application is required it is unlikely to be granted where the respond-

ent was acquitted in the criminal proceedings, except, for example, where there is material evidence that was not before the criminal court, or where important new evidence has since come to light (*First Capital East Ltd v Plana* [2015] EWHC 2982 (QB); [2016] 1 W.L.R. 1271, (Judge Hughes QC)).

VIII.   *General rules about committal applications, orders for committal and writs of sequestration*

Grounds and evidence relied on

Replace the first paragraph with:

81.28.4   In committal proceedings it is important that applicants be clear and consistent about the allegations they are making. And it is important that all involved should be clear about the type of contempt or contempts being alleged, for example, whether contempt for breach of court order, and/or contempt in the face of the court (see *In re L (A Child)* [2016] EWCA Civ 173, 22 March 2016, CA, unrep., where lack of clarity in this respect contributed to procedural error). A claim form or an application notice may be amended with the permission of the court but not otherwise (Practice Direction 81 paras 12(2) and 13.2(2)). Generally, the rule that, at the hearing, without the court's permission the applicant may not rely on any grounds or evidence not pleaded or served tends to be strictly applied by the courts. Too much leniency in that respect would lead to adjournments and prolonged trials. Obviously, as the relevant circumstances must vary enormously, apart from the consideration that the respondent must be treated fairly, there are no tests that could usefully be stated as to when the court may exercise its discretion.

Replace the fourth paragraph with:

A person accused of contempt, like the defendant in a criminal trial, has the right to remain silent (*Comet Products UK Ltd v Hawkex Plastics Ltd* [1971] 2 Q.B. 67, CA). It is the duty of the court to ensure that the accused person is made aware of that right and also of the risk that adverse inferences may be drawn from his silence (*Inplayer Limited v Thorogood* [2014] EWCA Civ 1511, 25 November 2014, CA, unrep., at para.41). The drawing of adverse inference in this context is consistent with the jurisprudence of the European Court of Human Rights (*Khawaja v Popat* [2016] EWCA Civ 362, 14 April 2016, CA, unrep., at para.30 per McCombe LJ). If the committal application is heard at the same time as other issues about which the alleged contemnor needs to give evidence, he is placed in the position where he is effectively deprived of the right of silence (ibid). That is a serious procedural error (see also *Hammerton v Hammerton* [2007] EWCA Civ 248; [2007] 2 F.L.R. 1133, CA). In the case of *In re L (A Child)* [2016] EWCA Civ 173, 22 March 2016, CA, unrep., in proceedings for enforcement of a collection order, the paternal uncle (D) of the child concerned was brought before the court on witness summons and gave evidence under compulsion (which was not believed). In proceedings brought by the local authority, in which it was alleged that D had not provided the court with all the information he had about the whereabouts of the child, D was committed for contempt. The Court of Appeal allowed D's appeal, principally on the ground that, at the committal hearing, use was made against him of "the evidence which had been extracted from him under compulsion".

In the fifth paragraph (beginning "A person against whom a committal application"), replace "where the applicant does not seeks" with "where the applicant seeks":

After the fifth paragraph (beginning "A person against whom a committal application"), add as a new paragraph:

In *Vis Trading Co Ltd v Nazarov* [2015] EWHC 3327 (QB), 18 November 2015, unrep. (Whipple J), where an application was made by the claimant (C) to commit for contempt a defendant (D) on the ground of his failure to comply with a disclosure order ancillary to a post-judgment freezing order, the judge explained (at para.31) that the fact that D had produced some documents, in purported compliance with the order, did not determine the compliance issue in his favour; nor did it require C to make any application for cross-examination. Rather, the position was that D was on notice of C's case of non-compliance and C was entitled to continue to advance that case, even in the face of purported compliance by D since the date of the application. The burden of proof remained on C throughout, to the criminal standard, and C could invite the court to conclude, on the basis of all the evidence in the case, that D had not yet complied with the order. If a respondent chose to remain silent in the face of such a submission, the court could draw an adverse inference against him, if the court considered that to be appropriate and fair, and recalling that silence alone cannot prove guilt. This is not to put the burden of proof on the respondent; the burden remains on the applicant.

Application to be discharged from prison

Add new paragraph at end:

81.31.1   In *Swindon BC v Webb* [2016] EWCA Civ 152, 16 March 2016, CA, a respondent contemnor (committed for breach of an injunction imposed on him under the Enterprise Act 2002 s.213 as "a rogue trader") made no application for discharge but, for purposes he did not comprehend, was taken before the court for a hearing scheduled on its own initiative, and of which the applicant had no notice, was told that in order to purge his contempt he should apologise to the court, dutifully did so, and was discharged. In effect the contemnor was released after he had served only eight days of the four months sentence imposed. On appeal by the applicant (who submitted that the procedure adopted by the court was irregular) the Court of Appeal stressed the importance of ordinarily insisting in cases of this sort that the procedure provided by r.81.31 is followed where a contemnor seeks his discharge (para.24). Ordinarily an application for discharge should where possible be listed before the judge who imposed the order for committal (ibid).

Discharge of a person

Replace the second paragraph with:

81.31.4

In most cases, an application for discharge under r.81.31 by a contemnor who has been committed to prison involves the contemnor in "purging" his contempt by apologising to the court for his past misbehaviour. Further, in most cases, where the contempt consists of a breach of an order of the court, it will also involve a promise to comply in future with the court's orders. But a credible promise of future good behaviour is not always necessary as there may come a point where even the most obdurate refusal to comply will nonetheless not prevent a contemnor's discharge (see *Harris v Harris* [2001] Fam. 502, at [28] per Munby J, and authorities referred to there). Thus the court can effectively cut short a term of imprisonment imposed on a contemnor for coercive purposes, if satisfied that the desired end will not be achieved.

Add new paragraph at end:

In *Swindon BC v Webb* [2016] EWCA Civ 152, 16 March 2016, CA, for the purpose of drawing the attention of judges to the guidance available to them when considering whether contemnors should be released before the expiry of the term of their sentences, the Court of Appeal explained the relevant authorities.

PART 83

WRITS AND WARRANTS—GENERAL PROVISIONS

Forms

Replace list with:

83.0.20

- **Form 53** Writ of control
- **Form 54** Writ of control on order for costs
- **Form 56** Writ of control (of Part)
- **Form 58** Writ of fieri facias de bonis ecclesiasticis
- **Form 59** Writ of sequestrari de bonis ecclesiasticis
- **Form 62** Writ of control to enforce Northern Irish or Scottish judgment
- **Form 63** Writ of control to enforce foreign registered judgment
- **Form 64** Writ of specific delivery: delivery of goods, damages and costs
- **Form 65** Writ of delivery of goods or value, damages and costs
- **Form 66** Combined writ of possession and control
- **Form 66A** Combined writ of possession and control for costs of action
- **Form 67** Writ of sequestration
- **Form 68** Writ of restitution
- **Form 69** Writ of assistance
- **Form 71** Notice of the extension of a writ of execution
- **N42** Warrant of control
- **N46** Warrant of delivery and of control for damages and costs
- **N49** Warrant for possession of land
- **N50** Warrant of restitution
- **N51** Warrant of Restitution (trespass)
- **N52** Warrant for Possession of Land (Trespassers)
- **N244** Application notice
- **N245** Application for suspension of warrant (and for variation of an instalment)
- **N246** Claimant's reply to defendant's application to vary instalment order
- **N246A** Claimant's reply to defendant's application to suspend warrant
- **N293A** Combined certificate of judgment and request for writ of control or writ of possession
- **N322** Order for recovery of money awarded by tribunal
- **N322A** Application for order to recover money awarded by tribunal or other body

- **N322H** Request to register a High Court judgment or order for enforcement
- **N323** Request for a warrant of control
- **N324** Request for warrant of delivery of goods
- **N325** Request for warrant of possession
- **N326** Notice of issue of warrant of control
- **N327** Notice of issue of warrant of control to enforce a judgment or order
- **N328** Notice of transfer of proceedings to the High Court
- **N444** Details of sale under a warrant of control
- PF 92 Order for permission to issue a writ of possession in the High Court to enforce a Judgment or Order for giving of possession of land in proceedings in the County Court (other than a claim against trespassers under Part 55) (Rule 83.13(2) and (8))

III.   Writs

Effect of rule

Replace the first paragraph with:

83.13.1   Under this rule, permission is required to enforce a judgment or order for the giving of possession of land, subject to the important exceptions listed in r.83.13(3) and (5)—which in practice cover a minority of cases—and r.83.13(6), which deals with mortgages/security. Whilst rr.83.13(3) and (4) incorporate the position in respect of warrants in possession proceedings against trespassers into the body of the provision for possession, it is important to stress that in other cases permission is required (r.83.13(2)). This is a point stressed by 'The Senior Master Practice Note 21.3.2016—Applications for transfers for enforcement of possession orders to the High Court', which recognises problems arising from the identified misuse of the procedure at r.83.19(1)(b). CPR r.83.19(1)(b) only applies to the enforcement of those possessions orders where the possession claim arises against trespassers. The Practice Note stresses this and reiterates that in possession claims the Queen's Bench Enforcement Section and court staff in District Registries will only accept **Form N293A** in respect of possession orders against trespassers. (Note this has no relevance to the use of **Form N293A** in respect of execution against goods—r.83.19(1)).

Replace the second paragraph with:

Rule 81.4 applies to the enforcement by committal orders of judgments, orders or undertakings to do or abstain ffrom doing an act, and r.81.20 applies to their enforcement by writs of sequestration. (As explained above, those rules replaced provisions formerly found in Ord.45.) A judgment or order to give possession of land will not be enforceable by an order of committal or by writ of sequestration unless it specifies the time within which this act is required to be done, and the defendant refuses or neglects to do it within that time (see r.81.4). Accordingly, as a judgment or order to give possession of land will not in practice specify the time within which this act is required to be done, it will not ordinarily be enforceable by an order of committal or by writ of sequestration, but only by a writ of possession, which will normally be sufficient to enforce the judgment. If, however, in an extreme case, it is desired to enforce the judgment against a recalcitrant defendant by an order of committal or writ of sequestration, it will be necessary first to apply to the court for an order to fix the time within which the defendant is required to give possession of the land, and to serve that order upon the defendant under r.81.5 (formerly r.7 of this Order), and then to apply under r.81.4 or r.81.20 for the order of committal or writ of sequestration.

Permission to issue writ of possession

Add new paragraphs at end:

83.13.6   Notice of any application for permission to issue a writ of possession under CPR r.83.13(2) must be given to the occupants of the property (r.83.13(8)). A failure to do so provides a sufficient ground upon which the court will set aside a writ of possession after it has been executed (see r.83.13.(8) and para.83.13.9 below and *Secretary of State for Defence v Nicholas* [2015] EWHC 4064 (Ch)).

From April 2016 there is a draft form of order (PF 92) for use when the court gives permission to enforce a judgment or order for giving possession of land in the County Court (other than in respect of trespassers)—see the commentary at para.83.13.9.

Notice of the proceedings

To the end of the first paragraph, add:

83.13.9   Failure to give notice of the application has been held to provide a sufficient ground upon which the court will set aside a writ of possession after it has been executed (see r.83.13(2) and para.83.13.6 above and *Secretary of State for Defence v Nicholas* [2015] EWHC 4064 (Ch)).

To the end of the second paragraph, add:

PF 92, introduced in April 2016, reinforces this, as it contains a standard paragraph that the court is satisfied that every person in occupation of the whole or part of the land has received such notice that "appears to the court sufficient to enable the occupant to apply to the court for any relief to which the occupant may be entitled".

IV. Warrants

Procedure on Transfer

Replace with:

Note that r.83.19 only applies to requests to transfer for enforcement (i) by execution against **83.19.2** goods (where the judgment is £600 or more) and/or (ii) of possession orders for possession of land made in claims against trespassers (cases where permission to issue writs of control or of possession is not required). **Form N293A** and this procedure is not required if the judgment creditor asks for, and receives, an order for transfer to the High Court under s.42 of the County Courts Act 1984 at the time judgment is given.

Add new paragraphs at end:

The grant of a certificate by the court takes effect as an order to transfer the proceedings to the High Court. Given identified misuse of this procedure (particularly in the case of orders for possession against tenants), the Senior Master issued a Practice Note 21.3.2016 'Applications for transfers for enforcement of possession orders to the High Court', clearly stating that the Queen's Bench Division Enforcement Section will not accept **Form N293A** for transfer to the High Court for enforcement of a possession order of the County Court other than in respect of possession orders against trespassers and requested that the same instructions were given to staff in the District Registries.

An earlier Practice Note from the Senior Master 14.12.2015 effectively brought to an end applications made 'not on notice' under s.41 of the County Courts Act 1984 (Transfer to High Court by order of the High Court) by High Court Enforcement Officers seemingly to avoid both perceived delays in the County Court and an apparent reluctance by that court to complete Form **N293A** without explanation. The note concluded '...that the QB Masters will not make Orders for Transfer for Enforcement under S.41 unless on notice, and therefore all applications for transfer of County Court Orders and Judgments for Enforcement should be made either by an application under S.42 to the District Judge making the order, or, if for a Writ of Control or of Possession in a claim against Trespassers, by lodging a properly completed Form N293A at a County Court Office.' The Practice Note in March 2016 took this a stage further by stating that the Queen's Bench Masters would not entertain any applications at all under s.41 in possession proceedings and that, where an order was required, applications should be made under s.42 to a judge of the hearing centre where the possession order was made.

For the procedure where permission is required to issue a writ of possession see the commentary to CPR r.83.13(2) and (8) above.

Add two new Practice Notes after Practice Direction 83:

SENIOR MASTER PRACTICE NOTE 14 DECEMBER 2015 TRANSFERS FOR ENFORCEMENT TO THE HIGH COURT

Form N293A (Combined Certificate for judgment and request for writ of **83PN.1** control or writ of possession) (*http://hmctsformfinder.justice.gov.uk/courtfinder/forms/n293a-eng.pdf*) is used when a judgment creditor with a County Court judgment of £600 or more, or in receipt of a possession order against trespassers, wishes to transfer the claim to the High Court for enforcement, so that they can instruct a High Court Enforcement Officer, ("HCEO") (rather than the County Court bailiffs) to enforce the judgment either by a writ of control or a writ of possession.

The procedure to be adopted, (unless the judgment creditor/party with the benefit of a possession order asks the County Court District judge for an order for transfer under S. 42 of the County Courts Act 1984 when judgment is given), is to use Form N293A. This is submitted to the County Court (and now that there is a single County Court in theory this can be done by any County Court Office), with Part 1 of the form completed by the Judgment Creditor's legal representative. Part 2 is then completed by a court officer. The HCEO then completes Part 3, and takes the completed and certified N293A to the Central Office or a District Registry of the High Court and obtains a Writ of Control and/or a Writ of Possession.

In the last 12 months, instead of the Claimant making an application under

S.42 at the hearing, or submitting Form N293A, a number of HCEOs have been making applications on a regular basis to the Practice Master in QBD under S. 41 of the County Courts Act 1984 to transfer the County Court claim for enforcement to the High Court. The HCEOs have informed the Masters that that County Court officers are refusing to certify Form 293As, without explanation. We have also been told that when applications are made under S. 42, some County Courts can take some 6-8 weeks to deal with them, and in the case of possession orders this means a significant loss of rental income to the judgment creditors. Thus it is much more efficient for judgment creditors/ parties with the benefit of a possession order, to enforce through a HCEO rather than via County Court bailiffs, so the HCEOs have no alternative but to make applications under S.41, where they can get an immediate order and issue a Writ of Control/Possession straight away.

The QB Practice Masters have been dealing with such applications, and making S.41 orders. However, as the County Court file and log for the case is not available to the QB Masters, in a number of cases their orders have conflicted with orders made by judges in the County Court. This has caused considerable problems in some cases. Accordingly, after consultation with the Deputy Head of Civil Justice, the President of the Queen's Bench Division, and the appropriate policy officials of the Ministry of Justice and of HM Courts & Tribunal Services, I have determined that the QB Masters will not make orders for transfer for enforcement under S.41 unless on notice, and therefore all applications for transfer of county court orders and judgments for enforcement should be made either by an application under S. 42 to the District judge making the order, or, if for a Writ of Control or of Possession in a claim against trespassers, by lodging a properly completed Form N293A at a County Court office.

Barbara Fontaine
The Senior Master
14 December 2015

SENIOR MASTER PRACTICE NOTE 21 MARCH 2016 APPLICATIONS FOR TRANSFERS FOR ENFORCEMENT OF POSSESSION ORDERS TO THE HIGH COURT

83PN.2   I have received complaints that some High Court Enforcement Officers ("HCEOs") have been using Form N293A to transfer County Court Possession Orders against tenants for enforcement to the High Court. This procedure is wrong because:

1.   The Form is intended for enforcement of possession orders against trespassers only (as stated in the notes at the bottom of the form; and
2.   CPR 83.13(2) requires the permission of the High Court before a High Court Writ of Possession can be issued; and
3.   CPR 83.13(8) (a) requires sufficient notice to be given to all occupants of the premises to enable them to apply to the court for any relief to which they may be entitled.

There have also been recent decisions where the misuse of Form N293A has been identified, e.g. *Birmingham City Council v Mondhlani* [2015] EW Misc (CC) (6 Nov. 2015); and lack of notice required under CPR 83.13(8) e.g. *Nicholas v Secretary of State for Defence* [2015] EWHC 4064 (Ch) (24 August 2015) Rose J. (unrep.).

In order to ensure that this practice does not continue:

1.   The Queen's Bench Division Enforcement Section will not accept Form N293A for transfer to the High Court for enforcement of a possession order of the County Court other than for possession orders against trespassers. By distributing a copy of this note to Designated Civil Judges in District Registries I shall request that the same instructions be given

to court staff in District Registries.

2. The Queen's Bench Masters will not accept applications under Section 41 of the County Court Act 1984 for transfer of a County Court possession claim for enforcement and such applications must be made under Section 42 of the County Court Act 1984 to a judge of the hearing centre of the County Court where the possession order was made, so that judge can satisfy themselves that the appropriate notice has been given under CPR 83.13(8).

3. The Civil Procedure Rule Committee ("CPRC") subcommittee on court forms has:

(i) re-drafted Form N293A with greater emphasis on the restriction of the use of the form to requests for writs of control and writs of possession against trespassers only; and

(ii) drafted a new form of draft order (PF92) giving permission to enforce a judgment or order for giving possession of land in the County Court (other than a claim against trespassers under Part 55), which make it clear that applications for such permission must provide evidence to satisfy the judge determining such application that the requirements of Rule 83.13(8) are met.

It is anticipated that these will be available for use in April 2016.

The Senior Master

SECTION C   PRE-ACTION CONDUCT AND PROTOCOLS

The Pre-action Conduct PD

Replace the second paragraph with:

The Practice Direction was amended and came into force in April 2015. The new version is **C1A-015** shorter and the main changes are:

- sections I, III and IV are omitted and the content of Sections III and IV are summarised into 4 short paragraphs (6-8 and 11);
- the aims are set out succinctly in paras 1–3 (consistent with the specific protocols);
- there are new paragraphs 4–5 on proportionality;
- there are new paragraphs 8–9 on settlement and ADR;
- there are new short paragraphs on expert evidence, 7, and the need for a stocktake, 12, to narrow the issues if the dispute does not resolve without proceedings;
- the section on compliance, paragraphs 13–16, is shortened.

PRE-ACTION PROTOCOL FOR LOW VALUE PERSONAL INJURY CLAIMS IN ROAD TRAFFIC ACCIDENTS FROM 31 JULY 2013

Section I — Introduction

Definitions

Replace paragraph 1.1 with:

1.1   In this Protocol—   **C13-001**

(A1) "accredited medical expert" means a medical expert who—

(a) prepares a fixed cost medical report pursuant to paragraph 7.8A(1) before 1 June 2016 and, on the date that they are instructed, the expert is registered with MedCo as a provider of reports for soft tissue injury claims; or

(b) prepares a fixed cost medical report pursuant to paragraph 7.8A(1) on or after 1 June 2016 and, on the date that they are instructed, the expert is accredited by MedCo to provide reports for soft tissue injury claims;

(1)   "admission of liability" means the defendant admits that—
   (a)   the accident occurred;
   (b)   the accident was caused by the defendant's breach of duty;
   (c)   the defendant caused some loss to the claimant, the nature and extent of which is not admitted; and
   (d)   the defendant has no accrued defence to the claim under the Limitation Act 1980;

(1A)   "associate" means, in respect of a medical expert, a colleague, partner, director, employer or employee in the same practice and "associated with" has the equivalent meaning;

(2)   "bank holiday" means a bank holiday under the Banking and Financial Dealings Act 1971;

(3)   "business day" means any day except Saturday, Sunday, a bank holiday, Good Friday or Christmas Day;

(4)   "certificate of recoverable benefits" has the same meaning as in rule 36.22(1)(e)(i) of the Civil Procedure Rules 1998.

(5)   "child" means a person under 18;

(6)   "claim" means a claim, prior to the start of proceedings, for payment of damages under the process set out in this Protocol;

(7)   "claimant" means a person starting a claim under this Protocol unless the context indicates that it means the claimant's legal representative;

(8)   "CNF" means a Claim Notification Form;

(9)   "deductible amount" has the same meaning as in rule 36.15(1)(d) of the Civil Procedure Rules 1998;

(10)   "defendant" means the insurer of the person who is subject to the claim under this Protocol, unless the context indicates that it means—
   (a)   the person who is subject to the claim;
   (b)   the defendant's legal representative;
   (c)   the Motor Insurers' Bureau ('MIB'); or
   (d)   a person falling within the exceptions in section 144 of the Road Traffic Act 1988 (a "self-insurer");

(10A) "fixed cost medical report" means a report in a soft tissue injury claim which is from a medical expert who, save in exceptional circumstances—
   (a)   has not provided treatment to the claimant;
   (b)   is not associated with any person who has provided treatment; and
   (c)   does not propose or recommend treatment that they or an associate then provide;

(11)   "legal representative" has the same meaning as in rule 2.3(1) of the Civil Procedure Rules 1998;

(12)   "medical expert" means a person who is—
   (a)   registered with the General Medical Council;
   (b)   registered with the General Dental Council; or
   (c)   a Psychologist or Physiotherapist registered with the Health Care Professions Council;

(12A) "MedCo" means MedCo Registration Solutions;

(13)   "motor vehicle" means a mechanically propelled vehicle intended for use on roads;

(14)   "pecuniary losses" means past and future expenses and losses;

(15)   "road" means any highway and any other road to which the public has access and includes bridges over which a road passes;

(16)   "road traffic accident" means an accident resulting in bodily injury to any person caused by, or arising out of, the use of a motor vehicle on

a road or other public place in England and Wales unless the injury was caused wholly or in part by a breach by the defendant of one or more of the relevant statutory provisions[1] as defined by section 53 of the Health and Safety at Work etc Act 1974;

(16A) "soft tissue injury claim" means a claim brought by an occupant of a motor vehicle where the significant physical injury caused is a soft tissue injury and includes claims where there is a minor psychological injury secondary in significance to the physical injury;

(17) "Type C fixed costs" has the same meaning as in rule 45.18(2) of the Civil Procedure Rules 1998; and

(18) "vehicle related damages" means damages for—

  (a) the pre-accident value of the vehicle;

  (b) vehicle repair;

  (c) vehicle insurance excess; and

  (d) vehicle hire.

---

[1] See — Control of Substances Hazardous to Health Regulations 2002 (S.I. 2002/2677) Lifting Operations and Lifting Equipment Regulations 1998 (S.I. 1998/2307) Management of Health and Safety at Work Regulations 1999 (S.I. 1999/3242) Manual Handling Operations Regulations 1992 (S.I. 1992/2793) Personal Protective Equipment at Work Regulations 1992 (S.I. 1992/2966) Provision and Use of Work Equipment Regulations 1998 (S.I. 1998/2306) Work at Height Regulations 2005 (S.I. 2005/735) Workplace (Health, Safety and Welfare) Regulations 1992 (S.I. 1992/3004). The Construction (Design and Management) Regulations 2007 (S.I 2007/320).

SECTION A1   PROCEDURAL GUIDES

15.   INSOLVENCY

15.2   Proceedings under s.6 of the Company Directors Disqualification Act 1986 (CDDA 1986)

Report of office-holder

Replace entry with:

A1.15-002

CDDA 1986 s.6(1), s.7(3)   If it appears to the office holder acting in the company insolvency that the conditions in CDDA, s.6(1) are present (i.e. that a person has been a director of a company which has become insolvent, and that his conduct as a director (either taken alone or taken together with his conduct as a director of any other company or companies) makes him unfit to be concerned in the management of a company), he shall forthwith report the matter to the Secretary of State. Detailed provisions as to the form and timing of the report are set out in the Insolvent Companies (Reports on Conduct of Directors) (England and Wales) Rules 2016.

The first hearing of the disqualification application/directions hearing

Replace entry with:

Directors Disqualification Proceedings PD paras 4.3 and 9
Disqualification Rules 1987 r.7
Insolvency Rules 1986 r.13(2)
Courts and Legal Services Act 1990 s.74

The first hearing is before a registrar in open court, and shall be not less than eight weeks from the date of issue of the claim form. The registrar can either determine the case (if it is uncontested, and does not merit a period of disqualification longer than five years), or give directions and adjourn it.

Where an uncontested case merits a period of disqualification of longer than five years it will be disposed of at the second hearing, provided there is sufficient time.

Evidence directions will normally simply provide for evidence in answer from defendants, and evidence in reply from the Secretary of State. Further rounds of evidence are possible, but unusual.

Expert evidence is rarely ordered, and expert evidence on questions such as whether a company was insolvent will almost never be appropriate.

In the context of the disqualification proceedings, "registrar" includes a district judge of a High Court District Registry or of a county court.

SECTION 2   SPECIALIST PROCEEDINGS

SECTION 2A   COMMERCIAL COURT

PART 58—COMMERCIAL COURT

Related sources

2A-3 *Replace "The Admiralty and Commercial Courts Guide 9th edn 2011 (updated January 2016), (see para.2A-39 et seq)." with:*

- The Admiralty and Commercial Courts Guide 9th edn 2011 (updated March 2016), (see para.2A-39 et seq).

ADMIRALTY AND COMMERCIAL COURTS GUIDE

APPENDIX 5

FORMS OF FREEZING INJUNCTION AND SEARCH ORDER
adapted for use in the Commercial Court

** FREEZING INJUNCTION **

PENAL NOTICE

FREEZING INJUNCTION

[FOR EITHER FORM OF INJUNCTION]

Replace paragraph (where the citation for JSC BTA Bank v Ablyazov in the first footnote has changed) with:

2A-162 **6.**   Paragraph 5 applies to all the Respondent's assets[1] whether or not they are in his own name, whether they are solely or jointly owned [and whether the Respondent is interested in them legally, beneficially or otherwise][2]. For the purpose of this order the Respondent's assets include any asset which he has the power, directly or indirectly, to dispose of or deal with as if it were his own. The Respondent is to be regarded as having such power if a third party holds or controls the asset in accordance with his direct or indirect instructions.

ADDRESSES AND CONTACT DETAILS

Replace paragraph with:

2A-215   The individual telephone and fax numbers are as follows:

The Admiralty Marshal:
Tel: 020 7947 6111
Fax: 020 7947 7671

---

[1] In *JSC BTA Bank v Ablyazov* [2015] UKSC 64; [2015] 1 W.L.R. 4754; [2016] 1 All E.R. 608; [2016] 1 All E.R. (Comm) 97; [2015] 2 Lloyd's Rep. 546 the Supreme Court held that the proceeds of a loan agreement were "assets" within the definition contained in the standard Commercial Court form of freezing order. Under that definition, the term "assets" included any asset which a defendant had power, directly or indirectly, to dispose of, or deal with as if it were his own. A loan agreement gave a borrower the power to dispose of or deal with the assets as if they were his own and a borrower who instructed a lender to pay the lender's money to a third party was dealing with the lender's assets as if they were his own.

[2] Whether this wider wording should be included in relation to the Order and/or the provision of information will be considered on a case by case basis—see generally *JSC BTA Bank v Kythreotis and Others* [2010] EWCA Civ 1436.

The Admiralty & Commercial Registry:
Tel: 020 7947 6112
Fax: 020 7947 6245
DX 160040 Strand 4

The Admiralty & Commercial Court Listing Office:
Tel: 020 7947 6826
Fax: 020 7947 7670
DX 160040 Strand 4

The Secretary to the Commercial Court Committee:
Mr Joseph Quinn
Tel: 020 7947 6826
Fax: 020 7947 7670
DX 160040 Strand 4[1]

SECTION 2B   MERCANTILE COURTS

MERCANTILE COURT GUIDE

APPENDIX A

COURT ADDRESSES AND OTHER INFORMATION

1.   LONDON AND SOUTH EAST

Judge

Replace "Clerk—Adham Harker" with:
　　Clerk—Adam Wilcox

2B-35

Replace "Email: Adham.Harker@hmcts.gsi.gov.uk" with:
　　Email: adam.wilcox@hmcts.gsi.gov.uk

5.   NORTH WEST (LIVERPOOL)

Judges

Replace paragraph with:

　　His Honour Judge Moulder
　　His Honour Judge Bird

2B-39

6.   NORTH WEST (MANCHESTER)

Judges and Listing

Replace paragraph with:

　　His Honour Judge Moulder
　　His Honour Judge Bird
　　Manager of Mercantile Listing—Lesley Armstrong
　　Clerk to Mercantile Judges: 0161 240 5305
　　Email: manchester.mercantile@hmcts.gsi.gov.uk
　　Fax (Goldfax): 01264 785034

2B-40

---

[1] The Secretary to the Commercial Court Committee is now Joseph Quinn. Contact details are unchanged.

7.   SOUTH WEST (BRISTOL)

Address

Replace paragraph with:

2B-41

The Bristol Civil and Family Justice Centre
2 Redcliff Street
Bristol England
BS1 6GR
DX 95903 Bristol 3

Judge and Listing

Replace paragraph with:

His Honour Judge Havelock-Allan QC (Court 12 on the 2nd floor)
Specialist Listing Officers—Debbie Thal-Jantzen and Amy Smallcombe
Telephone number 0117 366 4866 and 4833
Email: bristolmercantilelisting@hmcts.gsi.gov.uk
General switchboard: 0117 366 4860
Fax: 0117 366 4801 (not a dedicated fax so clearly mark "Mercantile Court")
Dedicated email: bristolmercantilelisting@hmcts.gsi.gov.uk

8.   WALES (CARDIFF)

Judge

Replace paragraph with:

2B-42

His Honour Judge Keyser QC
Clerk—Barry Sharples
Email: barry.sharples@hmcts.gsi.gov.uk
Tel: 02920 376411
Fax: 02920 376475
Listing Clerk—Amanda Barrago
Email: amanda.barrago@hmcts.gsi.gov.uk
Tel: 029 20376412
Fax: 029 20376475

SECTION 2E   ARBITRATION PROCEEDINGS

PART 62—ARBITRATION CLAIMS

Add new paragraph 2E–6.1:

Family Court claims

2E-6.1   Pending rule/practice direction amendments special provision has been made for arbitration claims arising out of family court cases. On 23 November 2015 the President of the Family Court, Sir James Munby, issued *Practice Direction (Family Court: Interface with Arbitration)* [2016] 1 W.L.R. 59. This concerns the interface between the Family Court and arbitrations conducted in accordance with the provisions of the Arbitration Act 1996 where the parties to a post-relationship breakdown financial dispute have agreed to submit issues for decision by an arbitrator whose award is to be binding upon them. The text of the guidance is at:
https://www.judiciary.gov.uk/publications/practice-guidance-arbitration-in-the-family-court/ [Accessed 17 May 2016].

Arbitration Act 1996

Onus of showing that claim should proceed

Replace the second paragraph (where the citation for Salford Estates (No.2) Ltd v Altomart Ltd has changed) with:

2E-112   In *Wealands v C.L.C. Contractors Ltd* [1998] C.L.C. 808, the court held on an application by a sub-contractor for third party proceedings against it by the contractor to be stayed under s.9 of the Arbitration Act 1996 that despite the disadvantages of the claim against the third party going to arbitration (if the plaintiff did not join the third party as a defendant) the 1996 Act gave priority to party autonomy and entitled the third party as of right to the stay which is sought (affirmed [1999] 2 Lloyd's Rep. 739, CA. However, in *Salford Estates (No.2) Ltd v Altomart Ltd* [2014] EWCA Civ 1575; [2015] Ch. 589; [2015] 3 W.L.R. 491; [2015] B.C.C. 306, the Court of Appeal held that where a number of disputes concerning liability for the payment of service charges and insurance rent were referred to arbitration under the provisions of a lease, the Arbitration Act 1996 s.9 did not apply to a winding-up petition presented by the lessor based on the lessee company's inability to pay its debts, because the substance of the dispute was the existence of a particular debt mentioned in the petition.

Unless otherwise agreed ... the following provisions apply

Add new paragraph at end:
In *Pearl Petroleum Co Ltd v Kurdistan Regional Government of Iraq* [2015] EWHC 3361 (Comm) **2E-184** Burton J held that when making a peremptory order under s.41(5), arbitrators did not have to state that the order was necessary for the "proper and expeditious conduct of the arbitral proceedings". Section 41(5) could be invoked for a failure to comply with "any" order of the tribunal and was not to be construed only in the context of s.41(1) of the Act.

Note

Replace the third paragraph (where the citation for Emirates Trading Agency LLC v Sociedade de Fomento Industrial Private Ltd has changed) with:
Arbitrators have to be appointed in compliance with any applicable procedure for appointment. **2E-256** Any irregularity in appointment invalidates the arbitration. There is no room in arbitration for the common law doctrine which can sometimes validate the acts of an apparent or reputed judge. See *Sumukan Ltd v Commonwealth Secretariat* [2007] EWCA Civ 1148; [2008] Bus L.R. 858; [2008] 2 All E.R. (Comm); [2008] 1 Lloyd's Rep. 40, CA; [2007] 2 C.L.C. 821; *Dallah Estate and Tourism Holding Co v Ministry of Religious Affairs of the Government of Pakistan* [2010] UKSC 46; [2011] 1 A.C. 763; [2011] 1 All E.R. 485; [2011] 1 All E.R. (Comm) 383; [2010] 2 Lloyd's Rep. 691; [2010] 2 C.L.C. 793. In *Emirates Trading Agency LLC v Sociedade de Fomento Industrial Private Ltd* [2015] EWHC 1452 (Comm); [2016] 1 All E.R. (Comm) 517; [2015] 2 Lloyd's Rep. 487 Popplewell J held that an application under this section to set aside a final merits award for lack of jurisdiction should be refused where the tribunal had already made a partial award on jurisdiction which was binding and had not been challenged.

"On the ground of serious irregularity"

In the first paragraph, after "813, Flaux J.", delete ", FlauxJ.".   **2E-262**

After the second paragraph (beginning "In BV Scheepswerf Damen Gorinchem v Marine Institute"), add as a new paragraph:
In *Larus Australia v Agrocorp International Pte Ltd* [2015] EWHC 3774 (Comm) Knowles J rejected a submission that arbitrations had committed misconduct within s.68(2)(a) where they did not invite a defendant to make an application under s.41 of the Act having considered the point and concluded that had such an application been made they would have concluded that the delay was not inexcusable.

Replace the eighth paragraph (where the citation for Maass v Musion Events Ltd has changed) with:
In cases under s.68(2)(d), there are four questions for the court: (i) whether the relevant point or argument was an "issue" within the meaning of the sub-section; (ii) if so, whether the issue was "put" to the tribunal; (iii) if so, whether the tribunal failed to deal with it; and (iv) if so, whether that failure has caused substantial injustice. Per Andrew Smith J. in *Petrochemical Industries Co v Dow Chemical* [2012] EWHC 2739 (Comm); [2012] 2 Lloyd's Rep 691 at [15], *Primera Maritime Hellas v Jiangsum Eastern Heavy Industry* [2013] EWHC 3066 (Comm); [2014] 1 Lloyd's Rep. 255; [2013] 2 C.L.C. 901, [2014] 1 All E.R. (Comm) 813 Flaux J., *Transition Feeds LLP (formerly Advanced Liquid Feeds LLP) v Itochu Europe Plc* [2013] EWHC 3629 (Comm); [2013] 2 C.L.C. 920 Field J. The test for whether such an irregularity caused, or would cause, a substantial injustice was whether the irregularity caused the arbitrator to reach a conclusion which, but for the irregularity, he might not have reached, as long as the alternative was reasonably arguable: *Maass v Musion Events Ltd* [2015] EWHC 1346 (Comm); [2016] 1 All E.R. (Comm) 292; [2015] 2 Lloyd's Rep. 383 (Andrew Smith J.). For there to be a serious irregularity under s.68(2)(d) because the arbitrators failed to deal with an issue put to them, it was necessary to establish that they had failed to deal at all with a fundamental issue which was essential to the decision: *Abuja International Hotels Ltd v Meridien SAS* [2012] EWHC 87 (Comm); [2012] 1 Lloyd's Rep. 461, Hamblen J. See also *Fidelity Management SA v Myriad International Holdings BV* [2005] EWHC 1193 (Comm); [2005] 2 All E.R. (Comm) 312. A failure to address central issue by GAFA constituted a serious irregularity within s.68(2)(d), see *Ascot Com-*

modities NV v Olam International Ltd [2002] C.L.C. 277. An issue is not "put to" the arbitrator when the question of fact is not supported by any evidence sufficient to require a conclusion and without a relevant factual finding, the point of law is of hypothetical interest only: *Cordoba Holdings v Ballymore Properties* [2011] EWHC 1636 (Ch) per Morritt C. Likewise a failure to make a declaratory award thereby depriving a party of a set off will not be a serious irregularity where it was clear to the parties that a money award was to be made, and the set off would have come too late: *L v R* [2012] EWHC 2894 (Comm), Hamblen J.

Appeals to the Court of Appeal

2E-268

Replace the last paragraph (where the citation for Michael Wilson & Partners Ltd v Emmott has changed) with:

In *CGU International Insurance plc v Astra Zeneca Insurance Co Ltd* [2006] EWCA Civ 1340; [2007] 1 Lloyd's Rep. 142; [2007] 1 All E.R. (Comm) 501; [2006] 2 C.L.C. 441, and *Philip Hanby Ltd v Clarke* [2013] EWCA Civ 647, March 20, 2013, CA the court has held that there is a residual discretion to permit an appeal despite the judge's refusal of leave where the refusal could be challenged on the ground that the decision had been arrived at as the result of some unfair or improper process such that that decision could not properly be called a decision at all or on the ground of unfairness under art.6 of the European Convention on Human Rights. Courts would however not allow such power which existed to ensure that injustice was avoided to become itself an unfair instrument for subverting statute and undermining the process of arbitration. See too *ASM Shipping Ltd of India v TTMI Ltd of England* [2006] EWCA Civ 1341; [2007] 1 Lloyd's Rep. 136; [2006] 2 C.L.C. 471 (residual discretion not involved; no overarching principle in Human Rights Convention that an award tainted by apparent bias must be set aside: application of margin of appreciation in domestic court). The recent cases of *Philip Hanby* (above) and *Bunge SA v Kyla Shipping Co Ltd* [2013] EWCA Civ 734; [2013] 3 All E.R. 1006; [2013] 2 All E.R. (Comm) 577; [2013] 2 Lloyd's Rep. 463 confirm that this is "an extraordinarily high hurdle to surmount" (per Longmore L.J. in the latter case) and has never, to date, been surmounted. An appeal from the High Court to the Court of Appeal based on this "residual jurisdiction" is an "appeal" for the purposes of s.16(1) of the Senior Courts Act 1981 (para.9A-57 below), and it follows from that that such an appeal is an appeal for which permission to appeal is required by r.52.3 (*Michael Wilson & Partners Ltd v Emmott* [2015] EWCA Civ 1285; [2016] 1 W.L.R. 857).

Note

2E-278

Add new paragraph at end:

It will only be in exceptional cases that a court faced with proceedings which require it to determine the jurisdiction of arbitrators will be justified in exercising its inherent power to stay those proceedings to enable the arbitrators themselves to decide the question: *Albon (t/a NA Carriage Co) v Naza Motor Trading Sdn Bhd* [2007] EWHC 665 (Ch) approved *Hashwani v OMV Maurice Energy Ltd* [2015] EWCA Civ 1171.

Subsection (5)

2E-361

In the first paragraph, replace "IPCO (Nigeria) v Nigerian National Petroleum [2015] EWCA Civ 1144" with:

IPCO (Nigeria) v Nigerian National Petroleum [2015] EWCA Civ 1144; [2016] 1 Lloyd's Rep. 36

Replace s.105(6) with:

PART IV

GENERAL PROVISIONS

Meaning of "the court": jurisdiction of High Court and county court

2E-364

(6) An order under this section for Northern Ireland shall be a statutory rule for the purposes of the [S.I. 1979/1573 (N.I. 12).] Statutory Rules (Northern Ireland) Order 1979 which shall be subject to negative resolution (within the meaning of section 41(6) of the Interpretation Act (Northern Ireland) 1954).

Note

2E-365

Add new paragraph at end:

Subsection (6) amended by the Northern Ireland Act 1998 (Devolution of Policing and Justice Functions) Order 2010 (SI 2010/976) Sch.18(1) para.50(2), with effect from 12 April 2010 subject to transitional provisions specified in SI 2010/976 art.28.

SECTION 2FA FINANCIAL LIST

PART 63A—FINANCIAL LIST

Editorial introduction

Replace the first paragraph with:
As is explained in the CPR Glossary, for administrative purposes, cases are allocated to different **2FA-1.1**
"lists" depending on the subject-matter of the case and may have their own procedures and judges.
CPR r.2.3 (Interpretation) para.(2) states that a reference in the CPR to a "specialist list" is a reference to a list that has been designated as such by a rule or practice direction (see further Vol. 1
para.2.3.14). Part 63A (rr.63A.1 to 63A.4) was inserted in the CPR by the Civil Procedure (Amendment No.4) Rules 2015 (SI 2015/1569). Rule 63A.2 creates a new "specialist list" known as the
Financial List. Part 63A is supplemented by Practice Direction 63AA (Financial List) published in
CPR Update 81 (August 2015). The rules and the Practice Direction came into effect on October 1,
2015.

The objectives of the Financial List

In the first paragraph, after the first instance of "the High Court", add:
, the Commercial Court and Chancery Division, to **2FA-1.2**

Replace the fourth paragraph with:
A "Financial List claim" is a claim exhibiting the features stated in r.63A.1(2). Such a claim "may
be started in the Financial List" (r.63A.4(1)). The "administrative office" for a particular Financial
List claim will be the Admiralty and Commercial Registry in the Royal Courts of Justice if it is com-
menced in the Commercial Court, or the Chancery Registry if it is commenced in the Chancery
Division (Practice Direction 63AA para.1.4).

Sources

*In the fourth paragraph (beginning "The objective of retaining the procedures"), after "answers is: https://
www.judiciary.gov.uk/publications/financial-list-faq[Accessed", replace "December 6, 2015" with:*
6 April 2016 **2FA-1.3**

Delete the sixth paragraph (beginning "In Part 30 (Transfer)").

Financial List claims

To the end of the first paragraph, add:
Paragraph 2.3 of the Financial List Guide recognises that whilst an insurance, professional **2FA-2.1**
negligence or Companies Court case will not generally fall within the definition of Financial List
claims, if such a case were to require financial market expertise to resolve the matter or raise issues
of general market importance, then it may be appropriate for the claim to be considered in the
Financial List.

Replace the second paragraph with:
At the time of writing, seventeen cases have been issued in the Financial List and three cases
transferred into the List, with four cases recently leading to final judgment. The Royal Bank of
Scotland Group issued the first four cases on 21 October 2015. The proceedings consist of claims
against four energy companies and the case type is described as "derivative and financial products".
There is currently limited publically available information on the matters.

*In the third paragraph (beginning "The first substantive judgment"), after "Association (the "LMA")", replace
"standard form documents. Given that the LMA standard forms are" with:*
facility documentation. Given that the LMA documentation is

After the fourth paragraph (beginning "There were two key issues in the case"), add as a new paragraph:
Mr Justice Blair handed down the second substantive in the Financial List 4 March 2016. In
Banco Santander Totta SA v Companhia Carris de Ferro de Lisboa SA [2016] EWHC 465 (Comm), the
Defendant public sector Portuguese transport companies raised various defences to claims by the
Claimant bank under swap agreements. The Court had made findings in favour of the Claimant
and findings in favour of the Defendants but the overall decision was in favour of the Claimant.
The decision sets out helpful clarification on the construction of the terms of "exotic" snowball
swaps, an area where there hereto been limited legal authority. In addition, the decisions clarifies
the scope of the Article 3.3 of the Convention on the Law Applicable to Contractual Obligations
1980 (the Rome Convention) in light of the *Dexia Crediop Spa v Comune di Prato* [2015] EWHC 1746
(Comm) decision.

Replace the fifth paragraph with:

When Financial List claims start to lead to a wider body of published judgments, it should provide further clarification on the types of cases that are suitable for determination in the Financial List. The Financial List judgments are published on the Judiciary's website dedicated to the Financial List at the following webpage: *https://www.judiciary.gov.uk/court/financial-list/* [Accessed 6 April 2016].

Delete the sixth and seventh paragraphs (beginning "The Royal Bank of Scotland Group" and "The first case to be transferred").

Replace the last paragraph with:

The Judiciary intends to use the Claims Information Form to be completed by claimants issuing Financial List claims to gather statistics on Financial List Claims to improve the Financial List (Financial List Guide at para.10.2). The Judiciary may also publish this information to provide guidance to users. In the interim, parties have the opportunity to raise queries by writing to the Financial List Users' Committee (Committee), which will provide a forum in which the High Court will listen and respond to matters raised by litigators and others concerned with the financial markets (Financial List Guide at para.4.1). Anyone having views concerning the improvement of financial markets litigation is invited to make his or her views known to the Committee, preferably through the relevant professional representative on the Committee or its secretary. The Committee held its first meeting in early 2016. The matters discussed included the types of cases suitable for determination using the Financial Markets Test Case Scheme introduced under Practice Direction 51M. The introduction of the Committee reflects the Judiciary's commitment to listen to users so as to improve the Financial List where possible. An aim endorsed by the comments of the Lord Chief Justice Lord Thomas, who has been at the vanguard of the Financial List, at the official launch event on October 20, 2015 who explained that the procedure would be kept under review and that "I do hope this initial experiment will work and we will try and improve it wherever possible" (reported at (2015) 6 LS Gaz, 26 Oct.).

Add new paragraph 2FA–2.2:

Transfer of claims

2FA-2.2   The Financial List Guide provides at para.2.3 that the parties may apply to transfer a case into the Financial List under CPR 30, including where the case falls "within the spirit but not the letter" of the specified criteria.

CPR 30 (Transfer), r.30.5(2) states that a judge dealing with claims in a specialist list may order proceedings "to be transferred to or from that list". Under r.63A.4(5), the provision of r.30.5 apply to proceedings in the Financial List and a judge dealing with claims in that List may order, not only that claims be transferred to or from it, but may order that a claim be transferred from it "to any other specialist list". Particular provisions as to the transfer of claims to or for the Financial List are contained in paras 4.1 to 4.6 of Practice Direction 63A. CPR r. 30.3, to which reference is made in para.4.6 of PD63AA, provides that various matters should be taken into account by the court when considering whether to make an order for the transfer of proceedings. These include:

(1)   the financial value of the claim;
(2)   whether it would be more convenient or fair for hearings, including the trial, to be held in some other court;
(3)   the availability of a judge specialising in the type of claim in question;
(4)   whether the facts, legal issues, remedies or procedures involved are simple or complex;
(5)   the importance of the outcome of the claim to the public in general; and
(6)   the facilities available to the court at which the claim is being dealt with.

In deciding whether or not to transfer a case into a specialist list, including in the Financial List, regard is also given to the overriding objective in CPR Pt 1.

One of the most recent cases transferred into the Financial List is *Property Alliance Group Ltd v Royal Bank of Scotland* [2016] EWHC 207 (Ch). In considering the Defendant's application for the case to be transferred, the Chancellor, Sir Justice Etherton, set out useful guidance on the issues that judges are likely to consider when deciding whether to accede to applications to transfer existing proceedings into the Financial List. The issues included ten matters which are likely to be of particular significance in deciding whether to accede to a contested application to transfer existing proceedings into the Financial List:

(1)   the extent to which the case concerns matters of market significance, as distinct from factual and other matters relevant only to the case and the parties in question;
(2)   the relative importance of the issues of market significance;
(3)   whether the case has already been assigned to a judge;
(4)   whether, if transferred into the Financial List, the proceedings would require a change of judge;
(5)   the length of time in which the proceedings have already been on foot;
(6)   the extent to which an assigned judge has already conducted hearings and delivered judgments in the pending proceedings, and his or her general familiarity with the case;
(7)   the extent to which the familiarity of the existing assigned judge with the case would en-

able judicial trial pre-reading, and the trial itself, to be conducted in a more efficient and timely way than if a new Financial List judge were to be appointed;

(8)   whether or not the trial date has been fixed, and, if so, the proximity to the trial date;

(9)   whether the trial timetable would be disrupted by the transfer into the Financial List; and

(10)   whether, and if so, assigning a new Financial List judge would be disruptive to one or more other cases in the other lists, because the new judge would no longer be able to conduct those other proceedings, or for any other reason.

On the facts of the case, it was found to be appropriate to transfer the case into the Financial List. This was even though the transfer involved a change of judge. It was considered that the case would benefit from being determined by a Financial List Judge, representing a relatively small cadre of judges who are not only particularly expert in the law applicable to financial markets, but also abreast of important developments in financial markets.

A further reason for concluding that it would be appropriate to transfer the case into the Financial List was that the case involved issues of general market significance regarded as clearly relevant to other participants in the market. Allied to those considerations, was that the case could be viewed in a general sense as a test or lead case, which would therefore make it desirable for a Financial List judge to determine the case so that the judgment carries appropriate weight in the future. Another important consideration was that it was possible for an alternative Financial List judge, also from the Chancery Division, to conduct both the Pre-Trial Review and the trial. Sir Justice Etherton noted that it would have been preferable and possible for the Defendant to apply to transfer the case at an earlier time and that delay may carry consequences that are more significant on the facts of other cases.

Effect of rule

Replace "(1)" with:

(1)   a docketed Financial List judge will generally preside over the matter from the commence- **2FA-5.1** ment of the proceeding to the trial, through to enforcement if necessary (see further the Financial List Guide at paras 6.1 and 6.2 and Financial List website FAQ at para.14); and

After the first paragraph, add as a new paragraph:

The rule that a docketed judge will preside over a Financial List claim from start to finish is not an inflexible procedure. In that, in certain cases there may be good reason to allow a Financial List claim to be assigned from one Financial List judge to another. For example, to allow a trial at an earlier date when requested by the parties for reasons of expediency.

The Financial List judges

In the first list of judges, replace "Mr Justice Richards;" with:

Mr Justice Hildyard;

Replace the fifth paragraph with:

The Judge in charge of the Commercial Court, currently Mr Justice Blair;

Mr Justice Flaux;

Mr Justice Leggatt;

Mr Justice Knowles;

Mr Justice Popplewell; and

Mr Justice Phillips.

In the sixth paragraph, after "https://www.judiciary.gov.uk/you-and-the-judiciary/going-to-court/high-court/ financial-list [Accessed", replace "December 6, 2015" with:

6 April 2016

GUIDE TO THE FINANCIAL LIST
Issued 1st October 2015

By authority of The Chancellor of the High Court, Sir Terence Etherton, and The Hon. Mr Justice Flaux, Judge in charge of the Commercial Court

A   GENERAL

2   JURISDICTION

Replace paragraph 2.3 with:

2.3   **2.3** The court has the general power to transfer proceedings into the Financial List under **2FA-14** CPR Part 30. This permits the court to order cases into the Financial List which fall within the spirit but not the letter of the three criteria. Cases which fall outside the subject matter definition and/or the financial markets definition may nevertheless require comparable expertise or may be of comparable general importance. Thus, a case concerning insurance, re-insurance or professional negligence, or a case falling within the normal specialist jurisdiction of the Companies Court (insolvencies, capital reductions, schemes of arrangement as well as shareholder disputes like unfair prejudice petitions and equitable petitions) will not generally fall within the definition of Financial List Claims. However, if issues arising in such a case were to require financial market expertise or were issues of general market importance, then it may be appropriate to issue the claim in the Financial List or transfer such a case or part of it into the Financial List.

Editorial

To the end of the paragraph, add:

2FA-21.1   At the time of writing, no parties have yet issued proceedings using the procedure. If this remains the case at the end of the two-year period, it is expected that the scheme will nonetheless remain open for application.

Qualifying claim

After "51M at para.2.1).", add:

For example, the procedure may be a vehicle to consider the consequences of a potential exit of the United Kingdom from the European Union on finance contracts.

SECTION 3   OTHER PROCEEDINGS
SECTION 3A   HOUSING

Protection from Eviction Act 1977

Replace s.8(6) with:

PART III

SUPPLEMENTAL PROVISIONS

Interpretation

3A-86   (6)   Any reference in subsection (5) above to a variation affecting the amount of the rent which is payable under a tenancy or licence does not include a reference to—

    (a)   a reduction or increase effected under Part III or Part VI of the Rent Act 1977 (rents under regulated tenancies and housing association tenancies), section 78 of that Act (power of tribunal in relation to restricted contracts) or sections 11 to 14 of the Rent (Agriculture) Act 1976; or

    (b)   a variation which is made by the parties and has the effect of making the rent expressed to be payable under the tenancy or licence the same as a rent for the dwelling which is entered in the register under Part IV or section 79 of the Rent Act 1977.

Note

Replace with:

3A-87   Amended by the Agricultural Holdings Act 1986 Sch.14, para.61; the Housing Act 1988 s.33; the Local Government and Housing Act 1989 Sch.11, para.54; and the Agricultural Tenancies Act 1995 Sch., para.29; and the Transfer of Tribunal Functions Order 2013 (SI 2013/1036) Sch.1(1) para.35, with effect from 1 July 2013 subject to transitional provisions and savings specified in SI 2013/1036 art.6(3) and Sch.3.

Housing Act 1985

After paragraph 28, add:

SECTION 84A(9)   SCHEDULE 2A

ABSOLUTE GROUND FOR POSSESSION FOR ANTI-SOCIAL BEHAVIOUR: SERIOUS OFFENCES

Violent offences

Drug-related offences

29.   An offence under section 6 of that Act (restrictions of cultivation of cannabis plant) where **3A–532** the cultivation is for profit and the whole or a substantial part of the dwelling-house concerned is used for the cultivation.

29A   An offence under either of the following sections of the Modern Slavery Act 2015—
    (a)   section 1 (slavery, servitude and forced or compulsory labour),
    (b)   section 2 (human trafficking).

Note

Add new paragraph at end:
    Paragraph 29A inserted, in relation to Wales by the Housing Act 1985 (Amendment of Schedule **3A–533** 2A) (Serious Offences) (Wales) Order 2016 (SI 2016/173) art.2(2), with effect from 16 February 2016; and in relation to England by the Modern Slavery Act 2015 (Consequential Amendments) Regulations 2016 (SI 2016/244) reg.7, with effect from 17 March 2016).

Housing Act 1988

Notice of proceedings for possession

Replace the first paragraph with:
    Before bringing possession proceedings against assured tenants, landlords must either serve a **3A–791** "notice of proceedings for possession" in accordance with the Housing Act 1988 s.8, or (in cases other than Ground 8) persuade the court that it is just and equitable to dispense with that requirement. The relevant form is contained in the Assured Tenancies and Agricultural Occupancies (Forms) (England) (Amendment) Regulations 2016 (SI 2016/443). The relevant form (Form 3) states that the landlord must, inter alia, "give the full text ... of each ground which is being relied upon". It is similar to the form of notice used in connection with public sector secure tenancies (Housing Act 1985 s.83). An earlier form provided that "Particulars of the grounds relied upon have to be included as well as the ground itself. The current form requires a full explanation of why each ground is being relied upon".

Note

Replace with:
    Amended by the Regulatory Reform (Assured Periodic Tenancies) (Rent Increases) Order 2003 **3A–827** (SI 2003/259) and the Transfer of Tribunal Functions Order 2013 (SI 2013/1036) Sch.1 para.82 with effect from July 1, 2013. The amendment made by SI 2003/259 was designed to overcome the argument that a strict interpretation of former s.13(2)(c) rendered many rent increases made by registered social landlords invalid because, although increases may have occurred annually, in some years they may have purported to take effect a few days earlier than "the first anniversary of the date" when the last increase took effect. The effect of the amendment is to enable landlords to set a fixed day (e.g. the first Monday in April) on which rent increases are to take effect. The first time that the rent is increased after the Order came into force on February 10, 2003, the increase may take effect not less than 52 weeks after the start of the tenancy or, if the rent has already been increased, not less than 52 weeks after the date of the last increase. On the second and subsequent occasions, the increase may take effect not less than 52 weeks after the last increase, unless that would result in the increase taking effect on a date falling a week or more before the anniversary of the first increase after the date on which the Order comes into force. In such a case the increase may not take effect until 53 weeks after the date of the last increase. In England, the prescribed forms to be used by landlords when proposing new rents under s.13(2) are contained in the Assured Tenancies and Agricultural Occupancies (Forms) (England) (Amendment) Regulations 2016 (SI 2016/443). The Assured Tenancies and Agricultural Occupancies (Forms) (Amendment) (Wales) Regulations 2003 (SI 2003/307) (w.46) prescribe the forms to be used in Wales.

Change title of paragraph: **3A–851.1**

Transfer of tenancies under Localism Act 2011

Note

Replace "October 2015" with:
    1 October 2015   **3A–897.8**

Housing Act 1996

Replace s.185(2A) with:

ELIGIBILITY FOR ASSISTANCE

Persons from abroad not eligible for housing assistance

3A–1289   (2A)   No person who is excluded from entitlement to universal credit or housing benefit by section 115 of the Immigration and Asylum Act 1999 (exclusion from benefits) shall be included in any class prescribed under subsection (2).

Note

Add new paragraph at end:

3A-1290   Subsection (2A) amended by the Universal Credit (Consequential, Supplementary, Incidental and Miscellaneous Provisions) Regulations 2013 (SI 2013/630) reg.12(5), with effect from 29 April 2013.

Persons from abroad and priority need

Add at end:

3A-1297   In relation to this section, see *Mirga v Secretary of State for Work and Pensions* [2016] UKSC 1, 27 January 2016.

Commonhold and Leasehold Reform Act 2002

Replace s.168 with:

No forfeiture notice before determination of breach

3A-1593   168.—(1)   A landlord under a long lease of a dwelling may not serve a notice under section 146(1) of the Law of Property Act 1925 (c.20) (restriction on forfeiture) in respect of a breach by a tenant of a covenant or condition in the lease unless subsection (2) is satisfied.

(2)   This subsection is satisfied if—

    (a)   it has been finally determined on an application under subsection (4) that the breach has occurred,

    (b)   the tenant has admitted the breach, or

    (c)   a court in any proceedings, or an arbitral tribunal in proceedings pursuant to a post-dispute arbitration agreement, has finally determined that the breach has occurred.

(3)   But a notice may not be served by virtue of subsection (2)(a) or (c) until after the end of the period of 14 days beginning with the day after that on which the final determination is made.

(4)   A landlord under a long lease of a dwelling may make an application to the appropriate tribunal for a determination that a breach of a covenant or condition in the lease has occurred.

(5)   But a landlord may not make an application under subsection (4) in respect of a matter which—

    (a)   has been, or is to be, referred to arbitration pursuant to a post-dispute arbitration agreement to which the tenant is a party,

    (b)   has been the subject of determination by a court, or

    (c)   has been the subject of determination by an arbitral tribunal pursuant to a post-dispute arbitration agreement.

(6)   For the purposes of subsection (4), "appropriate tribunal" means—

    (a)   in relation to a dwelling in England, the First-tier Tribunal or, where determined by or under Tribunal Procedure Rules, the Upper Tribunal; and

(b)   in relation to a dwelling in Wales, a leasehold valuation tribunal.

Add new paragraph 3A–1593.1:

Note —Amended by the Transfer of Tribunal Functions Order 2013 (SI 2013/1036) Sch.1 **3A-1593.1** para.141 with effect from 1 July 2013.

Policing and Crime Act 2009

Add new paragraph 3A–1719.2:

Interim injunctions
As to the variation and discharge of interim injunctions, see *Murray v Chief Constable of Lancashire* **3A-1719.2** [2015] EWCA Civ 1174 (18 November 2015).

Note

After "Sub-section", add:
(2)(e)   **3A-1720.1**

Replace s.43(7) with the following, and add para.3A–1728.1:

ARREST AND REMAND

Arrest without warrant
(7)   In this Part "relevant judge", in relation to an injunction, means a judge **3A-1728** of the court that granted the injunction, except that where—
(a)   the respondent is aged 18 or over, but
(b)   the injunction was granted by a youth court,
it means a judge of the county court.

Note —Subsection (7) was amended by the Crime and Courts Act 2013 s.18(3), with effect from 1 **3A-1728.1** June 2015 (SI 2015/813) subject to savings and transitional provisions specified in 2013 c.22 s.15 and Sch.8.

Add new paragraphs 3A–1732.2 and 3A–1732.3:

Appeals against decisions of youth courts
46B.—(1)   An appeal lies to the Crown Court against a decision of a youth **3A-1732.2** court made under this Part.
(2)   On an appeal under this section the Crown Court may make—
(a)   whatever orders are necessary to give effect to its determination of the appeal;
(b)   whatever incidental or consequential orders appear to it to be just.
(3)   An order of the Crown Court made on an appeal under this section (other than one directing that an application be re-heard by a youth court) is to be treated for the purposes of section 42 as an order of a youth court.

Note —Inserted, together with preceding crossheading, by the Crime and Courts Act 2013 **3A-1732.3** Sch.12 para.2 with effect from 1 June 2015 (SI 2015/813).

Replace para.3A–1734 with paras 3A–1734 and 3A–1734.1:

MISCELLANEOUS

Supplemental
48.—(2)   Rules of court may provide that an appeal from a decision to **3A–1734** which this subsection applies may be made without notice being given to the respondent.
(3)   Subsection (2) applies—
(a)   to a decision under section 39(4)(a) that an application without notice be dismissed, and

(b)   to a decision to refuse to grant an interim injunction under section 41.

(4)   In relation to a respondent attaining the age of 18 after the commencement of proceedings under this Part, rules of court may—

(a)   provide for the transfer of the proceedings from a youth court to the High Court or the county court;

(b)   prescribe circumstances in which the proceedings may or must remain in a youth court.

3A-1734.1   *Note* —Subsection (1) was repealed by the Crime and Courts Act 2013 Sch.9 para.51(2), with effect from 22 April 2014 (SI 2014/954) subject to transitional provision specified in SI 2014/954 art.3.

Subsections (2) and (3) were amended by the Crime and Courts Act 2013 Sch.12 para.3, with effect from 1 June 2015 (SI 2015/813) subject to savings and transitional provisions specified in 2013 c.22 s.15 and Sch.8.

Subsection (4) was inserted by the Crime and Courts Act 2013 s.18(4), with effect from 1 June 2015 (SI 2015/813).

Interpretation

Replace s.49(1) with:

3A-1735   (1)   In this Part—

"application without notice" has the meaning given by section 39(2);

"consultation requirement" has the meaning given by section 38(2);

"court" (except in Schedule 5A)—

(a)   in the case of a respondent aged under 18, means a youth court, and

(b)   in any other case, means the High Court or the county court,

but this is subject to any provision in rules of court that is or could be made under section 48(4);

"drug-dealing activity" has the meaning given by section 34(7).

"judge", in relation to a youth court, means a person qualified to sit as a member of that court;

"local authority" has the meaning given by section 37(2);

"relevant judge" has the meaning given by section 43(7);

"respondent" means the person in respect of whom an application for an injunction is made or (as the context requires) the person against whom such an injunction is granted;

"review hearing" has the meaning given by section 36(5);

"specify", in relation to an injunction, means specify in the injunction;

"violence" includes violence against property.

Note

Replace with:

3A-1735.1   Definition "court" substituted by the Crime and Courts Act 2013 s.18(2), with effect from 1 June 2015 (SI 2015/813).Definition "drug dealing activity" inserted by the Serious Crime Act 2015 Sch.4 para.85, with effect from 1 June 2015.

Definition "judge" inserted by the Crime and Courts Act 2013 Sch.12 para.4, with effect from 1 June 2015 (SI 2015/813) subject to savings and transitional provisions specified in 2013 c.22 s.15 and Sch.8.

3A-1737   *Replace para.3A–1737 with paras 3A–1737 and 3A–1737.1:*

SECTION 46   SCHEDULE 5

I NJUNCTIONS : P OWERS TO R EMAND

Injunctions: Power to remand

1.—(1)   The provisions of this Schedule apply where the court has power to remand a person under section 43(5) or 44(4).

(2)   In this Schedule, "the court" means the High Court, the county court or a youth court and includes—

    (a)   in relation to the High Court, a judge of that court,

    (b)   in relation to the county court, a judge of that court, and

    (c)   in relation to a youth court, a judge of that court.

Note —Paragraph 1(2) was amended by the Crime and Courts Act 2013 Sch.9 para.51(3), with **3A-1737.1** effect from 22 April 2014 (SI 2014/954) subject to savings and transitional provisions specified in 2013 c.22 s.15 and Sch.8 and transitional provision specified in SI 2014/954 arts 2(c) and 3. Paragraph 1(2) further amended by the Crime and Courts Act 2013 Sch.12 para.5(a), with effect from 1 June 2015 (SI 2015/813) subject to savings and transitional provisions specified in 2013 c.22 s.15 and Sch.8.

Replace Part 1 of Schedule 5A with:

SECTION 46

SCHEDULE 5A

BREACH OF INJUNCTION: POWERS OF COURT IN RESPECT OF UNDER-18S

PART 1

INTRODUCTORY

Power to make supervision order or detention order

1.—(1)   Where—   **3A-1744**

    (a)   an injunction under Part 4 has been granted against a person under the age of 18,

    (aa)   the person is still under the age of 18, and

    (b)   on an application made by the injunction applicant, a youth court is satisfied beyond reasonable doubt that the person is in breach of any provision of the injunction,

that court may make one of the orders specified in sub-paragraph (2) in respect of the person.

(2)   Those orders are—

    (a)   a supervision order (see Part 2 of this Schedule);

    (b)   a detention order (see Part 3 of this Schedule).

(4)   Before making an application under paragraph 1(1)(b) the injunction applicant must consult—

    (a)   the youth offending team consulted under section 38(1) or 39(5) in relation to the injunction, and

    (b)   any other person previously so consulted.

(5)   In considering whether and how to exercise its powers under this paragraph, the court must consider a report made to assist the court in that respect by the youth offending team referred to in subparagraph (4)(a).

(6)   An order under sub-paragraph (1) may not be made in respect of a person aged 18 or over.

(7)   The court may not make a detention order under sub-paragraph (1) unless it is satisfied, in view of the severity or extent of the breach, that no other power available to the court is appropriate.

(8)   Where the court makes a detention order under sub-paragraph (1) it must state in open court why it is satisfied as specified in sub-paragraph (7).

(9)   In this Schedule—

    "defaulter", in relation to an order under this Schedule, means the person in respect of whom the order is made;

    "injunction applicant", in relation to an injunction under Part 4 or an order under this Schedule made in respect of such an injunction, means the person who applied for the injunction.

Note

Add new paragraph at end:

Paragraph 1 amended by the Crime and Courts Act 2013 Sch.12 para.7, with effect from 1 June **3A-1744.1** 2015 (SI 2015/813) subject to savings and transitional provisions specified in 2013 c.22 s.15 and Sch.8.

3A-1745 *Replace paras 3A–1745 to 3A–1756 with paras 3A–1745 to 3A–1756.1:*

PART 2

SUPERVISION ORDERS

Supervision orders

2.—(1)   A supervision order is an order imposing on the defaulter one or more of the following requirements—

(a)   a supervision requirement;

(b)   an activity requirement;

(c)   a curfew requirement.

(2)   Before making a supervision order the court must obtain and consider information about the defaulter's family circumstances and the likely effect of such an order on those circumstances.

(3)   Before making a supervision order imposing two or more requirements, the court must consider their mutual compatibility.

(4)   The court must ensure, as far as practicable, that any requirement imposed by a supervision order is such as to avoid—

(a)   any conflict with the defaulter's religious beliefs,

(b)   any interference with the times, if any, at which the defaulter normally works or attends school or any other educational establishment, and

(c)   any conflict with the requirements of any other court order or injunction to which the defaulter may be subject.

(5)   A supervision order must for the purposes of this Schedule specify a maximum period for the operation of any requirement contained in the order.

(6)   The period specified under sub-paragraph (5) may not exceed six months beginning with the day after that on which the supervision order is made.

(7)   A supervision order must for the purposes of this Schedule specify a youth offending team established under section 39 of the Crime and Disorder Act 1998.

(8)   The youth offending team specified under sub-paragraph (7) is to be—

(a)   the youth offending team in whose area it appears to the court that the respondent will reside during the period specified under sub-paragraph (5), or

(b)   where it appears to the court that the respondent will reside in the area of two or more such teams, such one of those teams as the court may determine.

Supervision requirements

3A-1746   3.—(1)   In this Schedule, "supervision requirement", in relation to a supervision order, means a requirement that the defaulter attend appointments with—

(a)   the responsible officer, or

(b)   another person determined by the responsible officer, at such times and places as may be instructed by the responsible officer.

(2)   The appointments must be within the period for the time being specified in the order under paragraph 2(5).

Activity requirements

3A-1747   4.—(1)   In this Schedule, "activity requirement", in relation to a supervision order, means a requirement that the defaulter do any or all of the following within the period for the time being specified in the order under paragraph 2(5)—

(a)   participate, on such number of days as may be specified in the order, in activities at a place, or places, so specified;

(b)   participate in an activity or activities specified in the order on such number of days as may be so specified;

(c)   participate in one or more residential exercises for a continuous period or periods comprising such number or numbers of days as may be specified in the order;

(d)   in accordance with sub-paragraphs (6) to (9), engage in activities in accordance with instructions of the responsible officer on such number of days as may be specified in the order.

(2)   The number of days specified in a supervision order in relation to an activity requirement must not, in aggregate, be less than 12 or more than 24.

(3)   A requirement referred to in sub-paragraph (1)(a) or (b) operates to require the defaulter, in accordance with instructions given by the responsible officer, on the number of days specified in the order in relation to the requirement—

(a)   in the case of a requirement referred to in sub-paragraph (1)(a), to present himself or herself at a place specified in the order to a person of a description so specified, or

(b)   in the case of a requirement referred to in sub-paragraph (1)(b), to participate in an activity specified in the order, and, on each such day, to comply with instructions given by, or under the authority of, the person in charge of the place or the activity (as the case may be).

(4)   Where the order includes a requirement referred to in sub-paragraph (1)(c) to participate in a residential exercise, it must specify, in relation to the residential exercise—

64

(a)   a place, or

(b)   an activity.

(5)   A requirement under sub-paragraph (1)(c) to participate in a residential exercise operates to require the defaulter, in accordance with instructions given by the responsible officer—

    (a)   if a place is specified under sub-paragraph (4)(a)—

        (i)   to present himself or herself at the beginning of the period specified in the order in relation to the exercise, at the place so specified to a person of a description specified in the instructions, and

        (ii)   to reside there for that period;

    (b)   if an activity is specified under sub-paragraph (4)(b), to participate, for the period specified in the order in relation to the exercise, in the activity so specified, and, during that period, to comply with instructions given by, or under the authority of, the person in charge of the place or the activity (as the case may be).

(6)   Subject to sub-paragraph (8), instructions under sub-paragraph (1)(d) relating to any day must require the defaulter to do either of the following—

    (a)   present himself or herself to a person of a description specified in the instructions at a place so specified;

    (b)   participate in an activity specified in the instructions.

(7)   Any such instructions operate to require the defaulter, on that day or while participating in that activity, to comply with instructions given by, or under the authority of, the person in charge of the place or, as the case may be, the activity.

(8)   If the supervision order so provides, instructions under sub-paragraph (1)(d) may require the defaulter to participate in a residential exercise for a period comprising not more than seven days, and, for that purpose—

    (a)   to present himself or herself at the beginning of that period to a person of a description specified in the instructions at a place so specified and to reside there for that period, or

    (b)   to participate for that period in an activity specified in the instructions.

(9)   Instructions such as are mentioned in sub-paragraph (8)—

    (a)   may not be given except with the consent of a parent or guardian of the defaulter, and

    (b)   operate to require the defaulter, during the period specified under that sub-paragraph, to comply with instructions given by, or under the authority of, the person in charge of the place or activity specified under paragraph (a) or (b) of that sub-paragraph.

(10)   Instructions given by, or under the authority of, a person in charge of a place under sub-paragraph (3), (5), (7) or (9)(b) may require the defaulter to engage in activities otherwise than at that place.

(11)   Where a supervision order contains an activity requirement, a youth court may on the application of the injunction applicant or the defaulter amend the order by substituting for any number of days, place, activity, period or description of persons specified in the order a new number of days, place, activity, period or description (subject, in the case of a number of days, to sub-paragraph (2)).

(12)   A court may only include an activity requirement in a supervision order or vary such a requirement under sub-paragraph (11) if—

    (a)   it has consulted the youth offending team which is to be, or is, specified in the order,

    (b)   it is satisfied that it is feasible to secure compliance with the requirement or requirement as varied,

    (c)   it is satisfied that provision for the defaulter to participate in the activities proposed can be made under the arrangements for persons to participate in such activities which exist in the area of the youth offending team which is to be or is specified in the order, and

    (d)   in a case where the requirement or requirement as varied would involve the co-operation of a person other than the defaulter and the responsible officer, that person consents to its inclusion or variation.

(13)   For the purposes of sub-paragraph (9) "guardian" has the same meaning as in the Children and Young Persons Act 1933 (subject to sub-paragraph (14)).

(14)   If a local authority has parental responsibility for a defaulter who is in its care or provided with accommodation by it in the exercise of any social services functions, the reference to "guardian" in sub-paragraph (9) is to be read as a reference to that authority.

(15)   In sub-paragraph (14)—

    (a)   "parental responsibility" has the same meaning as it has in the Children Act 1989 by virtue of section 3 of that Act;

    (b)   "social services functions" has the same meaning as it has in the Local Authority Social Services Act 1970 by virtue of section 1A of that Act.

5.—(1)   In this Schedule, "curfew requirement", in relation to a supervision order, means a **3A–1748** requirement that the defaulter remain, for periods specified in the order, at a place so specified.

(2)   A supervision order imposing a curfew requirement may specify different places or different periods for different days.

(3)   The periods specified under sub-paragraph (1)—

(a)   must be within the period for the time being specified in the order under paragraph 2(5);

(b)   may not amount to less than two or more than eight hours in any day.

(4)   Before specifying a place under sub-paragraph (1) in a supervision order, the court making the order must obtain and consider information about the place proposed to be specified in the order (including information as to the attitude of persons likely to be affected by the enforced presence there of the defaulter).

(5)   Where a supervision order contains a curfew requirement, a youth court may, on the application of the injunction applicant or the defaulter amend the order by—

(a)   substituting new periods for the periods specified in the order under this paragraph (subject to sub-paragraph (3)); or

(b)   substituting a new place for the place specified in the order under this paragraph (subject to sub-paragraph (4)).

3A–1749   6.—(1)   A supervision order containing a curfew requirement may also contain a requirement (an "electronic monitoring requirement") for securing the electronic monitoring of compliance with the curfew requirement during a period—.

(a)   specified in the order, or

(b)   determined by the responsible officer in accordance with the order.

(2)   In a case referred to in sub-paragraph (1)(b), the responsible officer must, before the beginning of the period when the electronic monitoring requirement is to take effect, notify—

(a)   the defaulter,

(b)   the person responsible for the monitoring, and

(c)   any person falling within sub-paragraph (3)(b),

of the time when that period is to begin.

(3)   Where—

(a)   it is proposed to include an electronic monitoring requirement in a supervision order, but

(b)   there is a person (other than the defaulter) without whose cooperation it will not be practicable to secure that the monitoring takes place,

the requirement may not be included in the order without that person's consent.

(4)   A supervision order imposing an electronic monitoring requirement must include provision for making a person responsible for the monitoring.

(5)   The person who is made responsible for the monitoring must be of a description specified in an order under paragraph 26(5) of Schedule 1 to the Criminal Justice and Immigration Act 2008.

(6)   An electronic monitoring requirement may not be included in a supervision order unless the court making the order—

(a)   has been notified by the youth offending team for the time being specified in the order that arrangements for electronic monitoring are available in the area where the place which the court proposes to specify in the order for the purposes of the curfew requirement is situated, and

(b)   is satisfied that the necessary provision can be made under the arrangements currently available.

(7)   Where a supervision order contains an electronic monitoring requirement, a youth court may, on the application of the injunction applicant or the defaulter, amend the order by substituting a new period for the period specified in the order under this paragraph.

(8)   Sub-paragraph (3) applies in relation to the variation of an electronic monitoring requirement under sub-paragraph (7) as it applies in relation to the inclusion of such a requirement.

3A–1750   7.—(1)   For the purposes of this Part of this Schedule, the "responsible officer", in relation to a supervision order, means—

(a)   in a case where the order imposes a curfew requirement and an electronic monitoring requirement, but does not impose an activity or supervision requirement, the person who under paragraph 6(4) is responsible for the electronic monitoring;

(b)   in any other case, the member of the youth offending team for the time being specified in the order who, as respects the defaulter, is for the time being responsible for discharging the functions conferred by this Schedule on the responsible officer.

(2)   Where a supervision order has been made, it is the duty of the responsible officer—

(a)   to make any arrangements that are necessary in connection with the requirements contained in the order, and

(b)   to promote the defaulter's compliance with those requirements.

(3)   In giving instructions in pursuance of a supervision order, the responsible officer must ensure, so far as practicable, that any instruction is such as to avoid the matters referred to in paragraph 2(4).

(4) A defaulter in respect of whom a supervision order is made must—

    (a) keep in touch with the responsible officer in accordance with such instructions as the responsible officer may from time to time give to the defaulter, and

    (b) notify the responsible officer of any change of address.

(5) The obligations imposed by sub-paragraph (4) have effect as a requirement of the supervision order.

8.—(1) A youth court may, on the application of the injunction applicant or the defaulter, **3A–1751** amend a supervision order by substituting a new period for that for the time being specified in the order under paragraph 2(5) (subject to paragraph 2(6)).

(2) A youth court may, on amending a supervision order pursuant to sub-paragraph (1), make such other amendments to the order in relation to any requirement imposed by the order as the court considers appropriate.

9.—(1) This paragraph applies where, on an application made by the injunction applicant or **3A–1752** the defaulter in relation to a supervision order, a youth court is satisfied that the defaulter proposes to reside, or is residing, in the area of a youth offending team other than the team for the time being specified in the order.

(2) If the application is made by the defaulter, the court to which it is made may amend the order by substituting for the youth offending team specified in the order the youth offending team for the area referred to in sub-paragraph (1) (or, if there is more than one such team for that area, such of those teams as the court may determine).

(3) If the application is made by the injunction applicant, the court to which it is made must, subject as follows, so amend the order.

(4) Where a court amends the supervision order pursuant to sub-paragraph (2) or (3) but the order contains a requirement which, in the opinion of the court, cannot reasonably be complied with if the defaulter resides in the area referred to in subparagraph (1), the court must also amend the order by—

    (a) removing that requirement, or

    (b) substituting for that requirement a new requirement which can reasonably be complied with if the defaulter resides in that area.

(5) Sub-paragraph (3) does not require a court to amend the supervision order if in its opinion sub-paragraph (4) would produce an inappropriate result.

(6) The injunction applicant must consult the youth offending team for the time being specified in the order before making an application under sub-paragraph (1).

10.—(1) Where a supervision order is made, the injunction applicant or the defaulter may ap- **3A–1753** ply to a youth court—

    (a) to revoke the order, or

    (b) to amend the order by removing any requirement from it.

(2) If it appears to the court to which an application under sub-paragraph (1)(a) or (b) is made to be in the interests of justice to do so, having regard to circumstances which have arisen since the supervision order was made, the court may grant the application and revoke or amend the order accordingly.

(3) The circumstances referred to in sub-paragraph (2) include the conduct of the defaulter.

(4) If an application made under sub-paragraph (1) in relation to a supervision order is dismissed, no further such application may be made in relation to the order by any person without the consent of a youth court.

(5) The injunction applicant must consult the youth offending team for the time being specified in the order before making an application under sub-paragraph (1).

11. If the responsible officer considers that the defaulter has complied with all the require- **3A–1754** ments of the supervision order, the responsible officer must inform the injunction applicant.

12.—(1) If the responsible officer considers that the defaulter has failed to comply with any **3A–1755** requirement of the supervision order, the responsible officer must inform the injunction applicant.

(2) On being informed as specified in sub-paragraph (1) the injunction applicant may apply to a youth court.

(3) Before making an application under sub-paragraph (2) the injunction applicant must consult—

    (a) the youth offending team for the time being specified in the order, and

    (b) any person consulted by virtue of section 38(2)(a) or (b).

(4) If on an application under sub-paragraph (2) the court to which it is made is satisfied beyond reasonable doubt that the defaulter has without reasonable excuse failed to comply with any requirement of the supervision order, the court may—

(7) The court to which an application under sub-paragraph (2) is made must consider representations made by the youth offending team for the time being specified in the order before exercising its powers under this paragraph.

13.—(1) The court by which a supervision order is made must forthwith provide a copy of the **3A–1756** order to—

(a)   the defaulter, and

(b)   the youth offending team for the time being specified in the order.

(2)   Where a supervision order is made, the injunction applicant must forthwith provide a copy of so much of the order as is relevant—

(a)   in a case where the order includes an activity requirement specifying a place under paragraph 4(1)(a), to the person in charge of that place;

(b)   in a case where the order includes an activity requirement specifying an activity under paragraph 4(1)(b), to the person in charge of that activity;

(c)   in a case where the order includes an activity requirement specifying a residential exercise under paragraph 4(1)(c), to the person in charge of the place or activity specified under paragraph 4(4) in relation to that residential exercise;

(d)   in a case where the order contains an electronic monitoring requirement, to—

(i)   any person who by virtue of paragraph 6(4) will be responsible for the electronic monitoring, and

(ii)   any person without whose consent that requirement could not have been included in the order.

(3)   The court by which a supervision order is revoked or amended must forthwith provide a copy of the revoking order, or of the order as amended, to—

(a)   the defaulter, and

(b)   the youth offending team for the time being specified in the order.

(4)   Where—

(a)   a copy of a supervision order (or part of a supervision order) has been given to a person under sub-paragraph (2) by virtue of any requirement contained in the order, and

(b)   the order is revoked, or amended in respect of that requirement,

the injunction applicant must forthwith give a copy of the revoking order, or of so much of the order as amended as is relevant, to that person.

3A-1756.1   *Note* —Paragraph 4(11) amended by the Crime and Courts Act 2013 Sch.12 para.8, with effect from 1 June 2015 (SI 2015/813) subject to savings and transitional provisions specified in 2013 c.22 s.15 and Sch.8.

Paragraph 5(5) amended by the Crime and Courts Act 2013 Sch.12 para.9, with effect from 1 June 2015 (SI 2015/813) subject to savings and transitional provisions specified in 2013 c.22 s.15 and Sch.8.

Paragraph 6(7) amended by the Crime and Courts Act 2013 Sch.12 para.10, with effect from 1 June 2015 (SI 2015/813) subject to savings and transitional provisions specified in 2013 c.22 s.15 and Sch.8.

Paragraph 8 amended by the Crime and Courts Act 2013 Sch.12 para.11, with effect from 1 June 2015 (SI 2015/813) subject to savings and transitional provisions specified in 2013 c.22 s.15 and Sch.8.

Paragraph 9(1) amended by the Crime and Courts Act 2013 Sch.12 para.12, with effect from 1 June 2015 (SI 2015/813) subject to savings and transitional provisions specified in 2013 c.22 s.15 and Sch.8.

Paragraph 10(1), (4) amended by the Crime and Courts Act 2013 Sch.12 para.13, with effect from 1 June 2015 (SI 2015/813) subject to savings and transitional provisions specified in 2013 c.22 s.15 and Sch.8.

Paragraph 12(2) amended and para.12(5), (6) repealed by the Crime and Courts Act 2013 Sch.12 para.14, with effect from 1 June 2015 (SI 2015/813) subject to savings and transitional provisions specified in 2013 c.22 s.15 and Sch.8.

Replace Part 3 of Schedule 5A with:

Part 3

Detention Orders

Detention orders

3A–1757   **14**(1)   A detention order is an order that the defaulter be detained for a period specified in the order in such youth detention accommodation as the Secretary of State may determine.

(2)   The period specified under sub-paragraph (1) may not exceed the period of three months beginning with the day after that on which the order is made.

(3)   In sub-paragraph (1) "youth detention accommodation" means—

(a)   a secure training centre;

(aa)   a secure college;

(b)   a young offender institution;

[(c)   a secure children's home, as defined by section 102(11) of the Legal Aid, Sentencing and Punishment of Offenders Act 2012.]

(4)   The function of the Secretary of State under sub-paragraph (1) is exercisable concurrently with the Youth Justice Board.

(5)   A person detained under a detention order is in legal custody.

Revocation of detention order

15(1)   Where a detention order is made, the injunction applicant or the defaulter may apply to a youth court to revoke it.

(2)   If it appears to the court to which an application under sub-paragraph (1) is made to be in the interests of justice to do so, having regard to circumstances which have arisen since the detention order was made, the court may grant the application and revoke the order accordingly.

(3)   The circumstances referred to in sub-paragraph (2) include the conduct of the defaulter.

(4)   If an application made under sub-paragraph (1) in relation to a detention order is dismissed, no further such application may be made in relation to the order by any person without the consent of a youth court.

(5)   Before making an application under sub-paragraph (1) the injunction applicant must consult—

    (a)   in the case of a detention order made under paragraph 1(1), the youth offending team referred to in paragraph 1(4)(a); or

    (b)   in the case of a detention order made under paragraph 12(4)(b), the youth offending team referred to in paragraph 12(3)(a).

Note

Add new paragraph at end:

Paragraph 15(1), (4) amended by the Crime and Courts Act 2013 Sch.12 para.15, with effect **3A-1758.1** from 1 June 2015 (SI 2015/813) subject to savings and transitional provisions specified in 2013 c.22 s.15 and Sch.8.

SECTION 3B   BUSINESS TENANCIES

Landlord and Tenant Act 1954

s.30(1)(g) intention of landlord to occupy the holding for the purposes of a business or as his residence

Before the third paragraph (beginning "The landlord need not intend"), add as a new paragraph:

Compare *Gulf Agencies Ltd v Ahmed* [2016] EWCA Civ 44, where the Court of Appeal held that **3B-183** two years occupation on the facts of that case would be more than "fleeting or illusory" and more than "short term" (para.42).

Replace s.63 with:

PART IV

MISCELLANEOUS AND SUPPLEMENTARY

Jurisdiction of court for purposes of Parts I and II and of Part I of Landlord and Tenant Act 1927

63.—(1)   Any jurisdiction conferred on the court by any provision of Part I **3B-280** of this Act shall be exercised by the county court.

(2)   Any jurisdiction conferred on the court by any provision of Part II of this Act or conferred on the tribunal by Part I of the Landlord and Tenant Act 1927, shall, subject to the provisions of this section, be exercised [by the High Court or the county court]

(3)   [...]

(4)   The following provisions shall have effect as respects transfer of proceedings from or to the High Court or the county court, that is to say—

    (a)   where an application is made to the one but by virtue of [an Order under section 1 of the Courts and Legal Services Act 1990] cannot be entertained except by the other, the application shall not be treated as improperly made but any proceedings thereon shall be transferred to the other court;

(b) any proceedings under the provisions of Part II of this Act or of Part I of the Landlord and Tenant Act 1927, which are pending before one of those courts may by order of that court made on the application of any person interested be transferred to the other court, if it appears to the court making the order that it is desirable that the proceedings and any proceedings before the other court should both be entertained by the other court.

(5) In any proceedings where in accordance with the foregoing provisions of this section the county court exercises jurisdiction the powers of the judge of summoning one or more assessors under subsection (1) of section 91 of the County Courts Act 1959, may be exercised notwithstanding that no application is made in that behalf by any party to the proceedings.

(6) Where in any such proceedings an assessor is summoned by a judge under the said subsection (1),—

(a) he may, if so directed by the judge, inspect the land to which the proceedings relate without the judge and report to the judge in writing thereon;

(b) the judge may on consideration of the report and any observations of the parties thereon give such judgment or make such order in the proceedings as may be just;

(c) the remuneration of the assessor shall be at such rate as may be determined by the Lord Chancellor with the approval of the Treasury and shall be defrayed out of moneys provided by Parliament.

(7) In this section the expression "the holding"—

(a) in relation to proceedings under Part II of this Act, has the meaning assigned to it by subsection (3) of section twenty-three of this Act,

(b) in relation to proceedings under Part I of the Landlord and Tenant Act 1927, has the same meaning as in the said Part I.

(8) [...]

(9) Nothing in this section shall prejudice the operation of section 41 of the County Courts Act 1984 (which relates to the removal into the High Court of proceedings commenced in the county court).

(10) In accordance with the foregoing provisions of this section, for section 21 of the Landlord and Tenant Act 1927, there shall be substituted the following section—

The Tribunal

21. The tribunal for the purposes of Part I of this Act shall be the court exercising jurisdiction in accordance with the provisions of section sixty-three of the Landlord and Tenant Act 1954.

Note

Add new paragraph at end:

3B-281   Subsections (2), (9) amended by the Crime and Courts Act 2013 Sch.9 para.52(1)(b), with effect from 22 April 2014 (SI 2014/954) subject to savings and transitional provisions specified in 2013 c.22 s.15 and Sch.8 and transitional provision specified in SI 2014/954 arts 2(c) and 3.

SECTION 3C CONTEMPT OF COURT

A. An Outline of the Law of Contempt of Court

2. Principal forms of contempt liability

(c) Interference with the due administration of justice

After the third paragraph (beginning "Instances of contempt which involve interference"), add as a new paragraph:

In the case of *In re West* [2014] EWCA Crim. 1480; [2015] 1 W.L.R. 109, CA, a judge sitting in **3C-9** the Crown Court found a barrister to be in contempt of court by failing (a) to attend an adjourned preliminary hearing as directed, and (b) to assist with the case management requests that were made of him. The Court of Appeal (Criminal Division) allowed the barrister's appeal for want of procedural irregularity (in particular, lack of compliance with rules in Pt 62 of the Criminal Procedure Rules 2011), but in doing so acknowledged (after reviewing the relevant authorities) that a failure by a party's legal representative to co-operate with the court or a refusal to attend court conceivably may amount to contempt of court, being conduct that interferes with the due administration of justice.

(e) Contempt of court and enforcement of judgments etc by order of committal

Replace the second paragraph with:

See further, CPR r.70.2 (and 70PD para.1.2), and rr.81.4, 81.20, 83.13 and 83.14. **3C-18**

To the end of the seventh paragraph (beginning "This dictum was applied by the House of Lords"), add:

The principle derived from these authorities was confirmed and applied by the Court of Appeal **3C-19** in *Khawaja v Popat* [2016] EWCA Civ 362, 14 April 2016, CA, unrep., at para.30 per McCombe LJ).

3. Jurisdiction

(c) County courts

Replace the fourth paragraph with:

In *Ex p Martin* (1879) 4 Q.B.D. 212, D.C., sub nom *Martin v Bannister* (1879) 4 Q.B.D. 491, CA, **3C-33** it was held that, by the Supreme Court of Judicature Act 1873 s.89, county courts (being inferior courts within the meaning of that section) were invested with the power to grant injunctions and to enforce obedience of them by committal "in as full and ample a manner" (as the section said) as the same power invested in the High Court. Nowadays, those powers are invested in county courts by the County Courts Act 1984 s.38(1) (see para.9A-468). By that sub-section (subject to exceptions), in any proceedings in a county court the court may make any order which could be made by the High Court if the proceedings were in the High Court. It follows that, so far as orders made by county court judges are concerned, those judges have the same power and authority to commit for their breach as a High Court judge would have in respect of the breach of any order made by him (*Jennison v Baker*, op cit, at 65 to 66 per Salmon LJ). (Before Pt 81 was inserted in the CPR (particularly Section II thereof) the existence of such jurisdiction was recognised by CCR Ord.29.)

B. Debtors Acts 1869 & 1878

Replace para.3C–43 with paras 3C–43 and 3C–43.1: **3C-43**

Saving of power of committal for small debts

5. Subject to the provisions herein-after mentioned, and to the prescribed rules, any court may commit to prison for a term not exceeding six weeks, or until payment of the sum due, any person who makes default in payment of any debt or instalment of any debt due from him in pursuance of any order or judgment of that or any other competent court. Provided—

(1) That the jurisdiction by this section given of committing a person to prison shall, in the case the county court—

    (a) Be exercised only by a judge of the court, and by an order made in open court and showing on its face the ground on which it is issued.

    (b) [Repealed by Bankruptcy Act 1883 (c.52), Sch.5.]

(2) That such jurisdiction shall only be exercised where it is proved to the satisfaction of the court that the person making default either has or has had

since the date of the order or judgment the means to pay the sum in respect of which he has made default, and has refused or neglected, or refuses or neglects, to pay the same.

Proof of the means of the person making default may be given in such manner as the court thinks just.

For the purpose of considering whether to commit a debtor to prison under this section, the debtor may be summoned in accordance with the prescribed rules.

Any jurisdiction by this section given to the High Court or family court may be exercised by a judge sitting in chambers, or otherwise, in the prescribed manner.

For the purposes of this section any court may direct any debt due from any person in pursuance of any order or judgment of that or any other competent court to be paid by instalments, and may from time to time rescind or vary such order.

This section, so far as it relates to the county court, shall be deemed to be substituted for sections ninety-eight and ninety-nine of the County Courts Act 1846, and that Act and the Acts amending the same shall be construed accordingly, and shall extend to orders made by the county court with respect to sums due in pursuance of any order or judgment of any court other than the county court.

No imprisonment under this section shall operate as a satisfaction or extinguishment of any debt or demand or course of action, or deprive any person of any right to take out execution against the lands, goods, or chattels of the person imprisoned, in the same manner as if such imprisonment had not taken place.

Any person imprisoned under this section shall be discharged out of custody upon a certificate signed in the prescribed manner to the effect that he has satisfied the debt or instalment of a debt in respect of which he was imprisoned, together with the prescribed costs (if any).

Section 31E(1)(b) of the Matrimonial and Family Proceedings Act 1984 (family court has county court's powers) does not apply in relation to the powers given by this section to the county court.

3C-43.1   *Note* —Amended by the Crime and Courts Act 2013 Sch.9(3) para.78, Sch.10(2) para.2, with effect from 22 April 2014 (SI 2014/954) subject to savings and transitional provisions specified in 2013 c.22 s.15 and Sch.8 and transitional provision specified in SI 2014/954 arts 2(c), (d) and 3.

C. Contempt of Court Act 1981

Term of imprisonment or fine for contempt

Replace the sixth paragraph (where the citation for VIS Trading Co Ltd v Nazarov has changed) with:

3C-87   Where the court is required to distinguish between the element of sentence to reflect punishment for past failures, and the element which reflects continuing non-compliance, it must make findings about whether one or both aspects are proven, before arriving at the appropriate sentence (and giving reasons for that sentence), and if there is a dispute about whether there is continuing non-compliance, that issue must be resolved on the evidence (*VIS Trading Co Ltd v Nazarov* [2015] EWHC 3327 (QB); [2016] 4 W.L.R. 1 (Whipple J) at para.29). A claimant is entitled to continue to advance the case that the respondent is in breach, even in the face of purported compliance by the respondent since the date of the committal application (ibid).

After the twenty-fourth paragraph (beginning "In South Wales Fire and Rescue Service v Smith"), add as a new paragraph:

Where under a statutory provision the High Court has power to punish a person for an act or omission which, if it had been an act or omission in the High Court, would have been contempt of court (see CPR r.81.15), the purpose of the statutory provision should determine the appropriate penalty. See, for example, *Secretary of State for Business, Innovation and Skills v Marshall* [2015] EWHC 3874 (Ch), 30 October 2015, unrep. (Judge Pelling QC), where it was said that, as the primary purpose of proceedings under the Companies Act 1985 s.453C was not to imprison people for contempt but to enable the secretary of state to make progress in an investigation that had to be carried out in the public interest, the appropriate course to adopt where a company director had failed to comply with various demands for delivery up of documents was to impose a prison term, suspended on condition that he produced the relevant documents by a specified date.

Add new paragraph 3C–87.1:

Personal injury claim dismissed for "fundamental dishonesty" – sentence in subsequent proceedings for contempt

In the circumstances provided for by the Criminal Justice and Courts Act 2015 s.57, a court **3C-87.1** should dismiss a personal injury claim in which the court has found that the claimant is entitled to damages where, on the application of the defendant, the court is satisfied on the balance of probabilities that the claimant has been "fundamentally dishonest" in relation to the claim, unless the court is satisfied that the claimant would suffer substantial injustice if the claim were dismissed. Where a court dismisses a claim for these reasons it must record the amount of damages that the claimant would have been awarded. It is expressly provided that if in any subsequent proceedings for contempt of court against the claimant in respect of that dishonesty the claimant is found guilty, then in sentencing the claimant or otherwise disposing of the proceedings the court "must have regard" to the dismissal of the claim (s.57(6) and (7)).

Replace s.19 with:

SUPPLEMENTAL

Interpretation

19. In this Act— **3C-96**

"court" includes any tribunal or body exercising the judicial power of the State, and"legal proceedings" shall be construed accordingly;

"publication" has the meaning assigned by subsection (1) of section 2, and"publish" (except in section 9) shall be construed accordingly;

"Scottish proceedings" means proceedings before any court, including the Courts-Martial Appeal Court and Employment Appeal Tribunal, sitting in Scotland, and includes proceedings before the Supreme Court in the exercise of any appellate jurisdiction over proceedings in such a court;

"the strict liability rule" has the meaning assigned by section 1;

"superior court" means Supreme Court, the Court of Appeal, the High Court, the Crown Court, the Courts-Martial Appeal Court, the Employment Appeal Tribunal and any other court exercising in relation to its proceedings powers equivalent to those of the High Court.

Note

After "2009 (SI 2009/1604)", add:

; and the Competition Act 1998 (Consequential Provisions) Order 2013 (SI 2013/294) Sch.1, **3C-97** with effect from 10 March 2013.

Replace Schedule 1 with:

SCHEDULE 1

TIMES WHEN PROCEEDINGS ARE ACTIVE FOR PURPOSES OF SECTION 2

Preliminary

1. In this Schedule "criminal proceedings" means proceedings against a person in respect of **3C-102** an offence, not being appellate proceedings or proceedings commenced by motion for committal or attachment in England and Wales or Northern Ireland; and "appellate proceedings" means proceedings on appeal from or for the review of the decision of a court in any proceedings.

1ZA. Proceedings under the Double Jeopardy (Scotland) Act 2011 (asp 16) are criminal proceedings for the purposes of this Schedule.

2. Criminal, appellate and other proceedings are active within the meaning of section 2 at the times respectively prescribed by the following paragraphs of this Schedule; and in relation to proceedings in which more than one of the steps described in any of those paragraphs is taken, the reference in that paragraph is a reference to the first of those steps.

Criminal proceedings

3C-103   3.   Subject to the following provisions of this Schedule, criminal proceedings are active from the relevant initial step specified in paragraph 4 or 4A until concluded as described in paragraph 5.

4.   The initial steps of criminal proceedings are—

(a)   arrest without warrant;

(b)   the issue, or in Scotland the grant, of a warrant for arrest;

(c)   the issue of a summons to appear, or in Scotland the grant of a warrant to cite;

(d)   the service of an indictment or other document specifying the charge;

(e)   except in Scotland, oral charge.

(f)   the making of an application under section 2(2) (tainted acquittals), 3(3)(b) (admission made or becoming known after acquittal), 4(3)(b) (new evidence), 11(3) (eventual death of injured person) or 12(3) (nullity of previous proceedings) of the Double Jeopardy (Scotland) Act 2011 (asp 16).

4A.   Where as a result of an order under section 54 of the Criminal Procedure and Investigations Act 1996 (acquittal tainted by an administration of justice offence) proceedings are brought against a person for an offence of which he has previously been acquitted, the initial step of the proceedings is a certification under subsection (2) of that section; and paragraph 4 has effect subject to this.

5.   Criminal proceedings are concluded—

(a)   by acquittal or, as the case may be, by sentence;

(b)   by any other verdict, finding, order or decision which puts an end to the proceedings;

(c)   by discontinuance or by operation of law.

(d)   where the initial steps of the proceedings are as mentioned in paragraph 4(f)—

(i)   by refusal of the application;

(ii)   if the application is granted and within the period of 2 months mentioned in section 6(3) of the Double Jeopardy (Scotland) Act 2011 (asp 16) a new prosecution is brought, by acquittal or, as the case may be, by sentence in the new prosecution.

6.   The reference in paragraph 5(a) to sentence includes any order or decision consequent on conviction or finding of guilt which disposes of the case, either absolutely or subject to future events, and a deferment of sentence under section 1 of the Powers of Criminal Courts (Sentencing) Act 2000, s.219 or 432 of the Criminal Procedure (Scotland) Act 1975 or Article 14 of the Treatment of Offenders (Northern Ireland) Order 1976.

7.   Proceedings are discontinued within the meaning of paragraph 5(c)—

(a)   in England and Wales or Northern Ireland, if the charge or summons is withdrawn or a *nolle prosequi* entered;

(aa)   in England and Wales, if they are discontinued by virtue of section 23 of the Prosecution of Offences Act 1985;

(ab)   in England and Wales, if they are discontinued by virtue of paragraph 11 of Schedule 17 to the Crime and Courts Act 2013 (deferred prosecution agreements);

(b)   in Scotland, if the proceedings are expressly abandoned by the prosecutor or are deserted *simpliciter*;

(c)   in the case of proceedings in England and Wales or Northern Ireland commenced by arrest without warrant, if the person arrested is released, otherwise than on bail, without having been charged.

(d)   where the initial steps of the proceedings are as mentioned in paragraph 4(f) and the application is granted, if no new prosecution is brought within the period of 2 months mentioned in section 6(3) of the Double Jeopardy (Scotland) Act 2011 (asp 16).

9.   Criminal proceedings in England and Wales or Northern Ireland cease to be active if an order is made for the charge to lie on the file, but become active again if leave is later given for the proceedings to continue.

9A.   Where proceedings in England and Wales have been discontinued by virtue of section 23 of the Prosecution of Offences Act 1985, but notice is given by the accused under subsection (7) of that section to the effect that he wants the proceedings to continue, they become active again with the giving of that notice.

10.   Without prejudice to paragraph 5(b) above, criminal proceedings against a person cease to be active—

(a)   if the accused is found to be under a disability such as to render him unfit to be tried or unfit to plead or, in Scotland, is found to be insane in bar of trial; or

(b)   if a hospital order is made in his case under section 51(5) of the Mental Health Act 1983 or Article 57(5) of the Mental Health (Northern Ireland) Order 1986 or, in Scotland, where an assessment order or a treatment order ceases to have effect by virtue of sections 52H or 52R respectively of the Criminal Procedure (Scotland) Act 1995

but become active again if they are later resumed.

11.   Criminal proceedings against a person which become active on the issue or the grant of a warrant for his arrest cease to be active at the end of the period of twelve months beginning with the date of the warrant unless he has been arrested within that period, but become active again if he is subsequently arrested.

Other proceedings at first instance

12.   Proceedings other than criminal proceedings and appellate proceedings are active from **3C-104** the time when arrangements for the hearing are made or, if no such arrangements are previously made, from the time the hearing begins, until the proceedings are disposed of or discontinued or withdrawn; and for the purposes of this paragraph any motion or application made in or for the purposes of any proceedings, and any pre-trial review in the county court, is to be treated as a distinct proceeding.

13.   In England and Wales or Northern Ireland arrangements for the hearing of proceedings to which paragraph 12 applies are made within the meaning of that paragraph—
    (a)   in the case of proceedings in the High Court for which provision is made by rules of court for setting down for trial, when the case is set down;
    (b)   in the case of any proceedings, when a date for the trial or hearing is fixed.

14.   [*Proceedings in Scotland.*]

Appellate proceedings

15.   Appellate proceedings are active from the time when they are commenced—   **3C-105**
    (a)   by application for leave to appeal or apply for review, or by notice of such an application;
    (b)   by notice of appeal or of application for review;
    (c)   by other originating process,
        until disposed of or abandoned, discontinued or withdrawn.

16.   Where, in appellate proceedings relating to criminal proceedings, the court—
    (a)   remits the case to the court below; or
    (b)   orders a new trial or a *venire de novo*, or in Scotland grants authority to bring a new prosecution,
        any further or new proceedings which result shall be treated as active from the conclusion of the appellate proceedings.

Note

Replace with:
    Amended by the Mental Health Act 1983 Sch.4 paras 57(c) and 59(c); the Prosecution of Of- **3C-106** fences Act 1985 s.31, Sch.1 paras 4 and 5; the Mental Health (Scotland) Act 1984 s.17, s.127(1), Sch.3 para.48; the Criminal Procedure and Investigations Act 1996 s.57; the Powers of Criminal Courts (Sentencing) Act 2000; and by the Double Jeopardy (Scotland) Act 2011 Sch.1 paras 2, 3, 4; the Armed Forces Act 2006 Sch.17 para.1, with effect from 31 October 2009 (SI 2009/1167); and by the Crime and Courts Act 2013 Sch.17 para.34, with effect from 24 February 2014 subject to transitional provisions and savings specified in 2013 c.22 s.15, Sch.8 and Sch.17 para.39.

SECTION 3E   INSOLVENCY PROCEEDINGS

Jurisdiction and distribution of business

Company insolvency

Replace "The county courts have concurrent jurisdiction where the company's registered office is within the relevant insolvency district and the capital paid up or credited as paid up does not exceed £120,000 (s.117(2) Insolvency Act 1986)." with:
    •   The county court has concurrent jurisdiction where the company's registered office is **3E-22** within the relevant insolvency district and the capital paid up or credited as paid up does not exceed £120,000 (s.117(2) Insolvency Act 1986).

Bankruptcy

Replace the third paragraph (from "Petitions in the London Insolvency District" to "r.6.9(2) Insolvency Rules 1986.") with:
    NB: Debtors' petitions
    With effect from 6 April 2016 debtors' petitions are no longer dealt with by the courts but by an official known as the adjudicator. Debtors' applications for a bankruptcy order must now be made to the adjudicator online. See the Enterprise and Regulatory Reform Act 2013

(Commencement No.9 and Savings Provisions) Order 2016 (SI 2016/191) which brought into force s.71 Enterprise and Regulatory Reform Act 2013 which repealed ss.272–274A Insolvency Act 1986 and inserted a new Chapter A1 into Part IX of the Act. The new provisions do not affect debtors' petitions presented before 6 April 2016 or petitions presented under the Administration of Insolvent Estates of Deceased Persons Order 1986 (SI 1986/1999) or the Insolvent Partnerships Order 1994 (SI 1994/2421).

Petitions in the London Insolvency District are presented to the High Court (in the Rolls Building, Fetter Lane, London EC4A 1NL) or the County Court at Central London (sitting in the Thomas More Building, Royal Courts of Justice, Strand, London WC2A 2LL). The work is split between the High Court and the County Court at Central London as follows: With effect from 6 April 2011 where the petition debt is £50,000 or more, the debtor has not resided or had a place of business in England or Wales for six months preceding the date of presentation of the petition, the debtor's residence or place of business cannot be ascertained or the petition is presented against a member of a partnership that is being wound up by the High Court, the petition should be presented to the High Court. Where the petition debt is less than £50,000, subject to the exceptions mentioned, the petition should be presented to the County Court at Central London. NB Some county court hearing centres have no insolvency jurisdiction.

Add new paragraph 3E–27:

Insolvency Express Trials

3E-27   From 6 April 2016 a new regime for insolvency cases began as a two year pilot in the registrars' courts in the Chancery Division of the High Court at the Rolls Building. Practitioners are referred to the Practice Direction 51P—Pilot for Insolvency Express Trials (Vol.1 para.51PPD.1).

Company voluntary arrangements (Part I Insolvency Act 1986)

Company voluntary arrangements without moratorium

Replace the first paragraph with:

3E-31   The directors of a company, its administrator (where an administration order is in force) or its liquidator (where the company is being wound up) may propose to the creditors of the company a composition in satisfaction of its debts or a scheme of arrangement (a company voluntary arrangement) (s.1). The proposal must be made to all the company's creditors, and it must be for a composition of debts or a scheme of arrangement (as to which see *March Estates plc v Gunmark Ltd* [1996] 2 B.C.L.C. 1). Within 28 days (or any longer period the courts allow) the nominee must submit a report to the court stating whether a meeting of creditors and members of the company should be summoned to consider the proposal (s.2). The meetings must then be held at the time, date and place proposed (s.3). The chairman of the meetings must report to the court the result of the meetings (s.4(6)). Members vote according to the rights attaching to their shares (r.1.18(1)) but are entitled to vote even where no voting rights attach to their shares (r.1.18(2)). A resolution may be passed by a majority of creditors in value, but any resolution to approve or modify the proposal must be passed by a majority of three-quarters or more in value of creditors present and voting in person or by proxy (r.1.19(1) and (2)).

SECTION 3F   PERSONAL INJURY

Add new paragraphs 3F–32.3 to 3F–32.5:

Criminal Justice and Courts Act 2015

(2015 c.2)

ARRANGEMENT OF SECTIONS

Personal injury claims: cases of fundamental dishonesty

3F-32.3   **57.**—(1)   This section applies where, in proceedings on a claim for damages in respect of personal injury ("the primary claim")—

(a)   the court finds that the claimant is entitled to damages in respect of the claim, but

(b) on an application by the defendant for the dismissal of the claim under this section, the court is satisfied on the balance of probabilities that the claimant has been fundamentally dishonest in relation to the primary claim or a related claim.

(2) The court must dismiss the primary claim, unless it is satisfied that the claimant would suffer substantial injustice if the claim were dismissed.

(3) The duty under subsection (2) includes the dismissal of any element of the primary claim in respect of which the claimant has not been dishonest.

(4) The court's order dismissing the claim must record the amount of damages that the court would have awarded to the claimant in respect of the primary claim but for the dismissal of the claim.

(5) When assessing costs in the proceedings, a court which dismisses a claim under this section must deduct the amount recorded in accordance with subsection (4) from the amount which it would otherwise order the claimant to pay in respect of costs incurred by the defendant.

(6) If a claim is dismissed under this section, subsection (7) applies to—

(a) any subsequent criminal proceedings against the claimant in respect of the fundamental dishonesty mentioned in subsection (1)(b), and

(b) any subsequent proceedings for contempt of court against the claimant in respect of that dishonesty.

(7) If the court in those proceedings finds the claimant guilty of an offence or of contempt of court, it must have regard to the dismissal of the primary claim under this section when sentencing the claimant or otherwise disposing of the proceedings.

(8) In this section—

"claim" includes a counter-claim and, accordingly, "claimant" includes a counter-claimant and "defendant" includes a defendant to a counterclaim;
"personal injury" includes any disease and any other impairment of a person's physical or mental condition;
"related claim" means a claim for damages in respect of personal injury which is made—

(a) in connection with the same incident or series of incidents in connection with which the primary claim is made, and

(b) by a person other than the person who made the primary claim.

(9) This section does not apply to proceedings started by the issue of a claim form before the day on which this section comes into force.

Commencement

13 April 2015 by Sch.1 to the Criminal Justice and Courts Act 2015 (Commencement No.1, Saving and Transitional Provisions) Order 2015 (SI 2015/778). **3F-32.4**

General Note

By subss.(1)-(3) a Claimant who is found by the court in a personal injury claim (namely either **3F-32.5** his or her own claim, counterclaim or a "related" personal injury claim such as that of a relative arising from the same incident or series of incidents) to have have acted in a fundamentally dishonest way in relation to that claim may face an application under this section for dismissal of the claimant's own claim (referred to as the "primary" claim in the section). If the court is satisfied that the test of fundamental dishonesty is met, and the court finds that the claimant is entitled to damages in respect of the claim, then the court must dismiss the primary claim unless to do so "would" cause the claimant to suffer "substantial injustice" if the claim were dismissed. The entire claim must be dismissed, not merely the part affected by the dishonesty in question.

The dismissal under this section does not, it appears, bring matters to an end entirely because the court must nonetheless make a decision (subs.(4)) as to the sum of damages which it would (but for the application under s.57) have awarded to the Claimant, and (by subs.(5)) must then deduct that amount from the sum of costs it orders the Claimant to pay to the Defendant, when detailed assessment takes place. In any criminal or committal proceedings the court dealing with the criminal proceedings or the committal must have regard to the dismissal of the primary claim when deciding sentence (subss.(6)-(7)). Note that the power under s.57 is similar but not identical to that in CPR r.44.16 which provides that in relation to Qualified One Way Costs Shifting, "orders for costs made against the claimant may be enforced to the full extent of such orders with the permission of the court where the claim is found on the balance of probabilities to be fundamentally dishonest".

Case law: in relation to s.57 see *Hughes, Kindon and Jones v KGM*, 1 April 2016, unrep., county court at Taunton, a decision at Deputy District Judge level in which three claimants alleged they had suffered injuries whose effects lasted for 12 months. The court concluded that such injuries as had been suffered would have lasted around two weeks and awarded the two remaining claimants £750 in damages. On application under s.57 the court held that the two claims in question had been fundamentally dishonest (the claim of the third claimant had been struck out for other reasons) and that there would be no substantial injustice in dismissing the claims in their entirety, triggering the removal of QOCS protection.

In *Gosling v Hailo*, 29 April 2014, unrep. (county court at Cambridge, circuit judge decision of HHJ Maloney, claim no. UD17868, Lawtel AC0142747) the court made use of the similar powers under CPR r.44.16 (which, notably, apply even where a claim has been discontinued). It held that investigate the question of fundamental dishonesty in relation to liability, raised after discontinuance of a claim, it would be inappropriate to proceed on the papers without oral hearing and that holding an oral hearing would be disproportionate. However the case on quantum was capable of being found to be fundamentally dishonest based on the evidence without the need for further hearing. It was observed that "fundamental dishonesty" should be considered purposively and contextually and that the test determined whether or not the claimant had the protection of QOCS put in place for social policy reasons. Collateral or minor matters not going to the heart of the claim should not expose the claimant to the costs penalty. Where a case was not a plain one the court would have to consider whether it was proportionate to pursue the allegation but in some cases the dishonesty would be sufficiently plain that an oral hearing was unnecessary. The Claimant was ordered to pay the Defendants' costs in full.

SECTION 3G   DATA PROTECTION ACT 1998

INTRODUCTION

Replace the first paragraph with:

3G-1   The Data Protection Act ("the Act" or "DPA") was passed to implement Directive 95/46 of October 24, 1995 on the protection of individuals with regard to the processing of personal data and the free movement of such data ("Directive 95/46"). It repealed the Data Protection Act 1984 which had been passed to enable the UK to ratify the Convention for the Protection of Individuals with regard to automatic processing of Personal Data ("Treaty 108"). The Act will be replaced by the proposed General Data Protection Regulation and the accompanying Directive applicable to personal data in the criminal justice system. Both instruments are due for final approval in 2016, and to be implemented 2018. The UK courts have referred to the Directive, Treaty 108 and the Convention Rights under the European Convention on Human Rights and Fundamental Freedoms, particularly art.8, in interpreting cases on the Act. In case law since the Act came into force the courts have tended to consider the tort of misuse of private information and rights under art.8 in conjunction with the Act. The CJEU has increasingly referred to the European Union Charter of Fundamental Rights when considering data protection cases. Further specific rights in relation to telecommunications services and electronic marketing are contained in the Privacy and Electronic Communications (EC Directive) Regulations 2003 (see para.3G-17). Retention of personal data derived from public telecommunications services was mandated by Directive 2006/24 EC. That directive was ruled to be invalid by the CJEU in April 2014 because it breaches Articles 7 and 8 of the EU Charter of Fundamental Rights, in joined cases C-293/12 and C-594/12. The UK has enacted the Data Retention and Investigatory Powers Act 2014 (DRIPA) to replace its earlier legislation. DRIPA is currently subject to legal challenge in the UK.

Editorial note

After the fourth paragraph (beginning "Additional provisions apply to marketing by telephone"), add as a new paragraph:

3G-17   The maximum fine for breach of this provision has been a fine of £200,000.00 imposed by the Information Commissioner on the LMLd for making unlawful automated calls, September 2015.

The eighth principle

Replace the last paragraph with:

3G-62.0.24   The decision of the CJEU left a serious lacunae in the arrangements of many major businesses for sending personal data to the US. However, in February 2016 agreement was reached between the Commission and the US Government over replacement arrangements, called the 'Privacy

Shield'. The final authorisation has not been given for this replacement arrangement but is expected by mid-2016.

SECTION 3H CONSUMER CREDIT AND CONSUMER LAW

Introductory note about procedure in consumer credit cases

Unenforceable agreements

Change title of sub-paragraph: **3H-17.3.1**

Agreements made before 1 April 2014

Change title of sub-paragraph:

Agreements made on or after 1 April 2014

Add new paragraph at end:
    The Designated Professional Body (Consumer Credit) Handbook became effective from 1 April 2016.

Consumer Credit Act 1974

Unfair relationships

Add new paragraphs at end:
    See *Axton v G E Money Mortgages Ltd* [2015] EWHC 1343 (QB) concerning PPI mis-selling— **3H-329** brokers as agents.
    Swift Advances Plc v Okokenu [2015] C.T.L.C. 302 lending to elderly consumers and loan sustainability—relevance of OFT guidance.

Unfair Contract Terms Act 1977

Note

Replace with:
    Amended by the Occupiers' Liability Act 1984 s.2; and by the Consumer Rights Act 2015 Sch.4 **3H-549** para.3 with effect from 1 October 2015 (other than for the purposes of a contract to supply a consumer transport service) subject to transitional provisions and savings specified in SI 2015/1630 arts 6–8, and from 1 October 2016 (for the purposes of a contract to supply consumer transport service) subject to transitional provisions and savings specified in SI 2015/1630 art.6.

Note

Replace with:
    Subsection (4) inserted by the Consumer Rights Act 2015 Sch.4 para.4 with effect from 1 **3H-552.1** October 2015 (other than for the purposes of a contract to supply a consumer transport service) subject to transitional provisions and savings specified in SI 2015/1630 arts 6–8, and from 1 October 2016 (for the purposes of a contract to supply consumer transport service) subject to transitional provisions and savings specified in SI 2015/1630 art.6.

Note

Replace with:
    Subsection (1) amended and subs.(3) inserted by the Consumer Rights Act 2015 Sch.4 para.5 **3H-555.1** with effect from 1 October 2015 (other than for the purposes of a contract to supply a consumer transport service) subject to transitional provisions and savings specified in SI 2015/1630 arts 6–8, and from 1 October 2016 (for the purposes of a contract to supply consumer transport service) subject to transitional provisions and savings specified in SI 2015/1630 art.6.

Note

Replace with:
    Repealed by the Consumer Rights Act 2015 Sch.4 para.6 with effect from 1 October 2015 (other **3H-557.1**

than for the purposes of a contract to supply a consumer transport service) subject to transitional provisions and savings specified in SI 2015/1630 arts 6–8, and from 1 October 2016 (for the purposes of a contract to supply consumer transport service) subject to transitional provisions and savings specified in SI 2015/1630 art.6.

Note

Replace with:

3H-568   Repealed by the Consumer Rights Act 2015 Sch.4 para.10 with effect from 1 October 2015 (other than for the purposes of a contract to supply a consumer transport service) subject to transitional provisions and savings specified in SI 2015/1630 arts 6–8, and from 1 October 2016 (for the purposes of a contract to supply consumer transport service) subject to transitional provisions and savings specified in SI 2015/1630 art.6.

Note

Replace with:

3H-574   Repealed by the Consumer Rights Act 2015 Sch.4 para.11 with effect from 1 October 2015 (other than for the purposes of a contract to supply a consumer transport service) subject to transitional provisions and savings specified in SI 2015/1630 arts 6–8, and from 1 October 2016 (for the purposes of a contract to supply consumer transport service) subject to transitional provisions and savings specified in SI 2015/1630 art.6.

Note

Replace with:

3H-576.1   Amended by the Consumer Rights Act 2015 Sch.4 para.12 with effect from 1 October 2015 (other than for the purposes of a contract to supply a consumer transport service) subject to transitional provisions and savings specified in SI 2015/1630 arts 6–8, and from 1 October 2016 (for the purposes of a contract to supply consumer transport service) subject to transitional provisions and savings specified in SI 2015/1630 art.6.

Note

Replace with:

3H-579   Amended by the Sale of Goods Act 1979 s.63(2) and Sch.2; and by the Consumer Rights Act 2015 Sch.4 para.13 with effect from 1 October 2015 (other than for the purposes of a contract to supply a consumer transport service) subject to transitional provisions and savings specified in SI 2015/1630 arts 6–8, and from 1 October 2016 (for the purposes of a contract to supply consumer transport service) subject to transitional provisions and savings specified in SI 2015/1630 art.6.

Note

Replace with:

3H-580.1   Amended by the Consumer Rights Act 2015 Sch.4 para.27 with effect from 1 October 2015 (other than for the purposes of a contract to supply a consumer transport service) subject to transitional provisions and savings specified in SI 2015/1630 arts 6–8, and from 1 October 2016 (for the purposes of a contract to supply consumer transport service) subject to transitional provisions and savings specified in SI 2015/1630 art.6.

Consumer Rights Act 2015

Add new paragraph 3H–1112:

Editorial note

3H-1112   See *Makdessi v Cavendish Square Holdings BV* [2015] UKSC 67 and *ParkingEye Ltd v Beavis* [2015] EWCA Civ 402.

Although the *ParkingEye Ltd v Beavis* [2015] EWCA Civ 402 case raises issue under the Unfair Terms in Consumer Contracts Regulations 1999 (SI 1999/2083) replaced by the Consumer Rights Act 2015, this case is still of relevance to Schedule 2—Consumer Contract Terms which may be Regarded as Unfair at para.3H–1102.

SECTION 3J   DIRECTORS DISQUALIFICATION PROCEEDINGS

PRACTICE DIRECTION—DIRECTORS DISQUALIFICATION PROCEEDINGS

Appeals

In the first paragraph, replace "para.35" with:
   para.32   **3J-63**

SECTION 3K   CIVIL RECOVERY PROCEEDINGS

PRACTICE DIRECTION—CIVIL RECOVERY PROCEEDINGS

Add new paragraph 3K–10.1:

Editorial note
   See Senior Master Practice Note dated 15 April 2016 (at para.3K-29) as to the details of the **3K-10.1**
procedure to be adopted when commencing a Part 8 Civil Recovery Claim.

Add new Practice Note at end of Section 3K:

SENIOR MASTER PRACTICE NOTE 15 APRIL 2016 POCA CIVIL RECOVERY CLAIMS UNDER CPR PART 8
Civil Recovery Proceedings Practice Direction

Introduction

1.   Civil Recovery claims commenced under Part 5 of the Proceeds of Crime **3K-29**
Act 2002 ("POCA") must be brought under CPR 8 in accordance with
paragraph 4.1 of the Civil Recovery Proceedings Practice Direction.
   2.   Part 8 is primarily designed for matters that are not factually contentious.
There are normally no statements of case and claims are litigated purely by
way of witness evidence.
   3.   Whilst this remains an appropriate procedure for civil recovery claims
that are unlikely to be disputed, where facts may be contested the Part 8
procedure is not necessarily suitable. See for example the note in the White
Book Vol 2 3K-4 (end of page 1996 to beginning page 1997) and the cases
mentioned; particularly *Director of Assets Recovery Agency v Creaven* [2006] 1
WLR 633 at [11] per Stanley Burnton J. (as he then was); *SOCA v Bosworth*
[2010] EWHC 645 (QB) at [26] to [29] per HHJ Seymour; *SOCA v Pelekanos*
[2009] EWHC 2307 per Hamblen J. at [3].
   4.   The court has power to order a case to proceed under Part 7 where appropriate under CPR 3.3 (see Hamblen J. in *SOCA v Pelekanos*). However, that
would not assist in civil recovery cases, as many are suitable for the usual Part 8
procedure, and for those where facts are in issue the Part 7 procedure would
be likely to unduly delay progress to trial.
   5.   To resolve these issues, a procedure has been put in place in the Queen's
Bench Division under the court's case management powers in CPR 3.3 to take
effect from 3 May 2016 for the case management of POCA civil recovery claims,
as set out in the Schedule to this Practice Note.
   The Senior Master

Schedule

1. Before issuing the Part 8 Claim Form, the enforcement authority (as defined in s.316 (1) of POCA) will consider whether to ask the court to make directions ("Initial Directions") on the papers or at a hearing.

2. If the enforcement authority decides to seek Initial Directions without a hearing, it will

(1) serve on the Defendant (unless evidence is provided to the court that there is good reason not to do so before Initial Directions are given) and

(2) lodge at court

the issued Part 8 Claim Form, accompanied by a short witness statement, with the following exhibits:

(i) Draft Points of Claim; and

(ii) Draft Initial Directions providing for:

a) The serving and filing of Points of Claim, Points of Defence and Points of Reply;

b) A directions hearing to be listed after service and filing of statements of case;

c) Permission to the Defendant(s) to apply to court to vary any of the Initial Directions.

3. Where either:

(i) the draft Initial Directions have been agreed with the Defendant(s) or their legal representatives; or

(ii) the court considers that a hearing is not required;

the court will make Initial Directions without a hearing ("the Initial Directions Order").

4. If the court makes the Initial Directions Order, the enforcement authority will serve on the Defendant(s) within 7 days of receipt of the Initial Directions Order from the court:

(i) Part 8 Claim Form and witness statement with exhibits (unless previously served);

(ii) Points of Claim;

(iii) the Initial Directions Order.

5. If either:

(i) the court considers it is not appropriate to make Initial Directions without a hearing; or

(ii) the enforcement authority considers that it is not appropriate to ask the court to deal with the matter without a hearing;

the court will list a directions hearing for 30 minutes (or longer if requested by either party) and will serve notice of the hearing on all parties.

SECTION 3L EUROPEAN PROCEDURES (CPR PART 78)

Part 78—European Procedures

Editorial introduction

3L-1 *Add new sub-paragraph at end:*

(iii) Future amendments—Both the EOP Regulation (see Annex 1 and section I of this Part) and the ESCP Regulation (see Annex 2 and section II of this Part) are amended by Regulation (EU) 2015/2421 in part from 14 January 2017 and otherwise from 14 July 2017.

Section I—European Order for Payment Procedure

Making a claim

Add new paragraph at end:

The scope and effect of art.20 (Review in exceptional cases) (see para.3L-76 below) was **3L-5** considered by the ECJ in *Thomas Cook Belgium NV v Thurner Belgium GmbH* (C-245/14) EU:C:2015:715; [2016] 1 W.L.R. 878, ECJ, where it was argued by the judgment debtor that the court issuing the EOP lacked jurisdiction due to the possible existence of a jurisdiction clause agreed between the parties and not referred to in the application form for the order. The ECJ ruled that this did not constitute "exceptional circumstances" within art.20(2) such as to justify a review of the order by the competent court in the Member State of origin.

SECTION 3M PREVENTION OF TERRORISM PROCEEDINGS (CPR PARTS 76, 79 AND 80)

PART 79—PROCEEDINGS UNDER THE COUNTER-TERRORISM ACT 2008 AND PART 1 OF THE TERRORIST ASSET-FREEZING ETC. ACT 2010

IV. General Provisions applicable to Sections 2 and 3 of this Part

Effect of rule

Add new paragraph at end:

In *Bank Mellat v HM Treasury* [2015] EWCA Civ 1052; [2016] 1 W.L.R. 1187, the Court of Ap- **3M-95** peal rejected an argument that, in the light of *Tariq v Home Office* [2011] UKSC 35; [2012] 1 A.C. 452, the AF standard of disclosure should be held to apply only where either personal liberty or an equally fundamental interest is at stake. Applying *Kiani v Secretary of State for the Home Department* [2015] EWCA Civ 776; [2016] 2 W.L.R. 788, at [23], the Court of Appeal held that the question whether the AF standard of disclosure applied depended on the context and circumstances. In the particular context of proceedings under the Counter-Terrorism Act 2008 by Bank Mellat, the exercise of the power to impose financial retractions would have extremely serious and possibly ir-reversible consequences and involved a sufficiently serious restriction on the Bank's freedom of ac-tion and business that the application of the AF standard of disclosure was called for (*Bank Mellat v HM Treasury*, at [23]-[25]).

PART 80—PROCEEDINGS UNDER THE TERRORISM PREVENTION AND INVESTIGATION MEASURES ACT 2011

I Application of this Part

Effect of rule

After "withhold disclosed material.", add:

CPR r.80.7.

3M-106

II Permission Applications, References and Appeals to the High Court Relating to TPIM Notices

Add new paragraph 3M–110.1:

Review hearings and appeals

In *EB v Secretary of State for the Home Department* [2016] EWHC 137 (Admin), 29 January 2016, **3M-110.1** unrep. (Cranston J), where an individual (D) was subject to a TPIM notice and a review under s.9 of the 2011 Act was pending, D appealed under s.16 of that Act against the Secretary of State's refusal to vary measures set out in the notice. The judge directed that the appeal should not be heard forthwith (as D submitted) but should be joined with the review (due to be heard some time hence) so that both could be properly and justly determined.

SECTION 3O   EMPLOYMENT

Employment Tribunals (Constitution and Rules of Procedure) Regulations 2013

Forms of Costs and Preparation Time Orders

Replace the fifth paragraph with:

3O-2.1   Note that if, as frequently occurs, representation arrangements change during the course of the litigation, the type of order available may differ in respect of each period. But the Tribunal cannot make both types of order in favour of the same party in the same proceedings. However, a party whose representation status has changed may apply for both types of order, leaving the Tribunal to decide entitlement to each, and, as appropriate, which to make. See: *Duhoe v Support Services Group Ltd (In Liquidation)* UKEAT/0102/15, 13 August 2015.

SECTION 4   SUPREME COURT OF THE UNITED KINGDOM AND JUDICIAL COMMITTEE OF THE PRIVY COUNCIL
SECTION 4A   SUPREME COURT OF THE UNITED KINGDOM APPEALS

PRACTICE DIRECTION 6—THE APPEAL HEARING

Judgment

Conditions under which judgments are released in advance

Replace paragraph 6.8.5 with:

4A-106 6.8.5   Accredited members of the media may on occasion also be given a copy of the judgment in advance by the Court's communications team. The contents of this document are subject to a strict embargo, and are not for publication, broadcast or use on club tapes before judgment has been delivered. The documents are issued in advance solely at the Court's discretion, and in order to inform later reporting, on the strict understanding that no approach is made to any person or organisation about their contents before judgment is given.

PRACTICE DIRECTION 10—DEVOLUTION JURISDICTION

General note

4A-135 *Add new paragraph 10.1.7:*
   10.1.7   In cases where the Court is asked to consider the provisions of Bills passed by devolved legislatures, it will usually be desirable for special directions to be given, particularly if there is some urgency. It is helpful if at an early stage the relevant officer making the reference notifies any relevant officer and any other person or body who has a potential interest in the proceedings, of the making of the reference and of any request for directions. All parties to the proceedings are expected to co-operate with one another in order that the Court can ensure that the proceedings are conducted efficiently and expeditiously.

SECTION 7   LEGAL REPRESENTATIVES—COSTS AND LITIGATION FUNDING
SECTION 7A1   LITIGATION FUNDING BEFORE APRIL 1, 2013

Access to Justice Act 1999

Add new paragraph 7A1–11:

Editorial introduction

Sections 29 and 30 have been repealed with effect from 1 April 2013 by the Legal Aid, Sentenc- **7A1-11** ing and Punishment of Offenders Act 2012 ss.46(2), 47 save in relation to proceedings relating to a claim for damages in respect of diffuse mesothelioma and publication and privacy proceedings: Legal Aid, Sentencing and Punishment of Offenders Act 2012 (Commencement No.5 and Saving Provision) Order 2013 (SI 2013/77). The repeals were deferred until 6 April 2016 in relation to certain insolvency proceedings: the Legal Aid, Sentencing and Punishment of Offenders Act 2012 (Commencement No.12) Order 2016 (SI 2016/345) art.2 (see further Vol.1 para.48.0.2.4). Section 29 continues to apply in relation to a costs order made in favour of a party to proceedings who took out a costs insurance policy in relation to the proceedings before 1 April 2013. Section 30 continues to apply in relation to a costs order made in favour of a person to whom a body gave an undertaking before 1 April 2013 if the undertaking was given specifically in respect of the costs of other parties to proceedings relating to the matter which is the subject of the proceedings in which the costs order is made.

FUNDING ARRANGEMENTS

Conditional Fees

Success fees

Add new paragraph at end:

A conditional fee agreement provided that it covered work done by the claimant's solicitors **7A1-58** before the date of the agreement. In disallowing success fees claimed on the work done before the date of the agreement on the basis that the risk assessment when instructions were given was differ-ent to that at the date of the agreement, the costs judge had erred: *Ghising v Secretary of State for the Home Department* [2015] EWHC 3706 (QB).

SECTION 7A2   LITIGATION FUNDING AFTER APRIL 1, 2013

INTRODUCTION

Replace the second paragraph with:

The amendments made by the 2012 Act will not apply to claims for damages in respect of dif- **7A2-1** fuse mesothelioma until the Lord Chancellor has carried out a review of the likely effect of the amendments in relation to such proceedings, and published a report of the conclusions of the review. The commencement of the amendments has also been deferred in relation to publication and privacy proceedings: see the Legal Aid, Sentencing and Punishment of Offenders Act 2012 (Commencement No.5 and Saving Provision) Order 2013 (SI 2013/77), which lists the proceedings excluded and provides a definition of "publication and privacy proceedings". The commencement of the amendments was deferred until 6 April 2016 in relation to certain insolvency proceedings: the Legal Aid, Sentencing and Punishment of Offenders Act 2012 (Commencement No.12) Order 2016 (SI 2016/345) art.2 (see further Vol.1 para.48.0.2.4).

Replace the sixth paragraph with:

Premiums for after the event insurance policies are not recoverable save insofar as provided by regulations made under s.58C of the Courts and Legal Services Act 1990 and save in limited classes of cases in respect of which the commencement of the amendments has been deferred. Sections 29 and 30 of the Access to Justice Act 1999 have been repealed (section 29 is repealed except in respect of claims for damages in respect of diffuse mesothelioma and publication and privacy proceedings). The repeal of section 29 was deferred until 6 April 2016 in respect of certain insolvency proceedings. The Recovery of Costs Insurance Premiums in Clinical Negligence Proceedings (No.2) Regulations 2013 (SI 2013/739) permit the recovery of that part of a premium which insures against the liability to pay for experts' reports on liability and causation in clinical negligence proceedings if the financial value of the claim for damages exceeds £1,000. The Supreme Court has confirmed that, in the absence of agreement or specific statutory provision to the contrary, a party cannot recover an ATE premium as part of the costs of legal expenses: *McGraddie v McGraddie* [2015] UKSC 1.

Courts and Legal Services Act 1990

Note

Replace the first paragraph with:

7A2-4   Substituted, together with s.58A, by the Access to Justice Act 1999 s.27. Amended by SI 2003/1887, SI 2005/3429 and (with effect from April 1, 2013) by the Legal Aid, Sentencing and Punishment of Offenders Act 2012 s.44 which inserted ss.58(4A) and (4B). The amendments made by the 2012 Act will not apply to claims for damages in respect of diffuse mesothelioma until the Lord Chancellor has carried out a review of the likely effect of the amendments in relation to such proceedings, and published a report of the conclusions of the review. The amendments made by the 2012 Act have also not been brought into force in relation to publication and privacy proceedings and, in respect of certain insolvency proceedings, were deferred until 6 April 2016. All proceedings which can be the subject of an enforceable conditional fee agreement under s.58, other than proceedings under s.82 of the Environmental Protection Act 1990, are specified for the purposes of s.58(4)(a) by r.2 of the Conditional Fee Agreements Order 2013. For the purposes of s.58(4)(c), r.3 of that Order prescribes a maximum success fee of 100 per cent. Regulations 4 and 5 of the Order provide that the additional conditions shall apply to claims for personal injuries and that the maximum limit of the success fee in such claims shall be 25 per cent in proceedings at first instance and 100 per cent in all other proceedings of general damages for pain, suffering, and loss of amenity and damages for pecuniary loss, other than future pecuniary loss, net of any sums recoverable by the CRU. The amendments made by the Legal Aid, Sentencing and Punishment of Offenders Act 2012 s.44 were brought into force for certain purposes by the Legal Aid, Sentencing and Punishment of Offenders Act 2012 (Commencement No.12) Order 2016 (SI 2016/345) art.2, with effect from 6 April 2016.

Note

Replace the penultimate sentence with:

7A2-6   The amendments made by the 2012 Act have also not been brought into force in relation to publication and privacy proceedings and, in respect of certain insolvency proceedings, were deferred until 6 April 2016.

Note

Replace with:

7A2-12   Inserted by the Legal Aid, Sentencing and Punishment of Offenders Act 2012 s.46(1) with effect from April 1, 2013, except in respect of claims for damages in respect of diffuse mesothelioma, certain insolvency proceedings and publication and privacy proceedings: The Legal Aid, Sentencing and Punishment of Offenders Act 2012 (Commencement No.5 and Saving Provision) Order 2013, SI 2013/77. Subsequently, the saving in relation to insolvency proceedings was removed, with effect from 6 April 2016, by the Legal Aid, Sentencing and Punishment of Offenders Act 2012 (Commencement No.12) Order 2016 (SI 2016/345) (see further Vol.1 para.48.0.2.4). The insertion of this section by the Legal Aid, Sentencing and Punishment of Offenders Act 2012 s.46(1) was brought into force for certain purposes by the Legal Aid, Sentencing and Punishment of Offenders Act 2012 (Commencement No.12) Order 2016 (SI 2016/345) art.2, with effect from 6 April 2016.

Editorial note

Replace the first paragraph with:

7A2-13   The Access to Justice Act 1999 s.29 (Recovery of insurance premiums by way of costs) is revoked by the Legal Aid, Sentencing and Punishment of Offenders Act 2012 s.46(2) with effect from April 1, 2013, subject to savings in ss.46(3) and 48. Costs orders made in favour of a party to proceedings who took out a costs insurance policy in relation to the proceedings before the commencement day are not affected by the repeal (s.46(3)). The repeal is postponed in respect of proceedings relating to claims for damages for diffuse mesothelioma pending a review by the Lord Chancellor (s.48). By the Legal Aid, Sentencing and Punishment of Offenders Act 2012 (Commencement No.5 and Saving Provision) Order 2013 (SI 2013/77) the amendments made by the 2012 Act were not brought into force in relation to certain insolvency proceedings and publication and privacy proceedings, but subsequently the exception in relation to insolvency proceedings was removed, with effect from 6 April 2016, by the Legal Aid, Sentencing and Punishment of Offenders Act 2012 (Commencement No.12) Order 2016 (SI 2016/345) (see further Vol.1, para.48.0.2.4).

SECTION 7C   SOLICITORS ACT 1974

Add new paragraph 7C–58.1:

Subsection (5)—"Unfair or unreasonable"
See para.7C-83.

7C-58.1

Subsection (2)—"Fair and reasonable"

Add new paragraph at end:
   When considering what is unfair and unreasonable for the purposes of s.57(5) (non-contentious **7C-83** business agreements) the court must consider fairness and reasonableness separately: *Bolt Burdon Solicitors v Tariq* [2016] EWHC 811 (QB) (following *Re Stuart*). A non-contentious business agreement under which the solicitors would receive 50 per cent of the compensation received under the Financial Conduct Authority Redress Scheme was held not to be unfair or unreasonable even though they would recover fees of about £400,000 for work valued at about £50,000 if billed at hourly rates.

SECTION 8   LIMITATION

Limitation Act 1980

Knowledge of plaintiff in negligence actions

To the end of the eighth paragraph (beginning "In applying the test propounded in Nash v Eli Lilly & Co"), add:
   In *Lenderink-Woods v Zurich Assurance Ltd* [2015] EWHC 3634 (Ch) it was held that the claim **8-43** would be statute-barred if someone with the characteristics of a person in the claimant's position might reasonably be expected to have acquired knowledge (a) of the material facts; (b) that the financial adviser could have considered alternatives, but had not made enquiries or recommended things that other competent financial advisers would have recommended; (c) that what the financial adviser had or had not done was causally relevant to her predicament. That knowledge would need to have been accompanied by enough confidence to prompt her to embark upon preparations for litigation.

Section 21—actions for breach of trust and actions for breach of fiduciary duty

Replace the first paragraph with:
   In *Haysport Properties Ltd v Ackerman* [2016] EWHC 393 (Ch) a director was in breach of his **8-60** fiduciary duty by causing two of his companies to grant security over their properties and/or make a substantial unsecured loan to enable a third company, which he also ran, to acquire a property. He had failed to ensure that his companies were properly advised and had failed to deal with the obvious conflict of interest. The limitation period for bringing a claim against him was disapplied by virtue of the Limitation Act 1980 s.21(1)(b). In *Green v Gaul* [2006] EWCA Civ 1124 the Court of Appeal held that the 12-year period under s.22(a) of the Act to bring an action in respect of any claim to the personal estate of a deceased had no application to a claim to remove a personal representative of the estate. Claims against the representative to provide an account of the deceased's assets and make payment due were claims that fell within s.21(1)(b) of the Act, and although the defence of laches to the claims was not excluded by s.21(1)(b), it was not made out on the facts.

Discretion to disapply relevant limitation period

Replace the fifth paragraph with:

8-92   The Act of 1980 does not lay down any specific procedure whereby the statutory power under s.33 ("to override time limits") is to be invoked. In order to preclude any undue prolongation of an action which it may not be equitable to permit to proceed and in seeking to limit the burden of costs which may be imposed on the defendant, an application by him to stay the claim under CPR r.3.1(f) would, provided that the plaintiff has given due notice of his intention to rely on the section, serve to initiate the investigation contemplated by s.33. In a clear case, the defendant may apply for summary judgment under CPR r.24.2(a)(i), though in some situations the substantive issues may be so intimately and inextricably bound up with the questions arising under s.33 as to make any summary resolution of the question impracticable (see per Shaw LJ in *Walkley v Precision Forgings Ltd* [1979] 1 W.L.R. 606 at 1238; [1979] 1 All E.R. 102, CA). It has however been observed that there is a "danger in the section 33 exercise of putting the cart before the horse, that is, determining the claim and relying on that determination in undertaking the balance of prejudice as to whether the claim should have preceded at all": see *KR v Bryn Alyn Community (Holdings) Ltd* [2003] EWCA Civ 85; [2003] Q.B. 1441; [2003] 3 W.L.R. 107; [2004] 2 All E.R. 7116, CA, at paras 74(viii) and 309. It was also held at para.74(vi), that "Whenever the judge considers it feasible to do so, he should decide the limitation point by a preliminary hearing by reference to the pleading and written witness statements and, importantly, the extent and content of discovery … It may not always be feasible or produce savings in time and cost for the parties to deal with the matter by way of preliminary hearing, but a judge should strain to do so whenever possible." In *Blue Water Recoveries Ltd v Secretary of State for Transport* [2014] QBD (TCC) 27 June 2014 it was held that it was not appropriate to order a hearing of preliminary issues in relation to limitation because such a hearing would concern contentious issues of fact that could only be determined by calling witnesses from each side to be cross-examined, all the issues would have to be decided in the defendant's favour for the case to be brought to an end, and it was unlikely that costs would be reduced. In *Re Kenyan Emergency Group Litigation* [2016] EWHC 600 (QB) numerous claimants were seeking damages for trespass to the person arising from the alleged actions of employees and agents of the British colonial administration in Kenya during a state of emergency in 1952. It was held that although it was appropriate for certain issues of limitation to be determined as preliminary issues, it was not appropriate for the court to decide, at a preliminary stage, whether to exercise its discretion under the Limitation Act 1980 s.33 to disapply the limitation period. If limitation was decided in the defendant's favour, there might be an appeal that could hold up the litigation for two to three years. That would be extremely unsatisfactory. The rest of the evidence, including doctors, corroborative witnesses and the defendant's evidence would probably be compromised. The vast majority of lay witnesses for both sides were very elderly and might not be capable of giving evidence in three to four years' time.

Dissolution of a company defendant

Replace the second paragraph (where the citation for County Leasing Asset Management Ltd v Hawkes has changed) with:

8-95   In *County Leasing Asset Management Ltd v Hawkes* [2015] EWCA Civ 1251; [2016] B.C.C. 102 it was held that the starting point to achieve the purpose of the discretion under s.1032(3) of the 2006 Act was to recognise that time would have run against the company if it had not been dissolved in exactly the same way as it had in fact run, while it was dissolved. The court had to ask itself whether had it not been dissolved, the company would have commenced the relevant proceedings within time; there must be a causative link between the company's dissolution and the failure to bring proceedings in time. The court then had to ask itself whether it would be just to provide the opportunity, after the event, by a limitation direction.

SECTION 9   JURISDICTIONAL AND PROCEDURAL LEGISLATION
SECTION 9A   MAIN STATUTES

Senior Courts Act 1981

Replace s.9(4) with:

OTHER PROVISIONS

Assistance for transaction of judicial business [...]

(4)   Without prejudice to section 24 of the Courts Act 1971 (temporary ap-   **9A–31** pointment of deputy Circuit judges [...]), if it appears to the Lord Chief Justice, after consulting the Lord Chancellor, that it is expedient as a temporary measure to make an appointment under this subsection in order to facilitate the disposal of business in the High Court or the Crown Court or any other court or tribunal to which persons appointed under this subsection may be deployed, he may appoint a person qualified for appointment as a puisne judge of the High Court to be a deputy judge of the High Court during such period or on such occasions as the Lord Chief Justice, after consulting the Lord Chancellor, thinks fit; and during the period or on the occasions for which a person is appointed as a deputy judge under this subsection, he may act as a puisne judge of the High Court.

Civil jurisdiction of the Court of Appeal

Replace list (where the citation for In re X (Court of Protection: Deprivation of Liberty) (Nos 1 and 2) has   **9A-51** *changed) with:*

(1)   *High Court*—Subject to exceptions, the Court of Appeal has jurisdiction to hear and determine any appeals from any judgment or order of any Division of the High Court (including the Family Division and including any part of a Division, e.g. the Commercial Court or the Patents Court (s.16)) (see para.9A-57 below). Statutory provisions in addition to s.16 affecting rights of appeal from the High Court to the Court of Appeal include the Insolvency Act 1986 s.375 (Appeals etc from courts exercising insolvency jurisdiction) (see para.3E-661+ above), and the Patents Act 1977 s.97 (Appeals from the comptroller).

(2)   *County Court*—Subject to exceptions, the Court of Appeal has jurisdiction to hear and determine appeals from determinations of the County Court (County Courts Act 1984 s.77) (see para.9A-568 below)

(3)   *Family Court*—Subject to exceptions, an appeal lies to the Court of Appeal from a decision of the Family Court (Matrimonial and Family Proceedings Act 1984 s.31K(1)).

(4)   *Court of Protection*—Section 53(1) of the Mental Capacity Act 2005 states that an appeal lies to the Court of Appeal "from any decision" of the Court of Protection. This is qualified by s.53(2) which states that Court of Protection Rules may provide that appeals from certain decisions of the court lie "to a prescribed higher judge of the court and not to the Court of Appeal" (s.53(2)). Such rules qualifying s.53(1) are found in Part 20 of the Court of Protection Rules 2007 (rr.169 to 182). For explanation of their effects on the Court of Appeal's jurisdiction under s.53(1), see commentary on r.169 (para.6B-399+ above). It is noteworthy that, unlike the statutory provisions providing for appeals to the Court of Appeal from the High Court or from the County Court, s.53(1) does not speak of appeals from "any judgment or order" or from "any determination", but from "any decision". In the case of *In re X (Court of Protection: Deprivation of Liberty) (Nos 1 and 2))* [2015] EWCA Civ 599; [2016] 1 W.L.R. 227, CA, the Court of Appeal held (contrary to the submission of all parties to the appeal) that the word "decision" in s.53(1) did not include a decision made by a judge of the Court of Protection in determining, not an issue in a case before him, but a hypothetical issue. For there to be a "decision" capable of supporting an appeal there must be the determination of an issue arising between two or more parties to proceedings before the court (at para.42 per Black LJ, and at para.156 per Moore-Bick LJ).

(5)   *Upper Tribunal*—By the Tribunal, Courts and Enforcement Act 2007 s.13 (para.9A-994 below), where the Court of Appeal is "the relevant appeal court" (see s.13(13)), an appeal lies to that Court, with permission, on a point of law arising from a decision made by the Upper Tribunal, other than an "excluded decision" (as defined, see s.3(8)). (By the 2007 Act the functions of several tribunals and bodies were transferred to the First-tier tribunal

and the Upper Tribunal created by that Act. Thereafter any statutory rights of appeal that lay to the Court of Appeal from the decisions of such tribunals or bodies (e.g. the Lands Tribunal and the Social Security Commissioner) under particular statutory provisions were incorporated within the arrangements for appeals from the Upper Tribunal to the Court of Appeal, and the particular statutory provisions granting rights of appeal were amended as necessary (e.g. the Social Security Act 1998 s.15).)

(6) *Employment Appeal Tribunal*—An appeal lies to the Court of Appeal on any question of law from any decision or order of the Employment Appeal Tribunal in proceedings in England and Wales (Employment Tribunals Act 1996 s.37).

Residual discretion to permit an appeal

Replace paragraph (where the citation for Michael Wilson & Partners Ltd v Emmott has changed) with:

9A-55.1   The Court of Appeal has recognised that it has a residual discretion to permit an appeal, despite the lower court's refusal of permission to appeal, where that refusal can be challenged on the grounds of unfairness pursuant to art.6 of the Convention on Human Rights, that is to say in those rare cases when it can be said that there was no decision at all or "misconduct or unfairness (or even mischance) in the decision-making process" such that the decision was so flawed as to be in breach of art.6 (see *CGU International Insurance Plc v Astrazeneca Insurance Co Ltd* [2006] EWCA Civ 1340; [2007] Bus. L.R. 1340, CA; *Patel v Mussa* [2015] EWCA Civ 434; [2015] 1 W.L.R. 4788. Most of the authorities on the scope of this discretion are concerned with appeals to the Court in arbitration claims (see para.2E-268 above). An appeal from the High Court to the Court of Appeal invoking this "residual jurisdiction" is an "appeal" for the purposes of s.16(1) of the Senior Courts Act 1981 (para.9A-57below) and it follows from that that such an appeal is an appeal for which permission to appeal is required by CPR r.52.3 (*Michael Wilson & Partners Ltd v Emmott* [2015] EWCA Civ 1285; [2016] 1 W.L.R. 857, CA, where single lord justice on the papers refused permission and recorded that the application was totally without merit with the result that, pursuant to r.52.3(4A)(a), the appellants, though invoking the residual jurisdiction, were not entitled to ask for the decision to be reconsidered at an oral hearing).

Court of Appeal jurisdiction to hear appeals from High Court

Add new paragraph at end:

9A-59   CPR r.52.15(1A) states that where permission to apply for judicial review has been refused by the High Court, and recorded by that Court as totally without merit (TWM) in accordance with r.23.12, an application by the applicant to the Court of Appeal for permission to appeal to it will be determined on paper without an oral hearing. Section 16(1) does not confer any right of appeal to the Court of Appeal against the High Court's TWM certification as such (*R. (Wasif) v Secretary of State for the Home Department* [2016] EWCA Civ 82, 9 February 2016, CA, unrep.).

Appeals are against orders, not reasoned judgments—"appeals from any judgment or order"

Replace the first paragraph (where the citation for In re X (Court of Protection: Deprivation of Liberty) (Nos 1 and 2) has changed) with:

9A-59.3   Section 16 of the Senior Courts Act 1981 states that the Court of Appeal shall have jurisdiction to hear and determine appeals "from any judgment or order of the High Court". Section 77 of the County Courts Act 1984 states that if any party to any proceedings in a county court "is dissatisfied with the determination of the judge" that party may "appeal from it" to the Court of Appeal (see para.9A-568 below). (In this context, "determination" has the same meaning as "judgment or order".) These statutory provisions are given effect to by r.52.10 which states, in para.(2)(a), that an appeal court has power to "affirm, set aside or vary any order or judgment made or given by the lower court". (See further "Meaning of 'judgment' and 'order'" Vol. 1 para.40.1.1). The use of the word "decision" in para.(1) of CPR r.53.2 (Permission) does not imply that the Court of Appeal has a jurisdiction to entertain appeals other than from judgments or orders or from determinations (*In re X (Court of Protection: Deprivation of Liberty) (Nos 1 and 2)*) [2015] EWCA Civ 599; [2016] 1 W.L.R. 227, CA, at para.43 per Black LJ).

Jurisdiction where proceedings raising "academic" or "hypothetical" point of law

Replace the fifth paragraph with:

9A-77   In modern times, the appellate courts have indicated a greater willingness to entertain proceedings which raise points of law which, although "academic" or "hypothetical", are points of general public interest (see cases cited arguendo in *R. v Canons Park Mental Health Review Tribunal Ex p. A* [1995] Q.B. 60, op. cit. at 63) but no general principle to this effect has emerged (see also *Don Pasquale v Customs & Excise* [1990] 1 W.L.R. 1108, CA; *Watford BC v Simpson* (2000) 32 H.L.R. 9901; (2000) 80 P. & C.R. D37; *Prudential Assurance Co Ltd v McBains Cooper* [2000] 1 W.L.R. 2000, CA; *Callery v Gray (No.2)* [2001] EWCA Civ 1246; [2001] 1 W.L.R. 2142, CA (Court deciding not to resolve hypothetical questions as to recovery of insurance premiums as costs)). The law is not settled. In *R. v Secretary of State for the Home Department Ex p. Salem* [1999] 2 W.L.R. 483, HL, it was held that the House of Lords has a discretion, to be exercised sparingly, to hear an appeal on an "academic" issue of public law involving a public authority where there was good reason in the public interest for doing so. Note also *R. v Secretary of State for Health, Ex p. Imperial Tobacco Ltd* [2001] 1 W.L.R. 127, HL; *R. v Secretary of State for Employment Ex p. Equal Opportunities Commission* [1995] 1 A.C. 1, HL; *R. (Barron) v Surrey CC* [2002] EWCA Civ 713; [2002] 20 E.G. 225 (C.S.); [2002] N.P.C. 78 (and cases cited therein); *Pridding v Secretary of State for Work and Pensions* [2002] EWCA Civ 306; *R. (Customs and Excise Commissioners) v Canterbury Crown Court*, 2002 S.L.T. 834 (court declaring that Crown Court judge had no jurisdiction to make order even though matter had become academic); *R. (W.) v Commissioner of Police for the Metropolis* [2006] EWCA Civ 458; [2006] All E.R. (D.) 144 (May), CA (Court determining meaning and effect of statutory provision affecting powers of police). It is not unusual for the Court of Appeal, especially in public law proceedings, to give permission to appeal in a case raising a short point of some practical importance set in a context in which there is some uncertainty as to related issues with the intention that the court should not only determine the short point, but also should carry out an authoritative review of the whole position and give guidance on matters which are (strictly speaking) academic (e.g. *R. (Davey) v Aylesbury Vale DC* [2007] EWCA Civ 1166; *The Times*, 21 November 2007, CA (successful respondent's recovery of pre-permission costs in judicial review proceedings)). In *R. (MD (Afghanistan)) v Secretary of State for the Home Department* [2012] EWCA Civ 194; [2012] 1 W.L.R. 2422, CA, where, before the hearing of an appeal to the Court of Appeal the parties had agreed a settlement of the proceedings, the Court, having of its own initiative raised certain jurisdictional and procedural issues of general importance affecting its own jurisdiction, gave judgment dealing with those issues (making certain assumptions). In *Portland Gas Storage Ltd v Revenue and Customs* [2015] EWCA Civ 559; [2015] B.T.C. 20, CA, the Court of Appeal ruled that it was not appropriate for the Court to proceed to hear an appeal brought by the Revenue in respect of the First-tier Tribunal's jurisdiction to consider a claim for repayment of stamp duty land tax where the underlying claim had since been withdrawn by the taxpayer. In the circumstances, although the appeal might raise points of some general significance, it could not be said that it was unlikely that the Court would again have the chance to consider the points raised on a proper inter partes basis. In *R. (Sisangia) v Director of Legal Aid Casework* [2016] EWCA Civ 24; [2016] 1 W.L.R. 1373, CA, the defendant's decision to refuse the claimant legal aid on the ground that her proposed action was not within the scope of the Legal Aid, Sentencing and Punishment of Offenders Act 2012 (in particular para.21 of Sch.1 to that Act) was quashed by a judge, whereupon the claimant was granted legal aid to pursue her claim. Though the matter had become academic, the Court of Appeal entertained an appeal by the defendant because of the wider implications of the judge's decision and, in the event, allowed the appeal.

Replace the tenth paragraph with:

In the case of *In re X (Court of Protection: Deprivation of Liberty) (Nos 1 and 2))* [2015] EWCA Civ 599; [2016] 1 W.L.R. 227, CA, where two mental health patients and an intervening party appealed to the Court of Appeal against rulings of the President of the Court of Protection made in managing unrelated deprivation of liberty cases, in particular a decision on the question whether a person lacking capacity must be joined as a party to any application for approval of measures depriving him of his liberty, the Court held that the President had no jurisdiction to proceed as he did and that the Court had no jurisdiction to entertain an appeal against his determinations. The particular decision of the President related to a "generic academic issue" and it was one which raised a question of considerable general importance. The Court considered whether it should as a matter of discretion hear the appeal, even though it had no jurisdiction, but in the event, after reviewing the modern authorities on the power of appeal courts to entertain "academic appeals", declined to do so; see para.46 and following per Black L.J., and para.157 and following per Moore-Bick L.J. Black L.J. said that the authorities do not go so far as to establish that the Court of Appeal should entertain an appeal in a case in which the lower court was itself only ever engaged upon a determination of hypothetical or academic issues, and do not constitute a licence to ignore jurisdictional and procedural rules completely or permit the courts to be used to determine issues "just because it would be useful to have an authoritative answer" (ibid).

Effect of this section

Replace the first paragraph with:

Section 37(1) puts on a statutory basis the High Court's jurisdiction to grant injunctions and to **9A-130** appoint receivers. In *Masri v Consolidated Contractors International (UK) Ltd (No. 2)* [2008] EWCA Civ 303; [2009] Q.B. 450, CA, the Court of Appeal held that there was no rule that the court could not ever make a receivership order by way of equitable execution in relation to foreign debts. Before that decision it had long been thought that the power in (what is now) s.37(1) could only be exercised in circumstances which would have enabled the court to appoint a receiver prior to 1873 when it was first put on a statutory basis. The *Masri (No. 2)* case confirmed or established the following principles: (1) the demands of justice are the overriding consideration in considering the scope of the jurisdiction under s.37(1); (2) the court has power to grant injunctions and appoint receivers in circumstances where no injunction would have been granted or receiver appointed before 1873; (3) a receiver by way of equitable execution may be appointed over an asset whether or not the asset is presently amenable to execution at law; and (4) the jurisdiction to appoint receivers by way of equitable execution can be developed incrementally to apply old principles to new situations. In addition, the *Masri (No. 2)* case confirmed that s.37(1) does not confer an unfettered power. The injunctive power is circumscribed by judicial authority dating back many years, and modern authorities confirm that the power to' appoint receivers is also not unfettered. See further *Tasarruf Mevduati Signorta Fonu v Merrill Lynch Bank and Trust Company (Cayman) Ltd* [2011] UKPC 17; [2011] 1 W.L.R. 1721, PC, and extensive citation of authorities there at [55] to [58]. It has been said that the power to grant an injunction, while placed on a statutory footing by s.37, does not derive solely from the legislature. Rather it is "a hybrid creation of the old equitable power and 19th century statutory intervention" and it is not a solecism to refer to the power as deriving from the inherent jurisdiction of the court, though it is a power clearly defined and regulated by s.37 of the 1981 Act alone, and therefore its exercise can only be effected under that section and the authorities decided under it (*L v K (Freezing Orders: Principles and Safeguards)* [2013] EWHC 1735 (Fam); [2014] 2 W.L.R. 914 (Mostyn J) at para.14).

Add new paragraph at end:

For a comparison of the powers granted to the court by s.37 of the 1981 Act and of the powers granted by the Matrimonial Causes Act 1973 s.37 (Avoidance of transactions intended to prevent or reduce financial relief), and of the relationship between those powers and their respective functions, see *C v C* [2015] EWHC 2795 (Fam), 30 September 2015, unrep. (Roberts J) at para.49 et seq.

"costs ... shall be in the discretion of the court"

After the fourth paragraph (beginning "The breadth of the discretion was emphasised"), add as a new paragraph:

9A-202   For a survey of the authorities concerning the making of orders for costs against insurers who fund the defence of a claim (beginning with *TGA Chapman Ltd v Christopher* [1998] 1 W.L.R. 12, CA), see *Legg v Sterte Garage Ltd* [2016] EWCA Civ 97, 23 February 2016, C.A., unrep., at para.49 et seq per David Richards LJ).

County Courts Act 1984

Add new paragraph 9A–481.1:

Transfer for enforcing orders for possession

9A-481.1   Part 83 (Writs and Warrants—General Provisions) was inserted in the CPR with effect from 6 April 2014, and replaced Orders formerly found in the RSC and CCR (see Vol.1 para.83.0.1). Rule 83.13 therein provides for the enforcement in the High Court of a judgment or order for the possession of land. Rule 83.19 makes particular provision for transfer to the High Court of certain County Court judgments for enforcement at the request of a creditor (and applies where the creditor makes a request for a certificate of judgment under r.40.14A(1) for the purpose of enforcement in the High Court). Following upon the emergence of some practical problems concerning the transfer of County Court possession orders to the High Court for enforcement, the Senior Master issued two detailed Practice Notes. They are: Senior Master's Practice Note—Transfers for Enforcement to the High Court (14 December 2015), and Senior Master's Practice Note—Applications for Transfer for Enforcement of Possession to the High Court (21 March 2016). The texts of these Practice Notes may be found in Vol.1 at, respectively, para.83PN.1 and para.83PN.2. See further relevant commentary in CPR Part 83.

Transfer of proceedings to High Court

After the second paragraph (beginning "For transfer of proceedings under the Arbitration Act 1996"), add as a new paragraph:

9A-485   For transfer to High Court for enforcement of County Court possession orders, see para.9A-481.1 above.

Power to enforce undertakings of solicitors

To the end of the last paragraph, add:

9A-705   For law on solicitors' liability on undertakings enforceable in the High Court generally, see Jackson & Powell on Professional Liability (7th edn 2015) Ch.11.

Tribunals, Courts and Enforcement Act 2007

"appeal...from a decision made by the Upper Tribunal"

Replace with:

9A-1007.2   In *Sarfraz v Disclosure and Barring Service* [2015] EWCA Civ 544; [2015] 1 W.L.R. 4441, the Court of Appeal stated that it is a principle of long-standing derived from authority (in particular from *Lane v Esdaile* [1891] A.C. 210, HL) that, in the absence of express statutory language to the contrary, a provision giving a court the power to grant or refuse permission to appeal should be construed as not extending to an appeal against a refusal of permission to appeal. The Court, in applying that principle to s.13, held that there was no jurisdiction in the Court for it to give permission to appeal against the refusal by the UT of permission to appeal to itself. In doing so the Court rejected that submission of the would-be appellant that the exceptions to the right of appeal provided by s.13(1) are set out exhaustively in s.13(8) and there is no room for a further exception, whether based on the principle or on some other ground, outside s.13(8). CPR r.52.15A(2) states that where permission to apply for judicial review has been refused by the Upper Tribunal, and recorded by that Tribunal as totally without merit (TWM), in accordance with the Tribunal Procedure (Upper Tribunal) Rules 2008 r.30(4A), an application by the applicant to the Court of Appeal for permission to appeal to it will be determined on paper without an oral hearing. Section 13 does not confer any right of appeal to the Court of Appeal against the Tribunal's TWM certification as such (*R. (Wasif) v Secretary of State for the Home Department* [2016] EWCA Civ 82, 9 February 2016, CA, unrep.).

SECTION 9B   OTHER STATUTES AND REGULATIONS

Civil Liability (Contribution) Act 1978

Note

Replace the first paragraph with:

The similarity in the language used in s.2(1) and in the Law Reform (Contributory Negligence) **9B-1092**
Act 1945 s.1(1) (see para.9B-1198.1 below) is striking and there is no reason why the principles applicable under the two provisions should be different in cases where the facts are themselves similar (*J (A Child) v Wilkins* [2001] R.T.R. 19). An apportionment made under s.2(1) by a trial judge will only be interfered with on appeal where it is clearly wrong or there has been an error of principle or mistake of fact (ibid.). As the discretion as to costs granted by the Senior Courts Act s.51 is not limited so as to exclude an order in contribution proceedings in respect of a sum paid to the original claimants in respect of their costs, the court is entitled to order a contribution in respect of the full sum paid by the person applying for contribution inclusive of any part referable to costs (*B.I.C.C. Ltd v Cumbrian Industrials Ltd* [2001] EWCA Civ 1621; October 30, 2001, unrep., CA). The ex turpi defence is not available against a claim under s.1(1) (*K v P* [1993] Ch 140 (Ferris J)).

After the fourth paragraph (beginning "Section 2(1) requires the court to have regard"), add as a new paragraph:

In *Mohidin v Commissioner of Police of the Metropolis* [2016] EWHC 105 (QB); [2016] 1 Costs L.R. 71 (Gilbart J), where individual claimants (C) brought proceedings for false imprisonment etc against the police, the defendant Commissioner (D) issued claims against the police officers concerned under s.1 of the 1978 Act and successfully applied to join them as additional parties pursuant to CPR r.20.7. After judgment had been given for C at trial (during which D adopted a neutral stance on the issue of liability to C) and damages awarded, D's application for an order against the additional parties indemnifying him for the damages and costs he was liable to pay to and in respect of C, was resisted by them on various grounds. In granting the orders sought against some of the additional parties the judge (1) explained (a) that while the issue of what is "just and equitable" is relevant, it is so within the confines of the discretion set out in s.2(1), that is to say, having regard to the extent of the responsibility of the person from whom contribution is claimed for the damage in question (para.27), and (b) that that discretion is not unfettered, and the court's power to exempt granted by s.2(2) is governed by the context set out in s.2(1) (para.35), and (2) ruled that the current financial means of the person from whom contribution is sought cannot be relevant to the issue of the contribution to the damages claim (ibid para.28). In *Dawson v Bell* [2016] EWCA Civ 96, 19 February 2016, CA, unrep. the Court of Appeal dismissed an appeal by the claimant for contribution made by one director (C) of a company against another (D) in a commercial dispute between them, holding that in the circumstances it was not just and equitable that D should pay a share of what C owed to the company having regard to the extent of her responsibility for the damage in question, even though she knew of the practice of unlawful use of the company's funds and, in breach of her own duty to the company, had failed to put a stop to it.

SECTION 10   COURT FEES

Civil Proceedings Fees Order 2008

Add new paragraph 10–1.2:

Editorial note

10-1.2   Fees are regularly reviewed. The most recent increases were effected by the Civil Proceedings, Family Proceedings and Upper Tribunal Fees (Amendment) Order 2016 (SI 2016/402) which was made on 17 March 2016 and came into force on 21 March 2016.

10-5   *Replace paras 10–5 and 10–5.1 with:*

Remissions and part remissions

5. (1)   Subject to paragraph (2), Schedule 2 applies for the purpose of ascertaining whether a party is entitled to a remission or part remission of a fee prescribed by this Order.

(2)   Schedule 2 does not apply to—

    (a)   fee 1.2 if the fee relates to proceedings to recover a sum of money in cases brought by Money Claim OnLine users; or

    (b)   fee 8.8 (fee payable on a consolidated attached of earnings order or an administration order).

10-5.1   *Note* —Substituted by the Courts and Tribunals Fee Remissions Order 2013 (SI 2013/2302) art.6(2) with effect from October 7, 2013 (for transitional provisions see art.13(1) thereof). Sub-section (2)(a) substituted by Civil Proceedings and Family Proceedings Fees (Amendment) Order 2015 (SI 2015/576) art.2(2) with effect from March 1, 2015.

Replace Schedule 1 with:

ARTICLE 3

SCHEDULE 1

FEES TO BE TAKEN

10-7

Column 1 Number and description of fee	Column 2 Amount of fee (or manner of calculation)
1 Starting proceedings (High Court and County Court)	
1.1 On starting proceedings (including proceedings issued after permission to issue is granted but excluding CCBC cases brought by Centre users or cases brought by Money Claim OnLine users) to recover a sum of money where the sum claimed:	
(a) does not exceed £300;	£35
(b) exceeds £300 but does not exceed £500;	£50
(c) exceeds £500 but does not exceed £1,000;	£70
(d) exceeds £1,000 but does not exceed £1,500;	£80
(e) exceeds £1,500 but does not exceed £3,000;	£115
(f) exceeds £3,000 but does not exceed £5,000;	£205
(g) exceeds £5,000 but does not exceed £10,000;	£455
(h) exceeds £10,000 but does not exceed £200,000;	5% of the value of the claim
(i) exceeds £200,000 or is not limited.	£10,000
1.2 On starting proceedings in CCBC cases brought by Centre users or cases brought by Money Claim OnLine users, to recover a	

Column 1 Number and description of fee	Column 2 Amount of fee (or manner of calculation)
sum of money where the sum claimed:	
(a) does not exceed £300;	£25
(b) exceeds £300 but does not exceed £500;	£35
(c) exceeds £500 but does not exceed £1,000;	£60
(d) exceeds £1,000 but does not exceed £1,500;	£70
(e) exceeds £1,500 but does not exceed £3,000;	£105
(f) exceeds £3,000 but does not exceed £5,000;	£185
(g) exceeds £5,000 but does not exceed £10,000;	£410
(h) exceeds £10,000 but does not exceed £100,000.	4.5% of the value of the claim
Fee 1.1	
Where the claimant does not identify the value of the claim when starting proceedings to recover a sum of money, the fee payable is the one applicable to a claim where the sum is not limited.	
Fees 1.1 and 1.2.	
Where the claimant is making a claim for interest on a specified sum of money, the amount on which the fee is calculated is the total amount of the claim and the interest.	
1.4 On starting proceedings for the recovery of land:	
(a) in the High Court;	£480
(b) in the County Court, other than where fee 1.4(c) applies;	£355
(c) using the Possession Claims Online website.	£325
1.5 On starting proceedings for any other remedy (including proceedings issued after permission to issue is granted):	
in the High Court	£480
in the County Court	£280
Fees 1.1, 1.4 and 1.5. Recovery of land or goods. Where a claim for money is additional or alternative to a claim for recovery of land or goods, only fee 1.4 or 1.5 is payable.	
Fees 1.1 and 1.5. Claims other than recovery of land or goods. Where a claim for money is additional to a non money claim (other than a claim for recovery of land or goods), then fee 1.1 is payable in addition to fee 1.5.	
Where a claim for money is alternative to a non money claim (other than a claim for recovery of land or goods), only fee 1.1 is payable in the High Court, and, in the County Court, whichever is greater of fee 1.1 or fee 1.5 is payable.	
Fees 1.1 and 1.5. Where more than one non money claim is made in the same proceedings, fee 1.5 is payable once only, in addition to any fee which may be payable under fee 1.1.	
Fees 1.1 and 1.5 are not payable where fee 1.8(b), fee 1.9(a), fee 3 or fee 10.1 applies.	
Fees 1.1 and fee 1.5. Amendment of claim or counterclaim. Where the claim or counterclaim is amended, and the fee paid before amendment is less than that which would have been payable if the document, as amended, had been so drawn in the first instance, the party amending the document must pay the difference.	
1.6 On the filing of proceedings against a party or parties not named in the proceedings.	£50
Fee 1.6 is payable by a defendant who adds or substitutes a party	

Column 1 Number and description of fee	Column 2 Amount of fee (or manner of calculation)
or parties to the proceedings or by a claimant who adds or substitutes a defendant or defendants.	
1.7 On the filing of a counterclaim.	The same fee as if the remedy sought were the subject of separate proceedings
No fee is payable on a counterclaim which a defendant is required to make under rule 57.8 of the CPR (a) (requirement to serve a counterclaim if a defendant makes a claim or seeks a remedy in relation to a grant of probate of a will, or letters of administration of an estate, of a deceased person).	
1.8(a) On an application for permission to issue proceedings.	£50
(b) On an application for an order under Part 3 of the Solicitors Act 1974 (b) for the assessment of costs payable to a solicitor by a client or on starting costsonly proceedings.	£50
1.9(a) For permission to apply for judicial review.	£140
1.9(b) On a request to reconsider at a hearing a decision on permission.	£350
Where fee 1.9(b) has been paid and permission is granted at a hearing, the amount payable under fee 1.9(c) is £350.	
Where the court has made an order giving permission to proceed with a claim for judicial review, there is payable by the claimant within 7 days of service on the claimant of that order:	
1.9(c) if the judicial review procedure has been started.	£700
1.9(d) if the claim for judicial review was started otherwise than by using the judicial review procedure.	£140
2 General Fees (High Court and County Court)	
2.1 On the claimant filing a pre-trial check list (listing question-naire); or where the court fixes the trial date or trial week without the need for a pre-trial check list; or where the claim is on the small claims track, within 14 days of the date of despatch of the notice (or the date when oral notice is given if no written notice is given) of the trial week or the trial date if no trial week is fixed a fee payable for the hearing of:	
(a) a case on the multi-track;	£1,090
(b) a case on the fast track.	£545
(c) a case on the small claims track where the sum claimed:	
(i) does not exceed £300;	£25
(ii) exceeds £300 but does not exceed £500;	£55
(iii) exceeds £500 but does not exceed £1,000;	£80
(iv) exceeds £1,000 but does not exceed £1,500;	£115
(v) exceeds £1,500 but does not exceed £3,000;	£170
(vi) exceeds £3,000.	£335
Fee 2.1 is payable by the claimant except where the action is proceeding on the counterclaim alone, when it is payable by the defendant: or	
within 14 days of the date of despatch of the notice (or the date when oral notice is given if no written notice is given) of the trial week or the trial date if no trial week is fixed.	
Where a case is on the multi-track or fast track and, after a hearing date has been fixed, the court receives notice in writing from the party who paid the hearing fee that the case has been settled or discontinued then the following percentages of the hearing fee will be refunded:	
(i) 100% if the court is notified more than 28 days before the hearing;	
(ii) 75% if the court is notified between 15 and 28 days	

Column 1 Number and description of fee	Column 2 Amount of fee (or manner of calculation)
before the hearing; (iii) 50% if the court is notified between 7 and 14 days before the hearing.	
Where a case is on the small claims track and, after a hearing date has been fixed, the court receives notice in writing from the party who paid the hearing fee, at least 7 days before the date set for the hearing, that the case has been settled or discontinued the hearing fee will be refunded in full.	
Fee 2.1 is not payable in respect of a case where the court fixed the hearing date on the issue of the claim.	
2.2 In the High Court on filing:	£240
an appellant's notice: or	
a respondent's notice where the respondent is appealing or wishes to ask the appeal court to uphold the order of the lower court for reasons different from or additional to those given by the lower court:	
2.3 In the County Court on filing:	
an appellant's notice, or	
a respondent's notice where the respondent is appealing or wishes to ask the appeal court to uphold the order of the lower court for reasons different from or additional to those given by the lower court:	
(a) in a claim allocated to the small claims track;	£120
(b) in all other claims.	£140
Fees 2.2 and 2.3 do not apply on appeals against a decision made in detailed assessment proceedings.	
2.4(a) On an application on notice where no other fee is specified, except for applications referred to in fee 2.4(b).	£255
2.4(b) On an application on notice where no other fee is specified made—	£155
(i) under section 3 of the Protection from Harassment Act 1997; or (ii) for a payment out of funds deposited in court.	
2.5(a) On an application by consent or without notice where no other fee is specified, except for applications referred to in fee 2.5(b).	£100
2.5(b) On an application made by consent or without notice where no other fee is specified made—	£50
(i) under section 3 of the Protection from Harassment Act 1997; or (ii) for a payment out of funds deposited in court. For the purpose of fee 2.5 a request for a judgment or order on admission or in default does not constitute an application and no fee is payable.	
Fee 2.5 is not payable in relation to an application by consent for an adjournment of a hearing where the application is received by the court at least 14 days before the date set for that hearing.	
Fees 2.4(a) and 2.5(b) are not payable in proceedings to which fees 3.11 and 3.12 apply.	
2.6 On an application for a summons or order for a witness to attend court to be examined on oath or an order for evidence to be taken by deposition, other than an application for which fee 7.2 or 8.3 is payable.	£50
2.7 On an application to vary a judgment or suspend enforcement, including an application to suspend a warrant of possession.	£50
Where more than one remedy is sought in the same application	

Column 1 Number and description of fee	Column 2 Amount of fee (or manner of calculation)
only one fee is payable.	
2.8 Register of judgments, orders and fines kept under section 98 of the Courts Act 2003:	
On a request for the issue of a certificate of satisfaction.	£15
3 Companies Act 1985 , Companies Act 2006 **and** Insolvency Act 1986 **(High Court and County Court)**	
3.1 On entering a bankruptcy petition:	
(a) if presented by a debtor or the personal representative of a deceased debtor;	£180
(b) if presented by a creditor or other person.	£280
3.2 On entering a petition for an administration order.	£280
3.3 On entering any other petition.	£280
One fee only is payable where more than one petition is presented in relation to a partnership.	
3.4 (a) On a request for a certificate of discharge from bankruptcy.	£70
(b) after the first certificate, for each copy.	£10
3.5 On an application under the Companies Act 1985 (c), the Companies Act 2006 (d) or the Insolvency Act 1986 (e) other than one brought by petition and where no other fee is specified.	£280
Fee 3.5 is not payable where the application is made in existing proceedings.	
3.6 On an application for the conversion of a voluntary arrangement into a winding up or bankruptcy under Article 37 of Council Regulation (EC) No 1346/2000.	£160
3.7 On an application, for the purposes of Council Regulation (EC) No 1346/2000, for an order confirming creditors' voluntary winding up (where the company has passed a resolution for voluntary winding up, and no declaration under section 89 of the Insolvency Act 1986 has been made).	£50
3.8 On filing: a notice of intention to appoint an administrator under paragraph 14 of Schedule B1 to the Insolvency Act 1986 (f) or in accordance with paragraph 27 of that Schedule; or a notice of appointment of an administrator in accordance with paragraphs 18 or 29 of that Schedule.	£50
Where a person pays fee 3.8 on filing a notice of intention to appoint an administrator, no fee is payable on that same person filing a notice of appointment of that administrator.	
3.9 On submitting a nominee's report under section 2(2) of the Insolvency Act 1986.	£50
3.10 On filing documents in accordance with paragraph 7(1) of Schedule A1(g) to the Insolvency Act 1986.	£50
3.11 On an application by consent or without notice within existing proceedings where no other fee is specified.	£50
3.12 On an application with notice within existing proceedings where no other fee is specified.	£155
3.13 On a search in person of the bankruptcy and companies records, in a County Court.	£45
Requests and applications with no fee: No fee is payable on a request or on an application to the Court by the Official Receiver when applying only in the capacity of Official Receiver to the case (and not as trustee or liquidator), or on an application to set aside a statutory demand.	
4 Copy Documents (Court of Appeal, High Court and County	

Column 1 Number and description of fee	Column 2 Amount of fee (or manner of calculation)
Court)	
4.1 On a request for a copy of a document (other than where fee 4.2 applies):	
(a) for ten pages or less;	£10
(b) for each subsequent page.	50p
Note: The fee payable under fee 4.1 includes:	
where the court allows a party to fax to the court for the use of that party a document that has not been requested by the court and is not intended to be placed on the court file;	
where a party requests that the court fax a copy of a document from the court file; or	
where the court provides a subsequent copy of a document which it has previously provided.	
4.2 On a request for a copy of a document on a computer disk or in other electronic form, for each such copy.	£10
5 Determination of costs (Senior Court and County Court) Fee 5 does not apply to the determination in the Senior Courts of costs incurred in the Court of Protection.	
5.1 On the filing of a request for detailed assessment where the party filing the request is legally aided, is funded by the Legal Aid Agency or is a person for whom civil legal services have been made available under arrangements made by the Lord Chancellor under Part 1 of the Legal Aid, Sentencing and Punishment of Offenders Act 2012 (h) and no other party is ordered to pay the costs of the proceedings.	£200
5.2 On the filing of a request for detailed assessment in any case where fee 5.1 does not apply; or on filing a request for a hearing date for the assessment of costs payable to a solicitor by a client pursuant to an order under Part 3 of the Solicitors Act 1974 where the amount of the costs claimed:	
(a) does not exceed £15,000;	£335
(b) exceeds £15,000 but does not exceed £50,000;	£675
(c) exceeds £50,000 but does not exceed £100,000;	£1,005
(d) exceeds £100,000 but does not exceed £150,000;	£1,345
(e) exceeds £150,000 but does not exceed £200,000;	£1,680
(f) exceeds £200,000 but does not exceed £300,000;	£2,520
(g) exceeds £300,000 but does not exceed £500,000;	£4,200
(h) exceeds £500,000.	£5,600
Where there is a combined party and party and legal aid, or a combined party and party and Legal Aid Agency, or a combined party and party and Lord Chancellor, or a combined party and party and one or more of legal aid, Legal Aid Agency or Lord Chancellor determination of costs, fee 5.2 will be attributed proportionately to the party and party, legal aid, Legal Aid Agency or Lord Chancellor (as the case may be) portions of the bill on the basis of the amount allowed.	
5.3 On a request for the issue of a default costs certificate.	£60
5.4 On commencing an appeal against a decision made in detailed assessment proceedings.	£210
5.5 On a request or application to set aside a default costs certificate.	£110
6 Determination in the Senior Court of costs incurred in the Court of Protection	
6.1 On the filing of a request for detailed assessment:	
(a) where the amount of the costs to be assessed (excluding VAT	

Column 1 Number and description of fee	Column 2 Amount of fee (or manner of calculation)
and disbursements) does not exceed £3,000;	£115
(b) in all other cases.	£225
6.2 On an appeal against a decision made in detailed assessment proceedings.	£65
6.3 On a request or application to set aside a default costs certificate.	£65
7 Enforcement in the High Court	
7.1 On sealing a writ of control/possession/delivery.	£60
Where the recovery of a sum of money is sought in addition to a writ of possession and delivery, no further fee is payable.	
7.2 On an application for an order requiring a judgment debtor or other person to attend court to provide information in connection with enforcement of a judgment or order.	£50
7.3(a) On an application for a third party debt order or the appointment of a receiver by way of equitable execution.	£100
(b) On an application for a charging order.	£100
Fee 7.3(a) is payable in respect of each third party against whom the order is sought. Fee 7.3(b) is payable in respect of each charging order applied for.	
7.4 On an application for a judgment summons.	£100
7.5 On a request or application to register a judgment or order, or for permission to enforce an arbitration award, or for a certificate or a certified copy of a judgment or order for use abroad.	£60
8 Enforcement in the county court	
8.1 On an application for or in relation to enforcement of a judgment or order of the County Court or through the County Court, by the issue of a warrant of control against goods except a warrant to enforce payment of a fine:	
(a) in CCBC cases or cases in which a warrant of control is requested in accordance with paragraph 11.2 of Practice Direction 7E to the Civil Procedure Rules (Money Claim OnLine cases);	£70
(b) in any other case.	£100
8.2 On a request for a further attempt at execution of a warrant at a new address following a notice of the reason for non-execution (except a further attempt following suspension and CCBC cases brought by Centre users).	£30
8.3 On an application for an order requiring a judgment debtor or other person to attend court to provide information in connection with enforcement of a judgment or order.	£50
8.4(a) On an application for a third party debt order or the appointment of a receiver by way of equitable execution.	£100
(b) On an application for a charging order.	£100
Fee 8.4(a) is payable in respect of each third party against whom the order is sought. Fee 8.4(b) is payable in respect of each charging order applied for.	
8.5 On an application for a judgment summons.	£100
8.6 On the issue of a warrant of possession or a warrant of delivery.	£110
Where the recovery of a sum of money is sought in addition, no further fee is payable.	
8.7 On an application for an attachment of earnings order (other than a consolidated attachment of earnings order) to secure payment of a judgment debt.	£100
Fee 8.7 is payable for each defendant against whom an order is sought.	

Column 1 Number and description of fee	Column 2 Amount of fee (or manner of calculation)
Fee 8.7 is not payable where the attachment of earnings order is made on the hearing of a judgment summons.	
8.8 On a consolidated attachment of earnings order or on an administration order.	For every £1 or part of a £1 of the money paid into court in respect of debts due to creditors - 10p
Fee 8.8 is calculated on any money paid into court under any order at the rate in force at the time when the order was made (or, where the order has been amended, at the time of the last amendment before the date of payment).	
8.9 On an application for the enforcement of an award for a sum of money or other decision made by any court, tribunal, body or person other than the High Court or a County Court.	£40
8.10 On a request for an order to recover a sum that is:	
a specified debt within the meaning of the Enforcement of Road Traffic Debts Order 1993 (i); or pursuant to an enactment, treated as a specified debt for the purposes of that Order.	£7
No fee is payable on: an application for an extension of time to serve a statutory declaration or a witness statement in connection with any such order; or a request to issue a warrant of control to enforce any such order.	
8A Service in the county court	
8A.1 On a request for service by a bailiff of an order to attend court for questioning	£100
9 Sale (County Court only)	
9.1 For removing or taking steps to remove goods to a place of deposit.	The reasonable expenses incurred
Fee 9.1 is to include the reasonable expenses of feeding and caring for any animals.	
9.2 For the appraisement of goods.	5p in the £1 or part of a £1 of the appraised value
9.3 For the sale of goods (including advertisements, catalogues, sale and commission and delivery of goods).	15p in the £1 or part of a £1 on the amount realised by the sale or such other sum as the district judge may consider to be justified in the circumstances
9.4 Where no sale takes place by reason of an execution being withdrawn, satisfied or stopped.	(a) 10p in the £1 or part of a £1 on the value of the goods seized, the value to be the appraised value where the goods have been appraised or such other sum as the district judge may consider to be justified in the circumstances; and in addition (b) any sum payable under fee 9.1 and 9.2.
FEES PAYABLE IN HIGH COURT ONLY	
10 Miscellaneous proceedings or matters	
Bills of Sale	
10.1 On filing any document under the Bills of Sale Acts 1878 (j) and the Bills of Sale Act (1878) Amendment Act 1882 (k) or on an application under section 15 of the Bills of Sale Act 1878 for an order that a memorandum of satisfaction be written on a registered	£25

Column 1 Number and description of fee	Column 2 Amount of fee (or manner of calculation)
copy of the bill.	
Searches	
10.2 For an official certificate of the result of a search for each name, in any register or index held by the court; or in the Court Funds Office, for an official certificate of the result of a search of unclaimed balances for a specified period of up to 50 years.	£45
10.3 On a search in person of the court's records, including inspection, for each 15 minutes or part of 15 minutes.	£10
Judge sitting as arbitrator	
10.4 On the appointment of:	
(a) a judge of the Commercial Court as an arbitrator or umpire under section 93 of the Arbitration Act 1996 (l); or	£2,455
(b) a judge of the Technology and Construction Court as an arbitrator or umpire under section 93 of the Arbitration Act 1996.	£2,455
10.5 For every day or part of a day (after the first day) of the hearing before:	
(a) a judge of the Commercial Court; or	£2,455
(b) a judge of the Technology and Construction Court, so appointed as arbitrator or umpire.	£2,455
Where fee 10.4 has been paid on the appointment of a judge of the Commercial Court or a judge of the Technology and Construction Court as an arbitrator or umpire but the arbitration does not proceed to a hearing or an award, the fee will be refunded.	
11 Fees payable in Admiralty matters	
In the Admiralty Registrar and Marshal's Office:	
11.1 On the issue of a warrant for the arrest of a ship or goods.	£225
11.2 On the sale of a ship or goods	
Subject to a minimum fee of £205:	
(a) for every £100 or fraction of £100 of the price up to £100,000;	£1
(b) for every £100 or fraction of £100 of the price exceeding £100,000.	50p
Where there is sufficient proceeds of sale in court, fee 11.2 will be payable by transfer from the proceeds of sale in court.	
11.3 On entering a reference for hearing by the Registrar.	£70
FEES PAYABLE IN HIGH COURT AND COURT OF APPEAL ONLY	
12 Affidavits	
12.1 On taking an affidavit or an affirmation or attestation upon honour in lieu of an affidavit or a declaration except for the purpose of receipt of dividends from the Accountant General and for a declaration by a shorthand writer appointed in insolvency proceedings: for each person making any of the above.	£11
12.2 For each exhibit referred to in an affidavit, affirmation, attestation or declaration for which fee 12.1 is payable.	£2
FEES PAYABLE IN COURT OF APPEAL ONLY	
13 Fees payable in appeals to the Court of Appeal	
13.1(a) Where in an appeal notice, permission to appeal or an extension of time for appealing is applied for (or both are applied for): on filing an appellant's notice, or where the respondent is appealing, on filing a respondent's notice.	£235
13.1(b) Where permission to appeal is not required or has been granted by the lower court:	£465

Column 1 Number and description of fee	Column 2 Amount of fee (or manner of calculation)
on filing an appellant's notice, or on filing a respondent's notice where the respondent is appealing.	
13.1(c) On the appellant filing an appeal questionnaire (unless the appellant has paid fee 13.1(b), or the respondent filing an appeal questionnaire (unless the respondent has paid fee 13.1(b)).	£465
13.2 On filing a respondent's notice where the respondent wishes to ask the appeal court to uphold the order of the lower court for reasons different from or additional to those given by the lower court.	£235
13.3 On filing an application notice.	£235
Fee 13.3 is not payable for an application made in an appeal notice.	

Note

Add new paragraph at end:

Entries 1.4(b), 1.4(c), 2.4, 2.5 and the entry beginning "Fees 2.4 and 2.5 are not payable" **10-7.1** amended by the Civil Proceedings, Family Proceedings and Upper Tribunal Fees (Amendment) Order 2016 (SI 2016/402) art.2, with effect from 21 March 2016.

SECTION 11   OVERRIDING OBJECTIVE OF CPR

E.   DUTY OF THE PARTIES (R.1.3)

To the end of the seventh paragraph (beginning "There is no general duty upon one party"), add:

And see *OOO Abbott v Econowall UK Ltd* [2016] EWHC 660 (IPEC), 23 March 2016, unrep. (HHJ **11-15** Hacon), where it was noted that while parties are not required to inform their opponents of mistakes they have made, this is subject to the overriding objective and the obligation to ensure that parties and the court have a clear, common understanding of the real issues in dispute and as to the proper procedural arrangements for the effective progress of the claim. A failure to ensure this is the case can lead to unnecessary and disproportionate cost and delay to the parties, to the court, and have an adverse effect on other litigants. Where parties become aware of a genuine misunderstanding on a significant issue they should take reasonable steps to dispel it.

SECTION 12   CPR: APPLICATION, AMENDMENTS AND INTERPRETATION

C.   STATUTORY INSTRUMENTS AMENDING CPR

4.   *Amendments and Transitional Arrangements in Amending Statutory Instruments*

(b)   2014 to date

Add new paragraph at the beginning:

The Civil Procedure (Amendment) Rules 2016 (SI 2016/234) contained amendments to the fol- **12-34** lowing rules: Pt 3, r.45.8 Table 5; Pt 66; Pt 70; Pt 73; Pt 75; and RSC Ord.115 rule 4(4). It introduced a new Pt 89 (attachment of earnings) and deleted CCR Ord.27. It came into force on 6 April 2016, subject to transitional provisions which provide for that the amendments to the following only take effect as to proceedings commended on or after 6 April 2016: rules 3.13; 45.8; 66.6(1), 70.1; 70.5; 73.17; 75.6(d); 75.10; RSC Ord.115 r.4(4); and Pts 73, 89 and CCR Ord.27.

SECTION 13   RIGHTS OF AUDIENCE

G.   RIGHT OF AUDIENCE GRANTED BY THE COURT IN RELATION TO THE PROCEEDINGS (SCH.3, PARA.1(2))

4.   Exercise of the Discretion

(c)   McKenzie friend

Replace the fifth paragraph with:

13-19   McKenzie friends do not have a right to conduct litigation or a right of audience. However, once a party acting in person is allowed to have the assistance of a McKenzie friend, the question might then arise whether the court should exercise its discretion under para.1(2) of Sch.3 and grant the assistant a right of audience. Guidance in the Practice Note deals with the considerations which then arise. The High Court has inherent jurisdiction to grant a right of audience on an ad hoc basis to a party's McKenzie Friend even where that party is a body corporate if the body corporate would otherwise have no one capable of speaking for it; see per Hildyard J. in *Bank of St Petersburg PJSC v Arkhangelsky* [2015] EWHC 2997 (Ch); [2016] 1 W.L.R. 1081.

SECTION 14   ALTERNATIVE DISPUTE RESOLUTION

A.   INTRODUCTION

1.   Negotiation, Mediation and Other Dispute Resolution Procedures

Replace the last paragraph with:

14-2   With reference to the Government's proposals on legal aid in 2011 Lord Neuberger, Master of the Rolls, as he then was, expressed concern about what some see as the prospect of replacing legal aid-funded cases with alternative dispute resolution. Lord Neuberger warned: "If we expand mediation beyond its proper limits as a complement to justice we run the risk of depriving particular persons or classes of person of their right to equal and impartial justice under the law." (See *http://webarchive.nationalarchives.gov.uk/20131202164909/http://judiciary.gov.uk/Resources/JCO/ Documents/Speeches/moj-speech-mediation-lectureA.pdf* [Accessed 15 April 2016]).

2.   Appellate Judges' Statements and Speeches on ADR—The Jackson Report—Proposals for Reform

Replace the second paragraph with:

14-3   Between 2007 and 2009, Lightman J., Lord Phillips C.J. and Sir Anthony Clarke M.R. (as they then were) each delivered speeches, out of court, all of which were predicated on the greater use of ADR. They will be referred to collectively below as the "Judicial Speeches" and the speech on May 8, 2008 will be referred to as Sir Anthony Clarke's Birmingham Speech. The speeches are available at *http://www.cedr.com/articles/?item=Mediation-an-approximation-to-justice-a-speech-by-The-Honour- able-Mr-Justice-Lightman* [Accessed 15 April 2016] (Lightman J); *http://webarchive.nationalarchives.gov. uk/20131202164909/http://judiciary.gov.uk/Resources/JCO/Documents/Speeches/lcj_adr_india_290308. pdf* [Accessed 15 April 2016] (Lord Phillips CJ); *http://webarchive.nationalarchives.gov.uk/ 20131202164909/http://judiciary.gov.uk/media/speeches/2008/speech-clarke-lj-mor-11042008* [Accessed 15 April 2016] (Sir Anthony Clarke M.R., Brighton); *http://webarchive.nationalarchives.gov.uk/ 20131202164909/http://judiciary.gov.uk/Resources/JCO/Documents/Speeches/mr_mediation_conference_ may08.pdf* [Accessed 15 April 2016] (Sir Anthony Clarke M.R., Birmingham); *http://webarchive. nationalarchives.gov.uk/20131202164909/http://judiciary.gov.uk/Resources/JCO/Documents/Speeches/mr- littleton-chambers-080609.pdf* [Accessed 15 April 2016] (Lord Clarke of Stone-Cum-Ebony M.R.). In

2011 Lord Dyson responded to some of the issues arising in the Judicial Speeches in a speech subsequently published under title of "A word on Halsey v Milton Keynes" (Arbitration 2011, 77(3), 337-341).

In the sixth paragraph (beginning "Lord Neuberger of Abbotsbury"), replace the quoted section with:
". better able to achieve a just or fair outcome for the parties, provided that they both have the will to settle their differences. Fair here not because the outcome necessarily reflects the substantive legal merits of the underlying dispute but rather because the parties have both participated in a consensual process and reached a mutually agreeable resolution" (*http://webarchive.nationalarchives.gov.uk/20131202164909/http://www.judiciary.gov.uk/Resources/JCO/Documents/Speeches/mr-keating-lecture-19052010.pdf* [Accessed 15 April 2016]).

Replace the last paragraph with:
Also in 2011 the Ministry of Justice announced the Dispute Resolution Commitment. This requires government departments and agencies to be proactive in the management of disputes, and to use effective, proportionate and appropriate forms of dispute resolution to avoid expensive legal costs or court actions. (See *https://www.gov.uk/government/news/government-supports-more-efficient-dispute-resolution* [Accessed 15 April 2016]).

B.   ADR IN THE CONTEXT OF THE CPR

1.   Case Management

(c)   Voluntary v compulsory/mandatory ADR and case management

Replace the first paragraph with:
It is often said that the hallmark of ADR procedures, and perhaps the key to their effectiveness **14-6** in individual cases, is that they are processes voluntarily entered into by the parties in dispute with outcomes, if the parties so wish, which are non-binding. Indeed, it is also a popular view that the voluntary nature of mediation lies at the very heart of mediation and that compulsory mediation is an oxymoron. Authoritative commentators such as Lord Phillips of Worth Matravers, Lord Chief Justice (as he then was) and Professor Dame Hazel Genn, have remarked that compulsory mediation has always been a controversial subject that promotes strong views and more than a little confusion. It is, however, clear beyond doubt, and this was noted in the Judicial Speeches referred to in para.14-3 above, that some jurisdictions (with more experience than our own in the deployment of ADR) do use compulsory mediation. Also, the fact that compulsory mediation is used in Europe can be inferred from the EU Mediation Directive 2008 which includes a provision that nothing in the Directive should prejudice a Member State making the use of mediation compulsory. (Directive 2008/52/EC of the European Parliament and of the Council of May 21, 2008 on certain aspects of mediation in civil and commercial matters, para.(14) of the preamble: *http://eur-lex.europa.eu/LexUriServ/LexUriServ.do?uri=OJ:L:2008:136:0003:0008:EN:PDF* [Accessed 28 January 2016]). More information about how and where compulsory mediation is used may be obtained from a most comprehensive review of ADR in the "*Consultation Paper on Alternative Dispute Resolution*" published by the Law Reform Commission in Ireland in July 2008 (see *http://www.lawreform.ie/2008/consultation-paper-on-alternative-dispute-resolution.186.html* [Accessed 28 January 2016]). One of the most controversial aspects of compulsory mediation is whether it is successful. There is evidence to suggest that compulsory mediation schemes can (fairly obviously) increase the rate of take up of mediation, but that this is at the expense of lowering both the success rate in relation to settlements and the client satisfaction rate in the process (see "Twisting arms: court referred and court linked mediation under judicial pressure" *https://www.ucl.ac.uk/laws/judicial-institute/files/Twisting_arms_mediation_report_Genn_et_al_1.pdf* [Accessed 15 April 2016]). Against that, however, Lord Phillips has commented that "Statistics show that settlement rates in relation to parties who have been compelled to mediate are just about as high as they are in the case of those who resort to mediation of their own volition." (See the Judicial Speeches referred to in para.14-3 above.) The Irish Consultation Paper (see above) assists our understanding of these issues by suggesting that the issue of "voluntary" or "compulsory" is not an "either, or" choice but that there is a range of options along a spectrum. The options identified by the Commission were:
1.   The parties themselves propose the idea for mediation as an option;
2.   The court encourages the parties to consider mediation;
3.   The court encourages the parties to consider mediation and warns of the possible imposition of cost sanctions for an unreasonable refusal to consider ADR;
4.   Access to court is denied, where mediation has not first been attempted.

(f)   Judicial speeches—ADR case management post Halsey—power to direct ADR

To the end of the first paragraph, add:
See also para.14–20.   **14-9**

(h)   Case management and cost sanctions

At the end of the fourth paragraph (beginning "Jackson L.J. reviewed costs sanctions"), replace "November 13, 2015" with:

14-11   15 April 2016

Replace the sixth paragraph with:

In *Lewicki v Nuneaton & Bedworth BC* [2013] UKUT 120 (LC) the court stated, in agreement with the view of Jackson L.J. immediately above, that in principle, the refusal of a party to participate in mediation might justify an adverse costs order on the indemnity basis. Indemnity costs were awarded by way of a sanction in *Garritt-Critchley v Ronnan* [2014] EWHC 1774 (Ch), *Reid v Buckinghamshire Healthcare NHS Trust*, 28 October 2015, unrep., WL 8131473 and *Bristow v Princess Alexandra Hospital NHS Trust*, 4 November 2015, unrep., WL 9298774. In *PGF II SA v OMFS Co* [2013] EWCA Civ 1288 the Court of Appeal clearly contemplated that an unreasonable refusal to mediate might be met by a range of sanctions. The court suggested that the otherwise successful party might be ordered to pay part of the unsuccessful party's costs, and only in the event of the most serious and flagrant failures to engage would it be appropriate to adopt the draconian sanction of depriving it of all of its costs.

(i)   Case management: facilitation of ADR procedures and criteria for referral to ADR

Replace list with:

14-12   (i)   By ensuring that the opportunity to explore ADR prospects is not prejudiced by the rigours of case management procedures generally. (For example, see *Electrical Waste Recycling Group Ltd v Philips Electronics UK Ltd* [2012] EWHC 38 (Ch) where the court considered how ordering a split trial might impact on the prospects of mediating the matter.) In *CIP Properties (AIPT) Ltd v Galliford Try Infrastructure Ltd* [2014] EWHC 3546 (TCC) Coulson J. suggested "A timetable for trial that allows the parties to take part in ADR along the way is a sensible case management tool."

(ii)   By acting as a source of information about professional and commercial bodies providing ADR services (for example, see *http://www.civilmediation.justice.gov.uk* [Accessed 28 January 2016] and paras 14–22, 14–24 and 14–27 below).

(iii)   By verbally encouraging the parties to consider ADR at a hearing or telephone conference, such as a case management conference or a pre-trial review. (see para.14-11)

(iv)   By ordering a stay of the whole or part of the proceedings, for mediation or some other ADR procedure, pursuant to the application of the parties or one of them (r.3.1(2)(f) and r.3.3(1) and see para.14-13 below).

(v)   By ordering such a stay of its own initiative (r.3.1(2)(f) and r.3.3(1)). An appropriate time to make such an order might be upon perusal of the parties' statements about ADR in their directions questionnaires. (See para. 14-13 below.)

(vi)   By ordering such a stay upon the written request of a party or of its own initiative when considering completed directions questionnaires (r.26.4). (See also Standard Directions Model Paragraph B05-stay for settlement which provides:

"1)   ....

2)   The claim is stayed until xxxx, during which period the parties will attempt to settle the matter or to narrow the issues.

3)   By 4pm on xxxx the Claimant must notify the court in writing of the outcome of negotiations (without disclosing any matters which remain subject to 'without prejudice' terms) and what, if any, further directions are sought. Failure to comply with this direction or to engage properly in negotiations may result in the application of sanctions. If settlement has been reached, the parties must file a consent order signed by all of them." (See *http://www.justice.gov.uk/courts/procedure-rules/civil/standard-directions/list-of-cases-of-common-occurrence/menu-of-sd-paragraphs* (B05-ADR.doc) [Accessed 28 January 2016]).

(vii)   By ordering the parties to consider ADR (including Mediation) using, for example a direction in the form of Standard Directions Model Paragraph A03-ADR.doc, whether at the time of giving standard directions or otherwise as follows:

"1)   ....

2)   At all stages the parties must consider settling this litigation by any means of Alternative Dispute Resolution (including Mediation); any party not engaging in any such means proposed by another must serve a witness statement giving reasons within 21 days of that proposal; such witness statement must not be shown to the trial judge until questions of costs arise.

'21 days' can be altered manually.

The words 'and not less than 28 days before trial' can always be added after the word 'proposal' by the managing judge if appropriate. Not necessary for every Order." (See *http://www.justice.gov.uk/courts/procedure-rules/civil/standard-directions/list-of-cases-of-common-occurrence/menu-of-sd-paragraphs* (A03-ADR.doc) [Accessed 28 January 2016]).

It might be particularly appropriate to consider directions of the type referred to immediately above when considering cost budgets and proportionality during the costs management and case management process. Such directions might be combined with directions designed to facilitate the holding of an immediate mediation. For example, provision could be made for early disclosure of a particular category of documents that would facilitate a mediation prior to full disclosure. See *SM v DAM* [2014] EWHC 537 (Fam) 2014 WL 795215 at para.525. In respect of directions for a stay in boundary disputes see the observations about *Bradley v Heslin* [2014] EWHC 3267 (Ch) in para.14-9.1 above.

(viii)   By making an order, whether on directions for allocation or a later stage, of the type referred to in the Multi-Track Practice Direction (sometimes referred to as an "Ungley Order"). (29PD4.10(9) and see para.14-13 below.)

(ix)   By making an ADR order on the basis of the draft in App.7 to the Admiralty and Commercial Courts Guide (see para.14-22). The draft order includes the following paragraph: "4. The parties shall take such serious steps as they may be advised to resolve their disputes by ADR procedures before the neutral individual or panel so chosen by no later than [*]." See para.14-9 above regarding the issue of the court's power to order parties to take part in a mediation process.

(x)   By making an ADR order on the basis of the draft order in App.E to and Section 7 of the Technology and Construction Court Guide (see para.14-22). Although these Guides refer to their particular courts there appears to be no reason why the type of ADR orders made in these courts could not be made, where appropriate, in other courts. Again, see para.14-9 above regarding the issue of the court's power to order parties to take part in a mediation process. See also paras 14-22 and 14-23 below regarding ADR in the Commercial Court and the Technology and Construction Court.

(xi)   By arranging, in the Admiralty and Commercial Court or the Technology and Construction Court, for the court to provide Early Neutral Evaluation (see the references to the respective Court Guides in sub-paras (vii) and (viii) immediately above). Further, in the Technology and Construction Court the court can provide a judge to act as a mediator. (See *http://www.justice.gov.uk/downloads/courts/tech-court/tech-con-court-guide.pdf* [Accessed October 31, 2014].)

(xii)   By, in a case which is suitable to be resolved by an ADR procedure except for one sticking point, ordering the hearing of that point as a preliminary issue with a view to the case then being referred to ADR (see s.8 of the Technology and Construction Court Guide, para.14-22, although, again, there is no reason why the approach taken by the Technology and Construction Court cannot be taken by other courts, where appropriate).

(xiii)   By referring a Small Claim to the Small Claims Mediation Service (see para.14-24).

(xiv)   By making an appropriate costs order (or advising that such an order might be made in the future) in respect of failure to give adequate consideration to ADR prior to the commencement of proceedings (para.14-21) or during proceedings (see paras 14-11 and 14-17).

3.   Costs where ADR Declined

Replace the fifth paragraph with:

In *Vale of Glamorgan Council v Roberts* [2008] EWHC 2911 an unsuccessful litigant claimed costs **14-17** against the successful defendant local authority. His application did not succeed. The court noted that the defendant had not positively suggested mediation and said that it would be going too far to disallow costs incurred by a local authority because that authority did not initiate suggestions for a mediation. Making contact with a mediation provider does not amount to an offer to mediate: *Park Promotion Ltd v Welsh Rugby Union Ltd* [2012] EWHC 2406 (QB).

Replace the eleventh paragraph with:

This was in fact the approach taken by the Court of Appeal in *Bray (t/a Building Co) v Bishop* 2009 WL 1657212 when it considered conduct in relation to costs and took into account a number of factors, including one party's rejection of a Pt 36 offer and the other's refusal to engage with a suggestion of mediation. See also *Sonmez v Kebabery Wholesale Limited* [2009] EWCA Civ 1386; 2009 WL 3197559; *Fitzroy Robinson Ltd v Mentmore Towers Ltd* [2010] EWHC 98 (TCC); 2010 WL 308605; *Brookfield Construction (UK) Limited, (formerly Multiplex Constructions (UK) LIMITED) v Mott MacDonald Limited* [2010] EWHC 659; (TCC) 2010 WL 910166; *Kayll v Rawlinson* [2010] EWHC 1789 (Ch); [2010] W.T.L.R. 1479; *Oliver v Symons* [2011] EWHC 1250 (Ch); 2011 WL 1151625*Camertown Timber Merchants Ltd v Sidhu* [2011] EWCA Civ 1041; 2011 WL 2748531, *Nelson's Yard Management Co v Eziefula* [2013] EWCA Civ 235, *Bristow v The Princess Alexander Hospital NHS Trust*, 4 November 2015, unrep., WL 9298774 and *Flanagan v Liontrust Investment Partners LLP* [2016] EWHC 446 (Ch).

Delete paragraph 14–17A.

Add new section 3A:

3A.   Disputes about costs

ADR is as relevant to disputes about costs as it is to all other types of litigation. In particular an   **14-17A** unreasonable refusal to mediate a costs dispute may, and in a number of cases has, resulted in a costs sanction. In *Lakehouse Contracts Ltd v UPR Services Ltd* [2014] EWHC 1223 (Ch) a failure to mediate was taken into account in dealing with the costs of a winding-up petition. In *Morris v Thay County Court*, February 2, 2015, unrep.(Kingston upon Hull) the defendant paying party received two CPR r.47.20 offers prior to a detailed assessment but did not respond to them. The District Judge found that the defendant failed to failure to make any offer and/or to actively consider dispute resolution and concluded that this was a conduct issue. He said, following *Halsey v Milton Keynes General NHS Trust* [2004] EWCA Civ 576; [2004] 1 W.L.R. 3002 and *PGF II SA v OMFS Co 1 Ltd* [2013] EWCA Civ 1288; [2014] 1 W.L.R. 1386, that the parties were expected to engage in alternative dispute resolution. He considered it likely that further mediation could have achieved a far speedier conclusion and at less cost and concluded that the defendant's conduct was also conduct contrary to the overriding objective.

See also *Reid v Buckinghamshire Healthcare NHS Trust*, 28 October 2015, unrep., WL 8131473 and *Bristow v The Princess Alexandra Hospital NHS Trust*, 4 November 2015, unrep., WL 9298774.

The fact that disputes about costs are being mediated is demonstrated by *Sugar Hut Group Ltd v A J Insurance Service* [2016] EWCA Civ 46; WL 00386250: the Court of Appeal judgment noted that Property Damage costs in the matter were agreed at a mediation.

4. Confidentiality, without Prejudice and "Mediation Privilege" in Relation to Mediation

(c) Confidentiality

Replace the fourth paragraph with:

14-18.2   Another particular point clarified by this case was the finding that the mediator could enforce the provisions relating to confidentiality, as against the parties. This means that where, as in *Farm Assist 2*, the parties have waived without prejudice privilege the mediator may nevertheless be able to require that confidentiality will be maintained. (As in *Farm Assist Ltd*, the Court may not always treat the mediator's word on this issue as decisive: see the comment by Nicol J in *Commodities Research Unit International (Holdings) Ltd v King and Wood Mallesons LLP* [2016] EWHC 63 (QB) at para.21.)

(d) Without prejudice

Replace the fourth paragraph with:

14-18.3   See also *Youlton v Charles Russell* 2010 WL 1649039, *Curtis v Pulbrook* 2011 WL 291736 and *Commodities Research Unit International (Holdings) Ltd v King and Wood Mallesons LLP* [2016] EWHC 63 (QB). These are solicitor's professional negligence claims where it was necessary for the court to enquire into the detail of proceedings of a prior mediation to deal with the subsequent claim against the solicitors.

6. Miscellaneous Matters

Add new paragraph at end:

14-20   Any agreement reached at mediation needs to be recorded carefully and arrangements need to be made to implement the agreement in a manner that reflects the outcome intended to be agreed between the parties. This involves consideration of all aspects relating to implementation eg the impact of any taxation provisions that may arise during implementation. See *Moore v Revenue and Customs Commissioners* [2016] UKFTT 115 (TC); 2016 WL 00750585.

7. Mediation and EU Directives

At the end of the fifth paragraph (beginning "An EU Directive on alternative dispute resolution"), replace "November 13, 2015" with:

14-20.1   15 April 2016

14-21 *Change title of part:*

C.   ADR IN PRE-ACTION PROTOCOLS, COURT GUIDES AND HANDBOOKS

14-22 *Change title of section:*

2. ADR in Court Guides and Handbooks

Replace the first paragraph with:

Several Court Guides make reference to ADR procedures. To an extent the Guides repeat what is said in CPR provisions and in practice directions. Necessarily, the Court Guides are more broadly focussed than the pre-action protocols and refer to the application of ADR procedures in claims falling across the court's jurisdiction. However, litigants in person and the legal representatives of parties engaged in proceedings before those courts that have issued Court Guides are well advised to read carefully what is said about ADR, particularly if they are unfamiliar with the subject. The jurisdiction of the TCC is more specific than the other courts and the coverage of ADR procedures in that Guide is rather more detailed than that provided in the other Guides (see further "ADR in Technology and Construction Court", below). References to ADR in the Court Guides are as follows (for complete texts, see Section 1 (Court Guides) and Section 2 (Specialist Proceedings) above):

- Chancery Guide, Ch.17 (Alternative Dispute Resolution) paras 17.1 to 17.6;
- Queen's Bench Guide, Section 6 (Preliminary Case Management) para.6.6 (ADR);
- Admiralty and Commercial Courts Guide, Section G1 (Alternative Dispute Resolution), G2 (Early neutral evaluation), and App.7 Draft ADR Order. See also the Commercial Court working party report on long trials, which includes a number of provisions about ADR at *https://www.judiciary.gov.uk/publications/longtrials-working-party-report* [Accessed 15 April 2016];
- Technology and Construction Court Guide, Section 7 (Alternative Dispute Resolution and ENE) paras 7.1 to 7.5), Section 8 (Preliminary Issues) para.8.5 (Use of PI (Preliminary Issues) as an adjunct to ADR), and App.E (Draft ADR Order).

Add new paragraph at end:
The numerous publications on ADR include "The Jackson ADR Handbook" (mentioned in the section above and by the Court of Appeal in *PGF II SA v OMFS Co 1 Ltd* [2013] EWCA Civ 1288) and "A Handbook for Litigants in Person". The latter, which includes a section on mediation, has been written by the six judges who comprise the Civil Sub-committee of the Committee of the Council of Circuit Judges and is accessible at *https://www.judiciary.gov.uk/wp-content/uploads/JCO/Documents/Guidance/A_Handbook_for_Litigants_in_Person.pdf* [Accessed 14 April 2016].

D.   ADR IN PARTICULAR COURTS

2.   *Mediation in County Courts*

Delete the first paragraph.   **14–24**

Replace the second paragraph with:
In 2007 HMCTS introduced the Small Claims Mediation Service to all court users.

Replace the third paragraph with:
In 2011 there were more than 11,000 mediations with an average 70 per cent settlement rate. Parties can self refer to the Mediation Service, or a judge will refer a suitable case at allocation and directions stage, when at least one party has requested this. Information about the service is provided at a website contributed by a private training organisation: *http://www.smallclaimscourtgenie.co.uk/small-claims-mediation-service/* [Accessed 15 April 2016].

Replace the fourth paragraph with:
For claims valued above the small claims limit, the Ministry of Justice provides a list of civil mediation providers who provide a service for a fixed fee. The list is accessible at *http://www.civilmediation.justice.gov.uk* [Accessed 15 April 2016].

SECTION 15   INTERIM REMEDIES

A.   INTERIM INJUNCTIONS

2.   *Principles and Guidelines to be Applied (American Cyanamid Co. Case)*

(c)   Interim relief pending appeal

After "(Warren J.), where", add:
in a supplemental judgment (given on 23 October 2015, after delivery of the main judgment on **15-9.1** 19 October 2015)

7.   Strength of Applicant's Case in Freezing Injunction Cases

To the end of the fourth paragraph (beginning "For an explanation of the provenance"), add:

15-23   For a review of the authorities on the point, see *Metropolitan Housing Trust v Taylor* [2015] EWHC 2897 (Ch), 19 October 2015, unrep. (Warren J) paras 17 to 26.

B.   FREEZING INJUNCTIONS

6.   "Worldwide" Freezing Injunctions

(f)   Permission to enforce abroad

Before the last paragraph (beginning "Where, as a quid pro quo"), add as a new paragraph:

15-87   Guidance as to the application of these guidelines from the courts has been sparse. In *Arcadia Petroleum Ltd v Bosworth* [2015] EWHC 3700 (Comm), 15 December 2015, unrep. (Males J), the claimants applied for permission to enforce the order which had been continued on the return date, and some protections for the defendants were justified under Dadourian Guideline 2 as follows: (i) The order granting permission should be explicit as to what the steps the claimants were being given permission to take in each relevant overseas jurisdiction; (ii) The claimants were required to give an undertaking that the benefit of the undertakings in the inter partes WFO should ensure for the benefit of any third party notified in the overseas jurisdictions; (iii) The claimants had to undertake to undo any enforcement steps in the overseas jurisdictions if the WFO was set aside, including paying any costs reasonably incurred by the defendants in connection with such undoing; (iv) The claimants were required to undertake to be co-operative in relation to the exceptions and protections in the WFO (e.g. in relation to living expenses and legal costs). In *Ikon International (HK) Holdings Public Co Ltd v Ikon Finance Ltd* [2016] EWHC 318 (Comm), 17 February 2016, unrep. (Phillips J) the judge accepted the general proposition advanced by the claimants that a party who has been granted a freezing injunction is entitled to police that injunction and to seek further assistance from the court in so doing, regardless of the fact that there are outstanding applications to discharge, or, indeed, that a without notice WFO has not yet been considered at an inter partes hearing, but held that in the circumstances it was wrong to grant the claimants permission to enforce a freezing order out of the jurisdiction or make an order for cross examination before the return date of the freezing order which had been made on a without notice application.

E.   INTERIM PAYMENTS

3.   Conditions to be Satisfied and Matters to be Taken into Account (CPR r.25.7)

(a)   Generally

After the second paragraph (beginning "An application for an interim payment order"), add as a new paragraph:

15-101   In *Smith v Bailey* [2014] EWHC 2569 (QB); [2015] R.T.R. 6 (Popplewell J), where a claim was made for personal injuries arising out of a road traffic accident, the defendant intimated a defence of contributory negligence, but produced no evidence in support of that defence for the hearing of the claimant's application for an interim payment. In dismissing D's appeal against a Master's award of an interim payment the judge held that, in the absence of evidence of contributory negligence, the Master was justified in treating the likely award of damages to be on the basis of full liability. In *Sellar-Elliott v Howling* [2016] EWHC 443 (QB), 3 March 2016, unrep. (Sweeney J), the hearing of the claimant's (C) application for an interim payment, in a clinical negligence claim to which the defendant (D) had pleaded a defence (putting causation in dispute), took place six weeks before the date scheduled for the exchange of the expert evidence. In advance of that hearing, C served her expert evidence. A Master granted C's application. In refusing D permission to appeal a judge (1) explained that (a) D was under no obligation to file evidence opposing C's application, and (b) as was her right, she had chosen in response only to serve limited evidence in response (not including her expert evidence), and (2) held that (a) the Master had to determine the application on the evidence before him, and (b) on that evidence he was entitled to conclude that C had proved, to the requisite standard, that the conditions in r.25.7(1)(c) were met.

(d)   Judgment "for a substantial amount of money" (CPR r.25.7(1)(c))

Replace the last paragraph with:

15-108   In *Deutsche Bank AG v Unitech Global Ltd* [2014] EWHC 3117 (Comm), October 3, 2014, unrep. (Teare J.), it was predictable that the claimants' (C) claim for repayment of a loan agreement might fail at trial because the defendant's (D) defence of rescission (though opposed by C) succeeded, but on terms that D pay C a substantial sum. It was held that in those circumstances, by obtaining judgment for counter-restitution, C would not obtain judgment for "a substantial amount of money" within the meaning of r.25.7(1)(c) and an interim payment order was refused accordingly.

In *Peak Hotels and Resorts Ltd v Tarek Investments Ltd* [2015] EWHC 1997 (Ch), July 17, 2015, unrep. (Barling J.), the court reached the same conclusion. In that case the circumstances left open the question whether the r.25.7(1)(c) condition could be satisfied by an order for rescission that was merely conditional on counter-restitution and the court held it could not because such an order was not a judgment for a sum money within the scope of r.25.7. Subsequently, on an appeal by C from the judge's decision in the Deutsche Bank case referred to above, the Court of Appeal allowed C's appeal; see *Deutsche Bank AG v Unitech Global Ltd* [2016] EWCA Civ 119, 3 March 2016, CA, unrep. The Court held that the definition of an interim payment, given in the Senior Courts Act 1981 s.32(5) and in r.25.1(1)(k), is sufficiently wide to cover a situation in which a claimant claims to enforce a contract according to its terms and the defendant responds by saying he is entitled to rescind the contract on grounds of misrepresentation, but would only be held to be able to rescind on condition that he gives restitution of sums received from the claimant; the words "other sum" in s.32(5) and r.25.1(1)(k) were very wide, and would plainly cover a requirement in this case that C should pay a sum by way of restitution (paras 57 and 64).

INDEX

LEGAL TAXONOMY

FROM SWEET & MAXWELL

This index has been prepared using Sweet and Maxwell's Legal Taxonomy. Main index entries conform to keywords provided by the Legal Taxonomy except where references to specific documents or non-standard terms (denoted by quotation marks) have been included. These keywords provide a means of identifying similar concepts in other Sweet & Maxwell publications and online services to which keywords from the Legal Taxonomy have been applied. Readers may find some minor differences between terms used in the text and those which appear in the index. Suggestions to *sweetandmaxwell.taxonomy@thomson.com*.

(All references are to paragraph numbers)

Paragraph numbers marked "+" denote online/CD content; those within [...] refer to Volume 2

Paragraph numbers marked "+" denote online/CD content; those within [...] refer to Volume 2

Paragraph numbers marked "+" denote online/CD content; those within [...] refer to Volume 2

Paragraph numbers marked "+" denote online/CD content; those within [...] refer to Volume 2

Paragraph numbers marked "+" denote online/CD content; those within [...] refer to Volume 2

NOTES